# Research on Enhancing the Interactivity of Online Learning

**A Volume in**
**Perspectives in Instructional Technology**
**and Distance Education**

*Series Editors:* Charles Schlosser and Michael Simonson
*Nova Southeastern University*

# Research on Enhancing the Interactivity of Online Learning

*Edited by*

**Vivian H. Wright**
**Cynthia Szymanski Sunal**
*and*
**Elizabeth K. Wilson**

**INFORMATION AGE**
PUBLISHING

80 Mason Street • Greenwich, Connecticut 06830 • www.infoagepub.com

**Library of Congress Cataloging-in-Publication Data**

Research on enhancing the interactivity of online learning /edited by Vivian H.
Wright, Cynthia Szymanski Sunal, and Elizabeth K. Wilson.
p. cm. – (Perspectives in instructional technology and distance learning)
Includes bibliographical references.
ISBN 1-59311-362-5 (pbk.) – ISBN 1-59311-363-3 (hardcover)
1. Education—Computer network resources. 2. Web-based instruction.
3. Internet in education. I. Wright, Vivian H. II. Sunal, Cynthia S.
III. Wilson, Elizabeth K. IV. Series.
LB1044.87.R47 2005
371.33'44678–dc22

2005020173

Printed in the United States of America

# CONTENTS

# LIST OF CONTRIBUTORS

## 1. Future Directions for Online Learning

*Dr. Vivian H. Wright* is an Assistant Professor of Instructional Technology in the College of Education at The University of Alabama in Tuscaloosa. She works with teacher educators on innovative ways to infuse technology in the curriculum to enhance teaching and learning and has helped initiate and develop projects for online learning and professional development.

*Dr. Cynthia Szymanski Sunal* is Full Professor of Curriculum and Instruction at The University of Alabama. She edits the *Journal of Interactive Online Learning*. Her research focus includes consideration of how electronic formats influence cooperative group work and teachers' examination of their personal teaching values.

*Dr. Elizabeth K. Wilson* is a Professor in the Department of Secondary, Curriculum, Teaching, and Learning at The University of Alabama. She works with classroom teachers to integrate technology into K–12 settings. Her research interests include social studies education, technology integration, and content literacy.

## 2. Learner Intent and Online Learning

*Dr. Randall S. Davies* is an Assistant Professor of Educational Research in the School of Education at Indiana University South Bend. His interests

*Research on Enhancing the Interactivity of Online Learning*, pages vii–xii
Copyright © 2006 by Information Age Publishing

include Web-based learning environments, assessment and program evaluation, and educational research involving data collection techniques and instrument design.

## 3. An Emerging Hybrid Model for Interactive Online Learning

*Dr. Martha Jeanne Yanes* is an Assistant Professor of Instructional Technology in the College of Education at the University of Texas Pan American. She works with preservice and inservice teachers to infuse technology into instruction and learning. She has published articles on online learning and maintains an active research agenda studying the use and effectiveness of electronic learning communities and electronic portfolios for teacher preparation.

*Dr. Carmen M. Peña* is an Assistant Professor of Curriculum & Instruction at the University of Texas Pan American. She has published several articles on online learning in teacher education and electronic mentoring of preservice teachers, and maintains an active research agenda involving the integration of technology in teacher education.

*Dr. James B. Curts* is an Assistant Professor of Instructional Methods in the College of Education at The University of Texas Pan American. He works with preservice and inservice teachers modeling the use of technology to achieve principles of learning with understanding. His research interests include cognitive progression of teachers through the use of metacognitive strategies.

## 4. Assessment in Online Learning: Are Students Really Learning?

*Dr. Jean Foster Herron* is Emeritus Associate Director of Academic Outreach in the College of Continuing Studies at The University of Alabama. She is responsible for instructional technology and academic services. Her research interests are evaluation and assessment, problem-based learning, and college teaching.

*Dr. Vivian H. Wright* is an Assistant Professor of Instructional Technology in the College of Education at The University of Alabama in Tuscaloosa. She works with teacher educators on innovative ways to infuse technology in the curriculum to enhance teaching and learning and has helped initiate and develop projects for online learning and professional development.

## 5. Authentic Assessment Through Problem-Based Learning in the Online Environment

*Susan M. Powers,* Ed.D., is Acting Associate Dean & Professor of Educational Technology, College of Education, Indiana State University. She has been teaching online since 1997 and has taught an online, graduate course about online learning for six years. Her focus is on the integration of technology to enhance teaching and learning, and effective applications of online learning.

*Lisa Dallas,* MS, Instructional Support Specialist, Eastern Illinois University currently works with faculty, staff, and administration concerning technology inclusion into courses, curriculum programs, and work environments. She has helped develop well over 50 online courses for both graduate and undergraduate programs. Currently she is enrolled in a Ph.D. program with a focus in Curriculum Instruction and Multi-media Technology.

## 6. Collaborating on an Interactive Online Study Guide

*Dr. Catherine Collier* is Associate Professor of Education and Director of Graduate Teacher Education at Roberts Wesleyan College in Rochester, NY. She works with teachers to infuse technology in the K–12 curriculum, with particular emphasis on improving literacy. Teachers in her online classes collaboratively develop high-order thinking activities that integrate Web, print and primary source materials.

## 7. Using Narrative Strategies to Enhance Interactivity Online

*Dr. Linda Lohr* is an Associate Professor of Educational Technology at the University of Northern Colorado. Her research and teaching interests include visual literacy, instructional design, and performance technology.

*Kathy Miller,* M.Ed., is a doctoral student in the adult education program at North Carolina State University. Her research interests include self-directed learning, learning communities, older learners, and contemplative practice. She teaches life-story writing.

*Dr. Donald Winiecki* is an Associate Professor in the Instructional & Performance Technology Department, in the College of Engineering at Boise State University. His research and teaching interests include the sociology of work; labor and technology; affects of technological media and technological systems on individual and group communication behaviors.

## 8. Enhancing Elementary Teachers' Understanding of Inquiry: Teaching and Learning Using Online Scientific Discourse

*Dr. Lea B. Accalogoun* is an Assistant Professor in the Master of Arts in Teaching (MAT) Program at The Empire State College in Long Island Center, Old Westbury. She works with adult career-changers and teacher-candidates in both online and face-to-face environments to prepare them for an effective transition to teaching profession. She collaborated in many research projects for online science learning and teaching, and currently is involved in an innovative Web-based Alternative Teacher Education Program.

*Dr. Dennis W. Sunal* is a Professor and Director of Science Education in the College of Education at The University of Alabama in Tuscaloosa. He is also a director of the National Center for Online Learning and Research (NCOLR) and NASA Opportunities for Visionary Academic (NOVA) at The University of Alabama. He works with science teacher educators, has conducted extensive investigations on best practices in online learning, and has developed models of online learning in science, engineering, and education.

*Dr. Sharon Nichols* is an Associate Profession of Science Education in the College of Education at The University of Alabama in Tuscaloosa. She works with science teacher educators on innovative ways to enhance science teaching and learning and has collaborated in projects for online learning and professional development.

## 9. Collaborative Learning Environments Across the Internet

*Dr. Michael J. Berson* is an Associate Professor of Social Science Education at the University of South Florida. He served as the Chair of the College and University Faculty Assembly of the National Council for the Social Studies. He has extensively published books, chapters, and journal articles and presented worldwide. Dr. Berson conducts research on global child advocacy and technology in social studies education.

*Dr. Cheryl Mason Bolick* is an Assistant Professor of Education Technology and Social Studies Education in the School of Education at the University of North Carolina at Chapel Hill. She works with inservice and preservice teachers to identify, develop, and research effective ways to integrate technology into social studies teaching and learning.

*Dr. Scott M. Waring* is a Visiting Assistant Professor of Social Science Education and Educational Technology at the University of South Florida Saint Petersburg. He is currently conducting research on the integration of technology in social studies education and the use of the blended course model and technology to enhance teaching in higher education.

*Shelli A. Whitworth* is an instructor and doctoral student in Curriculum & Instruction, Social Science Education at the University of South Florida. She is also a Social Science teacher within the School District of Hillsborough Country, Florida. She works with educators on infusing technology into social classrooms to enhance information literacy.

## 10. Problem-Solving and Coping Strategies Used in an Online Learning Environment

*Dr. Cheryl White Sundberg* is the Program Manager in the College of Continuing Studies at The University of Alabama in Tuscaloosa. Her research interests include interactive online learning environments, teacher professional development and effective science teaching.

*Dr. Dennis W. Sunal* is Professor of Science Education in the College of Education at The University of Alabama. His research interests are in professional development, alternative conceptions and conceptual change in teachers and faculty, student conceptions of the nature of science, and Web course design, pedagogy, and contextual factors in interactive online learning.

*Allison Mays* is a science teacher with the Tuscaloosa County Schools in Tuscaloosa, Alabama. She has provided extensive research support for online learning projects in the College of Education at The University of Alabama in Tuscaloosa.

*Dr. Michael R. L. Odell* is Chair of Curriculum and Instruction at Illinois State University and an Associate Professor of Science and Technology Education. He is currently involved in research to develop effective tools and strategies to improve online learning.

## 11. Concept Mapping and E-Learning: A Pathway Toward Thinking Dispositions

*Dr. Craig S. Shwery* is an Assistant Professor of Curriculum and Instruction-Elementary Education Programs at The University of Alabama in Tuscaloosa. He works with teacher candidates, as well as classroom teachers on ways to recognize personal teaching beliefs and attitudes in order to enhance effective teaching and learning perspectives. Dr. Shwery is currently the Practica Coordinator for the elementary Teacher Education Program.

# CHAPTER 1

# FUTURE DIRECTIONS FOR ONLINE LEARNING

**Vivian H. Wright, Cynthia Szymanski Sunal, and Elizabeth K. Wilson**
*University of Alabama*

Our goal with this book, *Research on Enhancing the Interactivity of Online Learning,* is to present a juried, scholarly, and accessible review of research, theory, and/or policy on specific issues of interactive online learning for K–16 educators, administrators, and students of online learning. Online learning has become the norm rather than the exception for many of today's students. Instructors are more willing to explore online learning options, students are enrolling in record numbers and colleges, as well as many K–12 institutions, are offering more online courses. As educators, we have more tools than ever to ensure online course success, but just as with a traditional class, we must continue to place emphasis on good pedagogy. To achieve good pedagogy, online teaching takes additional time and a restructuring of course content by the instructor. Student issues include coping strategies, ease of navigation, skills required to complete the course, availability of online resources, feedback from the instructor, and collaborative, interactive learning opportunities. Principles of interactive online learning are new to many, and this book provides a forum for interactive online learning research, while also including ideas that enhance both the practical and theoretical aspects of interactive online learning.

*Research on Enhancing the Interactivity of Online Learning,* pages 1–4
Copyright © 2006 by Information Age Publishing
All rights of reproduction in any form reserved.

The editors have included chapters that can further knowledge and understanding of emerging trends and foster debate regarding issues that surround interactive online learning.

As we offer more online courses and as more students enroll, how important is it to assess the students' intentions for learning? Davies, in his chapter "*Learner Intent and Online Learning*," offers an overview of conditions that de-emphasize learning and may adversely affect learner intent, while suggesting practices that help focus student learning. To make this process easier, many educators at schools and colleges begin their efforts in online learning by launching a hybrid or blended course. Yanes, Peña, and Curts, in their chapter, "*An Emerging Hybrid Model for Interactive Learning,*" explore the hybrid model, specifically the use of online discussion combined with face-to-face (F2F) discussion to enhance student interaction. These authors offer recommendations for planning and managing such a model, including how to plan for online discussions that can foster students' cognitive growth. As we consider the issues and potential solutions discussed in the Yanes, Peña, and Curts chapter, an important, persistent question arises for many of us when teaching a course online. How can we assess students' learning? In chapter four, "*Assessment in Online Learning: Are Students Really Learning?*" Herron and Wright present a content analysis of literature related to categories of assessment and assessment tools. The authors challenge readers to allow assessment to play a major role in the design of an online course. Powers and Dallas, in "*Authentic Assessment Through Problem-Based Learning in the Online Environment,*" further suggest that problem-based learning (PBL) is an excellent tool for authentic assessment in an online environment and offer pedagogical applications and implications of PBL and online learning.

Collier gives a glimpse of how a traditional writing assignment was transformed into an online interactive study guide and used for assessment, in "*Collaborating on an Interactive Online Study Guide.*" Her longitudinal research offers an idea of how students stretched their technical ability while gaining in their writing and research abilities. Collier also found that, compared to those writing the traditional paper, there was greater enthusiasm for learning among the group using online interactive strategies. Similarly, Lohr, Miller, and Winiecki explored the use of narrative strategies for enhancing interactivity online (*"Using Narrative Strategies to Enhance Interactivity Online"*) and found that interactivity increased with both the complexity of the assignment and increased teamwork. Accalogoun, Sunal, and Nichols investigated how elementary teachers used scientific discourse to support their learning to teach inquiry-based science using online media in their chapter, "*Enhancing Elementary Teachers' Understanding of Inquiry: Teaching and Learning Using Online Scientific Discourse.*" The authors share findings about how portfolio and discussion board use helped the teachers have positive attitudes about online environments and further promoted scientific discourse.

What are some of the challenges and rewards of interactive, collaborative education online? Using a telecollaborative model, Berson, Bolick, Waring, and Whitworth expand virtual walls in their study of two university social studies online classrooms and offer excellent advice and lessons learned from their experiences, in the chapter, "*Collaborative Learning Environments Across the Internet.*" Sundberg, Sunal, Mays, and Odell examine problem solving and coping strategies (*"Problem-Solving and Coping Strategies Used in an Online Learning Environment"*) used in an online learning environment in a study that included major universities in the Northwestern, Midwestern, and Southeastern United States. They found that students were creative in developing problem solving techniques and coping strategies and that those who used coping strategies actually finished the course. Shwery's findings, in the final chapter, "*Concept Mapping and E-Learning: A Pathway Toward Thinking Dispositions,*" also point to a need to implement online learning strategies that are challenging, interactive, and engage students in exploring their intellectual thinking dispositions.

The underlying theme of each chapter is the importance of pedagogy that is research-based and effective. It is our hope that the experiences, advice, and recommendations of the authors featured in this book will further your growth in effective interactive online learning and design as you continue to explore what enhances student learning.

# CHAPTER 2

# LEARNER INTENT AND ONLINE LEARNING

**Randall S. Davies**
*Indiana University South Bend*

Learning is a natural human activity that can be facilitated with online instruction. Yet while online instruction offers many potential benefits, it tends not to produce learning unless the participating student's main intention is to learn. When the design of an online course deliberately or inadvertently promotes course completion as a primary goal, students often abandon any real intention of learning. Implementing effective online instruction requires a fundamental shift in the way we think about the administration and design of online courses. The expectation that learning occurs must be communicated to students, not just through the instruction but through the administrative practices and policies that govern an online course.

Many developers and designers of online instructional systems seem to rely on the assumption that if you build it, students will learn. Quite often this attitude is qualified by the conviction that there exist certain basic principles of teaching and learning that always hold true; and that learning will be promoted in direct proportion to how well the instruction implements proven practices that are based on these principles (Merrill, 2002). While this may be true to some extent, Brentano (1973) has criticized educational practitioners and researchers for not capturing the true nature of

*Research on Enhancing the Interactivity of Online Learning*, pages 5–26
Copyright © 2006 by Information Age Publishing

5

the learner in the learning process. Too often designers of instruction place little emphasis on the fact that each learner approaches an educational opportunity with an assortment of abilities, interests, aspirations, expectations, habits, and preferences (Gibbs, 1992); their view of the learner tends to follow a largely passive model of individual functioning (Renninger, Hidi, & Krapp, 1992). The more we look closely at actual learning behavior, however, the more we are impressed with the complexity of factors influencing it. The assumption that students are largely passive participants educationally empowered to learn when provided with quality instruction becomes a clearly flawed supposition (Gibbs, 1992; Pervin, 1983).

With the advent of Internet technology, understanding students as learners becomes even more important. Since both teaching and learning are human performances, the outcome of any given learning opportunity may vary dramatically with the diversity of individuals participating and interacting in distinctive learning situations. A concern among educators who have considered online education as an alternative to traditional classroom teaching is the loss of personal contact between teachers and students (Weiss, 2000). Often, effective learning is the result of enthusiastic teachers who inspire their students to make exceptional learning efforts (Pratt, 1998). When the teacher is removed as the director of learning and students are required to learn more independently, they are no longer able to rely on the regulated learning controls and motivations that the traditional classroom previously provided. The act of simply providing quality instructional materials, online or otherwise, is not always enough to promote learning; a student's intentions for the expected learning determine whether learning will occur and how long that learning will last (Osguthorpe, 2000). Unfortunately, the design and administrative practices of some online courses tend to facilitate and even encourage students to complete courses without necessarily learning anything.

## LITERATURE REVIEW

The fundamental theory upon which the discipline of instructional design rests is based on the methodology associated with instructional systems design (ISD). In this methodology, a student's failure to learn is usually considered to be either the result of a skill deficiency or an unsuitable learning situation (Mager & Pipe, 1984). The solution is either to train the student or improve the instruction. Instructional designers, especially those creating online instruction, are typically charged with developing quality instructional materials that, when presented to students, will result in the desired learning (Richey et al., 2001). In the specific case of online learning, the instruction must not only cover the material, the material must be sufficiently self-contained, and intuitively uncomplicated enough for students to follow. A common complaint, however, is that students attempt to get through online courses without exerting the necessary intellectual activity and effort required (Davies, 2002; Sandberg & Barnard, 1997; Sierpinska, 1994). Students simply do not try hard enough to learn, and most online courses fail to inspire sufficient learning effort (Bates, 1994; Merrill, 2002; Stokes, 2000).

Sivasailam Thiagarajan suggests that this is because traditional ISD learning models "cling to a wrong world view" (as cited in Gordon & Zemke, 2000, p. 52). Thiagarajan's complaint is that current ISD learning models have adopted a fundamentally flawed view of the student. Designers tend to utilize a model that views individual student functioning as being primarily passive, without accounting for differences in students' goals and intentions, knowledge about themselves and their environment, and individual abilities to develop and change strategies of action (Renninger et al., 1992). This flawed view of the student becomes particularly evident and problematic in online learning situations, with asynchronous independent study courses being particularly vulnerable in this regard.

One might reasonably conclude that the goal of facilitating learning by emphasizing the impact of quality instructional materials is incomplete. Clearly, there are many factors other than instruction that affect learning. Key among these additional factors are the affective and conative characteristics of the learner (Anderson & Bourke, 2000). Those who design online courses may need to consider more thoroughly how the learner ultimately decides not just when he or she will attempt a learning activity, but also how much effort he or she will expend toward the complete capture of that learning.

In line with this thinking, recent research has focused on the development and measurement of affective character traits and how these traits influence motivation (Anderson & Bourke, 2000). Yet, while motivational elements may influence individuals to act, motivation typically emphasizes outward incentives rather than a student's innate desire to learn (Keller, 1983), and course designers who address motivation usually focus more on manipulating these external incentives than on stimulating a student's intentions to learn (Davies, 2002). Intentionality—one's ability to form intent volitionally and willfully act on a chosen intent (Rychlak, 1997)—makes it possible for learning to become an intended goal rather than an incidental outcome (Bereiter & Scardamalia, 1993). Yet, while many researchers have examined ways to improve learning, few have studied the effect of learner intent in online learning situations. Researchers and instructional designers have typically avoided the conative aspects of learning, considering them to be unimportant or too difficult to measure

(Rychlak, 1997; Snow, Corno, & Jackson, 1996). However, these more elusive components of learning and teaching may provide valuable insights leading to a better understanding of how we should teach (Osguthorpe, 2000).

## UNDERSTANDING THE IMPORTANCE OF LEARNER INTENT IN ONLINE LEARNING SITUATIONS

Intent is a relatively common term that appears to be readily understood by most people (Zimmerman, 1984). Nevertheless, despite its familiarity, our ability to characterize the true essence of a person's intentions has proven difficult. A basic definition of intent equates intent to the reason, motive, or purpose for one's action. We attribute purpose and reason to our own specific behavioral acts, as well as those of others, yet this definition of intent is incomplete. Intent as a conative construct is the result of the volitional decision-making process (Ryan, 1970; Rychlak, 1997; Tyler, 1973). Volitional aspects of intent include persistence, determination, willpower, effort investment, desire, work ethic, striving, mindfulness, and focus (Jackson, 1994; Kuhl, 1990; McCarty & Siccone, 2001; Ryan, 1970; Snow et al., 1996). Clearly, some of these aspects may be distinctions without a difference. However, none of these aspects of intent imply or indicate a reason, motive, or purpose for choosing to act. When a decision to willfully act is made, volitional aspects of intent associated with the resulting choice extend beyond purpose. As a result, intent not only describes the reason for acting, but it also represents a person's commitment to the chosen course of action (Jackson, 1994; Malle & Knobe, 2001; Ryan, 1970).

Constructs like intent are not considered to be behaviors; rather, they are aspects of human nature (Snow et al., 1996). Intent is an internal representation of a person's beliefs, values, aims, purposes, and commitment to a particular activity. Intentions are formed in the mind and are assumed to capture all the motivational factors that may have an impact on a behavior. Nevertheless, intent is separate from both motivation and action, even though learner intent often determines how hard a person is willing to try in order to learn (Ajzen, 1988; Bandura, 2001; Heckhausen & Kuhl, 1985). Not only do humans have the volitional ability to willfully choose specific actions, they do so with specific intentions that determine the persistence, striving, and effort with which they pursue that action (Rychlak, 1997).

## Learner Intent

[Learner intent is] what the individual wants to get out of the class and what the individuals intentions are for taking the class. Do they expect to learn or do they just expect to get the grade...what their goals are and what amount of effort they will put into it, that kind of thing. (student comment)

Learner intent is defined as a person's commitment and desire to learning what is expected of him or her when presented with a specific learning opportunity. It is a mental representation of commitment to learn separate from both motivation and effort (Bandura, 2001; Heckhausen & Kuhl, 1985). Learner intent can be wholehearted or somewhat less sincere. Learner intent characterizes individuals' aims and values as well as their reason and purpose for participating in the learning activity.

As with most abilities, an individual's capacity to make good decisions may vary depending on specific developmental stages and individual aptitudes. Children, for example, may have the capacity to willfully behave, but they are less likely to exercise this ability with the same control that adults do (Montessori, 1995). Gardner (1993) claims that the ability to control one's self in this way is a type of intelligence. This intrapersonal intelligence, as Gardner calls it, describes the degree to which an individual is able to efficaciously control motivational influences and accurately assess situations when making decisions and forming intent.

## Learner Intent and Motivation

Intent and motivation are considered by some to be similar concepts (Keller, 1983; Raven, 1992; Ryan, 1970). This is understandable, since the familiar definition of intent involves motive and the conative domain spans both motivational and volitional aspects of human behavior (Jackson & Snow, 1992). Heckhausen and Kuhl (1985), however, consider intentional states to be distinct from motivational states. The motivational state is a pre-decisional state. During this phase of the choice process, people deliberate and consider the motivational factors that will influence their choice. The motivational phase ends when a person makes a decision.

In contrast, the volitional state is post-decisional. Intent is considered to be fully formed at this point, and volitional aspects of intent come into play. Clearly, there is evidence that motivational influences do sometimes determine whether or not an individual will attempt an activity (Anderson & Bourke, 2000; Keller, 1983; Messick, 1979; Ryan, 1970). In addition, intrinsic motivations like innate interest or love for a subject have been found to be especially important in forming efficacious learner intent for a specific learning activity (Amabile, 2001; Green, 1999; Schiefele, 1991; Tyler, 1973). However, many factors simultaneously influence one's motivation to act, and no individual motivational element can adequately predict the quality of a student's effort. Fishbein and Ajzen (1975) believe this is because actual learning behavior is more accurately predicted by a learner's intent. Although motivation is important initially, it is learner intent that determines the quality of effort expended and, often, the quality of learning achieved (Osguthorpe, 2000; Warner, 2001).

While useful, Heckhausen & Kuhl's (1985) description of the decision-making process is an oversimplification in two important ways. First, intentions associated with a specific decision to act are not fixed (Tyler, 1973). As environmental circumstances change and motives are reconsidered, intent for a specific activity may fluctuate. Second, people routinely engage in a number of willful acts each day, forming intent for each activity. Thus, it could be said that an individual has multiple intentions in that he or she forms intent for multiple activities. Often these activities compete for important resources of time and attention. To manage available resources, individual students utilize specific self-regulatory strategies to accomplish their learning goals (Snow et al., 1996). These action-control strategies help handle competing intentions, manage distractions, and preserve persistence (Corno & Kanfer, 1993; Heckhausen & Kuhl, 1985; Kuhl & Kazen-Saad, 1989). In learning situations in which students are faced with conflicting intentions, often for learning activities not of their choosing yet important to their general educational goals, trade-offs and compromises are made. The trade-offs and compromises one makes are often situational. Understanding how this works for individual students is important.

## Intent and Self-Regulation

Zimmerman, Bonner, and Kovach (1996) have shown that students who self-regulate well tend to achieve scholastically. Possibly because self-regulated learners are aware of the information and skills they must possess, they take the necessary steps to acquire these items (Schunk & Zimmerman, 1994). Self-regulatory skills include the ability to set specific learning goals, use a variety of learning strategies, self-monitor learning progress, and systematically adapt efforts on the basis of learning outcomes. Eom and Reiser (2000) believe that self-regulatory skills can be learned. However, effective implementation of these skills is a matter of intrapersonal intelligence, and not all students self-regulate well even after receiving training (Gardner & Boix-Mansilla, 1994). Moreover, students who receive training and are believed to possess good self-regulatory skills may choose not to use their skills if they are not interested in the task (Schiefele, 1991).

Even capable students have to want to learn before they are willing to expend the effort required (Eom & Reiser, 2000; Mager & Pipe, 1984). Schiefele (1991) found that additional factors leading to students using specific self-regulatory learning strategies included students' beliefs about self-efficacy, locus of control, and task-orientation. One might conclude that having good self-regulatory skills will help a student learn more productively, but learners' intent for a learning activity ultimately determines the commitment and effort they are willing to make in order to learn what is expected of them.

## METHOD

### Research Approach

In experimental studies, researchers typically attempt to control for all the factors that affect learning in order to study a specific issue (Gay, 1996). Considering the complexity of factors that simultaneously influence learning, the practice of controlling for factors is not only difficult, it has limited our understanding of educational issues (Snow et al., 1996). Intent is a construct, an aspect of consciousness, and as such it is difficult to measure (Rychlak, 1997; Tyler, 1973). In addition, an individual's intent may vary depending on the specific educational situation the learner is experiencing. For this reason, some theorists argue that we will learn more about individual difference constructs through analyses of "person-situation" interactions using both general constructs and rich situational descriptions. In addition, generalizations about teaching and learning cannot be validated without studying personal differences and situational differences jointly (Snow et al., 1996). For both theoretical and practical reasons we need to study the function of learner intent as it exists in real educational settings. Therefore, this research used a hermeneutic phenomenological approach to explore the construct of intent in online learning situations. The focus of these phenomenological observations was to understand the phenomenon of learner intent by observing, questioning, and gathering stories from students involved in the experience as they attempt to learn online.

### Research Design

This study was implemented using four phases of investigation. The first phase was a pilot study, designed to help refine interview techniques and to determine interview questions that best led to a discussion about the phenomenon of intent. Phase 2 was carried out over an 8-week period and followed students as they completed an online course. In Phase 3, students who had recently completed an online course were interviewed and asked to reflect and comment on their experience. The final stage involved assembling, interpreting, and reporting the data.

### Participants

Participants were selected from willing students taking a semester online course. This was completed by e-mailing students currently enrolled in an online course and asking whether they would be willing to participate. Twenty students agreed to participate. Several of the student participants were enrolled in more than one online course, or had taken other semester online courses previously.

### Online Courses

Semester online courses are courses developed by the university to be taken online during the regular semester. Most of these courses were totally online with little or no instructor facilitation. A few of the online courses represented in this study did, however, contain a classroom component in the form of special lectures or optional labs with teaching assistants to help students with questions about assignments. In each case, the student participants were undergraduates or graduate students taking online courses as part of their regular course of study or as a required general elective.

### Data Collection

Because direct observation of students taking the online courses was impractical, this data collection included semistructured e-mail interview sessions with students as they studied online. Students were asked to provide responses once a week, with follow-up questions based on the insights they provided. Using e-mail interviews allowed students time to reflect on the questions before answering. It also allowed the researcher time to consider the response and decide on follow-up inquiries. The e-mail interviews consisted of one question each week, with follow-up questions as needed through the week to get students to elaborate on their answers. At the conclusion of the 8-week period of e-mail interviews, students were invited to participate in a face-to-face interview. During this interview they were asked to expand on their responses and comment on any interpretations the researcher had made about their experience.

### Data Analysis

Qualitative methods were used to analyze and present data from participant comments. Content analysis of these data was conducted using open coding and axial coding. Open coding entailed the initial breakdown of raw text into discrete conceptual categories that identified particular events. Axial coding was used to systematically link categories to contextual conditions, action/interaction strategies, and consequences, and to determine emergent themes. All student comments provided in this paper are a compilation of direct quotes from individual students.

## The Problematic Goal of Course Completion: Results and Discussion

While online and distance education courses have become more prevalent in both high school and postsecondary education, promised educational benefits have not always materialized. One of the major benefits of taking an online or distance education course is the control students have over the time, pace, and place of the instruction. Certainly this flexibility is an extremely important advantage for many students; one problematic side effect of this flexibility, however, is the likelihood that students will not find a convenient time to work on lessons. In fact, initial efforts to provide online courses were often deemed ineffective because large numbers of students failed to complete the courses they started (Bates, 1994; Stokes, 2000). As a result, much research has been done and a variety of techniques have been developed with the specific goal of getting students to complete their online courses. The efforts, techniques, and practices adopted by instructional designers, educational institutions, and teachers of online courses in general seem to have improved the completion rates of online and distance education courses (U.S. Department of Education, 2003). Yet while much concern and effort has gone into improving course completion rates, some solutions have had unanticipated adverse affects on learning. One should not assume that student learning is the natural outcome guaranteed as a result of course completion.

Unfortunately, students in formal learning situations often do not spontaneously engage in cognitive activities that foster understanding unless required (Sandberg & Barnard, 1997). And, while learning is often a reason students give for taking a specific online course, most students who enroll in these courses for academic credit plan on completing course requirements as quickly as possible while expending minimal effort on the learning expected of them (Davies, 2002). Compounding this problem is the fact that design strategies in many online courses tend to encourage students to complete assessments and assignments without requiring them to fully engage themselves in the content. As a result, more students now take and complete online courses, but many fail to take the time necessary to adequately practice and reflect on course material, resulting in only superficial, temporary learning.

Nelson and Stoltermann (2003) suggest that this is because students generally approach learning challenges either as a "design action" or a "problem action." Learner intent that is derived from a need to succeed or a fear of failure is a problem action; the learning effort expended as a result is draining, and seldom will a student do more than what is absolutely necessary. Learner intent that is based on a passion to learn, a hope of increasing one's abilities, or a love for the topic is a design action that generates synergetic energy and a desire to do more.

The problem with having course completion as a main focus or primary goal is that it is a problem action that tends to supplant any real desire to learn in favor of substitute forms of academic success. Students generally equate academic success with the understanding and retention of useful information and skills that benefit them in some way; complicating the issue is the fact that they also believe that getting high grades and completing courses indicates academic success. One involves learning, the other, grades and recognition of course completion.

Ideally, students say that they want to both learn and get good grades. However, when students find that they cannot obtain success in both learning and grades, they compromise; more often than not, that means sacrificing learning for grades. Clearly, academic success associated with grades is something students do not give up easily. The following student comments illustrate this point.

> I'm a little bit anal about grades...I really like to learn the material and I wish that I had, but at a certain point I felt like I wasn't getting [help from the instructor] and I wasn't clearly understanding it, so I just sort of thought, well I'm not going to learn this material as well as I would like to [and] I still want to get a good grade. Because, I mean, in classes you can not know the material and still do well in a lot of classes; so then I did want to learn it initially, but after a while it was like, forget it, I just want to get a good grade and get it over with. So definitely success is both grades and understanding. (student comment)

> When I can apply what I learned to real life and when I can remember it to apply it [then I've succeeded]. To be completely honest I usually study to pass and not to achieve successful learning. (student comment)

> [It's] not just the grade but yah it's like the grade; it reflects how much I've gained, how much I've got; it probably reflects how well I did in the class and probably I say oh I didn't learn well. So maybe it's like probably I took it for the wrong reason in the first place but still I think I need[ed] to take a class...when it came down to it. [I] had two reasons for taking the course but one became more important...you [do] what you need to do to get the grade

even though you couldn't do what you needed to do to learn the information. (student comment)

Ultimately, the goal of course completion adversely affects learning when instructional design strategies emphasize or focus too much on course completion. When this happens, a common unintended consequence is that students choose to complete rather than to learn. Goals are not synonymous with intentions, but understanding what students believe to be the focus of their striving helps us understand their intent for learning and why they choose not to learn when their goals conflict with their desire to learn.

## Promoting Online Learning

Reigeluth & Beatty (2003) point out that there are many reasons why students fail to learn; lacking the opportunity to receive a high-quality education is but one reason. In fact, students often learn in spite of severely inadequate instruction and less-than-perfect learning environments (Keller & Suzuki, 1988). Of educational importance is the fact that when a learner's intentions are centered on course completion, actually learning something becomes an expendable objective. When a student's intentions focus on learning, instructional imperfections are more easily overcome, students are energized and inspired, and course completion becomes a natural consequence of the experience, rather than an artificial indicator that learning may have occurred.

The purpose of providing instruction, online or otherwise, is to promote learning (Gagne, Briggs, & Wager, 1992). There are many reasons why an online course might be offered as a method for delivering instruction; few online courses, however, can be categorized as instructional, and fewer still as high-quality instruction (Merrill, 1997; Weiss, & Pasley, 2004). This is especially problematic with asynchronous online independent study courses taken for school credit when the instruction and testing are automated and largely unregulated. An abundance of independent study online courses seem to rely on the assumption that providing a course online empowers students to learn on their own. Unfortunately, most high school and college students who take independent study courses online take them for remedial course credit (i.e., they have failed a course and need to take it again) or accelerated graduation (i.e., they want to finish ahead of schedule, and the course fills a requirement); they do only the tasks assigned them, review only the material they know will be tested, and forget the material soon afterwards (Davies & Mendenhall, 1998; Davies, 2002; Martinez, 1998). A key factor in changing this trend is to promote learning as a primary goal with course completion dependant on student learning instead of task completion. This requires a fundamental shift in the way we think about online instruction and the administration practices currently being used to facilitate them.

## Conditions and Practices That De-emphasize Learning

In formal learning situations, the part of the course that provides students with learning resources, incorporates learning strategies and activities meant to accomplish learning objectives, or makes use of formative assessment and feedback to support learning, is called instruction. Course administration practices (i.e., rules and procedures) facilitate the instructional component of a course and help it happen. In different ways, certain practices in both these areas tend to de-emphasize learning and should be modified or discontinued so that learning, not task completion, becomes the primary objective of the course.

## Administrative Practices

Examples of administrative practices that tend to suppress learning include allowing students to overload their schedules, setting arbitrary course completion deadlines, and misusing assessment practices and policies.

### Schedule Overload

> I figured that if I took an online course then I could fit it in when it was convenient; I originally signed up for the course just because it was required. It was simply a way for me to squeeze in another class. [In the end] I just felt so pressured for time this semester; I didn't know if I was that motivated to take the course at all. (student comment)

> I didn't spend as much time [studying as] I thought [I should]....I realize I could have done better....I got really busy. (student comment)

Allowing students to overload their schedule is an administrative practice that increases the likelihood that students will have to limit the time and attention they spend on any particular course. Because students tend not to relinquish course completion goals when faced with conflicting intentions, students more often abandon learning in favor of task completion.

## Arbitrary Deadlines

> Do I want to learn or just graduate so I can go get a job? I think [I should say] what do I want to learn? Instead of saying—I need to get this done just before the deadline; see that's a hard thing because you want to get it done by the deadline. (student comment)

> I get easily distracted especially when my roommates are around....I easily forget about [my studies] and get behind; then I'd have to catch up and do like four quizzes in one day so I could go take the midterm or try to finish it before the deadline because I had forgotten about it. (student comment)

Forcing online courses to fit a semester-long program not only defeats the "at your own pace" benefit of taking an asynchronous independent study course, but in many educational institutions, most courses have completion deadlines set near or on the same day. Because students tend to procrastinate, setting arbitrary completion deadlines for such courses means students again are faced with the prospect of choosing between course completion and learning. On the other hand, the difficulty with allowing totally open completion deadlines is the possibility that students may never find the time to complete a course. Clearly, a compromise solution needs to be reached. Intermediate task and course completion deadlines need to be set realistically based on reasonable expectations of what students will be able to accomplish, keeping in mind that students often abandon learning goals for course completion when overwhelmed.

## Inadequate Assessment and Feedback Policies

> Do you realize how easy it is to cheat? One student completes the chapter and quiz then prints it off with all of the correct answers for the other students to use. (student comment)

> This course was first at the bottom of my priorities. The course itself is pretty easy, after all, the quizzes are open book and you can repeat the quizzes as many times as you would like, then simply use the best score. I feel that repeating the quiz is somewhat of a loophole in the program. Some people might just take the quizzes without reading the material and rely solely on the combination of luck and this loophole. (student comment)

> [The] e-mail [the instructor] sent out. He said please don't call me, this is an online course...and that's when I knew there was not going to be that support system. To tell you the truth I think that I will do OK in the course; I think I'll get a decent grade...but my attitude [for learning] was not as good. (student comment)

The use of formative assessment when linked with appropriate feedback can be an effective instructional strategy. Students can greatly benefit from an honest assessment of their learning gains throughout a course. However, students quickly figure out, and often take advantage of, loopholes to avoid learning if they are allowed.

## Instructional Practices

Along with the administrative practices that deter students from learning, the design and quality of online instruction may also promote the development of poor learner intent. Flawed instructional practices that impede learning include poor assessment and feedback, inappropriate levels of difficulty, and generally useless instructional strategies.

### Poor Assessment and Feedback

> Having the same kind of quiz after the end of each chapter instead of giving you a chance to write about your feelings or a paper about something you found interesting or how does this apply to me. It just got boring; so toward the end I just kind of went down and skimmed for the answers. I was just focused on finding the answer not on learning. (student comment)

> When I really sat down and started doing lessons, I did them as quickly as I could. I did it all in two days, which obviously wasn't very good. I probably would have gotten a lot more out of it if I had actually paced myself and tried to learn something from it; but if you're so rushed just trying to find the answers then you don't learn anything, which is what I was doing. (student comment)

> I never [went] back and reviewed and I [didn't] take notes. I feel I learned the material well enough for the tests and quizzes, they were easy, but I don't know how much I will retain when the class is over. Those new topics I learned, I have already forgotten. (student comment)

Assessment for any course is an extremely challenging task. It is difficult to accurately measure what a student knows or has learned. Given the practical limitations of using technology and the challenges of the online environment, online assessment is extremely difficult to do well. Many online courses inappropriately assume that students will utilize scores from multiple-choice self-check quizzes and practice assignments with automated scoring to regulate their study and improve their understanding. The scores from these flawed assessments are then used as an indicator of successful learning. Task completion indicators do not measure learning gains; more often they suppress them. Assessments that are too easy or that do not properly measure the learning objectives sterilize the experience for the learner.

### Inappropriate Level of Difficulty

If it's too easy you actually have to want to learn to learn the material...but I can't think of another word for it. Challenged perhaps; yah, be a little more challenged. Because that's when you learn the material a little bit more because you're thinking there must be something in here that the teacher really wants me to learn instead of the teacher saying we'll just give them all A's because we'll make this class really easy. (student comment)

When something becomes a struggle that's when I decide [it's] kind of getting hard and the time that I put into the lessons are less. (student comment)

For my Philosophy class, it was almost in one ear and out the other. I didn't understand many of the concepts while I was taking the course and I didn't feel like I got much help from my professor in clarifying. Either consciously or unconsciously I kind of gave up on trying to understand the ideas. (student comment)

I've had some experiences with other general elective [online] classes where the amount of work is over and above, I mean it's a 102 class and [the work in this class outweighs] my 470 class like two or three times; well maybe just two times, but it [gets] so [it's] just not fun. It's a lot of work and the amount of pressure that's on you to do some things makes the course and the ideas in the course not fun; that makes me just want to turn off you know turn off ever thinking about it again. (student comment)

Research suggests that tasks which students find too hard or too easy decrease motivation and performance (Torrance, 1970). Online courses that are too demanding or pedagogically lack rigor tend to encourage students to abandon any real intention to learn the course content. Designers of online instruction who reduce the difficulty (i.e., required rigor) of a course in order to increase course completion rates may limit or eliminate learning.

### Ineffective Instructional Material and Strategies

To get through the chapters they would tell us one to two hours but if you were just to get through it fast you could get through it in a half hour. I was getting through them as fast as I could, in a half hour; but probably every two to three days [I would] spend a few hours doing the assignments. I didn't want to do it at all or I did do it quickly and not pay attention I'd just get through it and take the quizzes and get my points. So most of the things I learned went in one ear and out the other. (student comment)

Sometimes the reading assignments online were a little lengthy; you just get kind of tired sitting forever. For this course, honestly, I didn't really study....I get to the point where I don't care. The "I don't care" is a release. It will work out; it doesn't matter. (student comment)

In the beginning I was really good about studying to see if I knew the answers before [taking the quizzes] but by the end it just got boring to me [reading and taking a quiz] so toward the end I just skimmed for the answers. (student comment)

Not all instruction is, or ever will be, enjoyed by students; after all, learning can be hard work. Still, when online courses use telecommunications technology to deliver independent study courses but fail to utilize instructional technologies and strategies that facilitate learning, students may as well be given a textbook to read. Most high school and postsecondary online courses are offered as glorified or convenient self-study options. Too many of these courses provide information in the form of required reading, check that the reading was completed using unregulated, automated, self-check quizzes and assignments, and then use these assessments and a similar final exam as evidence that learning occurred; this is not instruction (Merrill, 1997). Rarely do students taking this type of online course choose to learn; their intent to learn is diminished by the tedious task of fulfilling course requirements they see as irrelevant or boring.

## Conditions and Practices That Promote Learning

Compare the comments about online learning above with comments of students taking an online accounting course.

In accounting, I hated it at first. I thought it was a really dumb idea [taking it online] because I felt that I was getting robbed because I wasn't in class with a teacher where I could ask questions; but as it went along, it was an easier way to learn....I got into it after I saw that it was a good idea. Once I believed that [it was] a great learning experience...it was awesome. (student comment)

The first course, accounting, it grabbed me; it was a very attractive course to me and it kept my attention the whole way through. I was always wanting to pick it up again. [My other online] class really, it was more of a thing that I just needed to do, something I needed to get done, where accounting I wanted to do it...[my other class] sits on the back burners until I have time for it. It is important that I get it done, but it doesn't matter to me. (student comment)

This instructor's actions facilitated learning and encouraged student reflection about his or her own intent. Reflective reasoning, actually thinking about one's commitment to learning and the quality of that learning, can be a catalyst in the formation of intent (Davies, 2003). What may be missing in many learning situations is the component of students reflecting on themselves as learners, specifically, reflecting on their true intentions for the learning expected of them. What is it about this accounting course that made students excited about learning? The key difference was the instructor's intentions. The individual who designed the instruction and taught the course made it clear to students in a number of ways that the purpose and function of this online course was to facilitate student learning. Unlike other courses, students indicated that this instructor emphasized the fact that the course content was not easy, but he expected them to be able to learn. Students understood that should the online instruction fail to facilitate their learning, they could contact the instructor for assistance by phone, e-mail, or by appointment. In fact, he invited and encouraged them to do so. The instructor used technology not just to deliver information, but also to enhance the instruction (e.g., video clips of interesting guest speakers and special explanations of challenging topics). The assignments and assessments used a variety of appropriate formats and were both challenging and comprehensive. Most everything the instructor did for this course conveyed to the students the message that learning was important, not just getting the course done.

There are no simple solutions or course templates that can guarantee students will be intent on learning. The curricular content and learning objectives of each course must be used to determine which instructional and assessment strategies are best. Certain practices, when adopted together, encourage students to focus on learning rather than on course completion. They include (a) having a policy of individualized acceptance into a course based on the expectation that students maintain reasonable course loads as much as possible; (b) setting intermediate task and course completion deadlines reasonably based on course content, not semester timelines, then make students responsible for any changes that need to be made for them personally; (c) basing the evaluation of administrative practices, policies, and decisions for online courses on whether they focus the student on learning instead of course or task completion; (d) ensuring test security (e.g., proctored exams, test banks); (e) using assessment instruments that measure the learning objectives, even if they are not convenient; (f) providing individualized formative feedback and monitoring that is focused on learning; and (g) making sure the online course provides instruction with practice, not just information, especially for difficult concepts.

Some of these suggestions are not cost-effective or easily implemented, but many online courses sacrifice learning for less-expensive practices and convenient policies. Overall, the design and implementation of any online course must make it clear to students that they are expected to learn, and that course completion is the result of them learning, not just finishing tasks.

## CONCLUSION

Some students are more diligent than others; they are better able to manage their time and put off motivationally enticing activities that are counterproductive to learning. Some students are more capable, more intelligent, or more able to learn than others. But having intent to learn does make a difference in a learner's effort. It often determines whether or not learning occurs and, as Osguthorpe (2000) affirms, it is a key factor to learning that lasts.

Online learning offers many potential benefits but tends not to produce learning unless the participating students' main intention is to learn and not merely to complete the course. Simply providing interesting information covering specific curricular content is not enough to promote learning. When the design of online courses deliberately or inadvertently promotes course completion as a primary goal, students often abandon any real intention of learning.

Some examples of how learner intent, and learning, can be adversely affected are as follows:

(a)  testing policies that do not require students to study;
(b)  allowing students to overload their schedule;
(c)  expecting students to learn within arbitrary deadlines unrelated to the course content;
(d)  setting an inappropriate level of difficulty for the course;
(e)  allowing assessment instruments to be used that fail to measure learning objectives adequately; and
(f)  the use of ineffective instructional strategies given the nature of the curricular content

In general, asynchronous online independent study courses are notoriously problematic (Merrill, 1997; Weiss, & Pasley, 2004). One should not assume that students have learned simply because they have completed the task requirement for this type of online course. Educational institutions that support and promote these types of courses often do so regardless of the fact that these online courses rarely offer an effective alternative to quality classroom instruction. The result is that more students now take and complete online courses, but many of these students achieve only superficial, temporary knowledge.

Learning is a natural human activity that can be facilitated with online instruction. Instructional technology can enhance instructional activities when the technology is used efficaciously and appropriately given the curricular content, and not just as a convenient delivery system for information. As those who design online instruction focus on instruction that promotes learning, and are aware of how certain conditions and practices may affect a student's intentions to learn, learning online will improve. A key factor in making this change is to promote learning as a primary goal with course completion dependent on student learning, rather than on task completion. This requires a fundamental shift in the way we think about online instruction and administration practices currently being used.

Suggested practices that help focus students on learning include: (a) ensuring that students maintain reasonable course loads so they have time to learn; (b) setting completion deadlines reasonably based on course content rather than on semester timelines; (c) evaluating all administrative practices, policies, and decisions based on whether they focus the student on learning; (d) ensuring test security and validity; (e) providing individualized formative feedback and monitoring; and (f) making sure the online course provides pedagogically sound instruction.

If online instruction is to be effective, along with quality instruction the main focus of the course must be learning. While it is important to ensure a reasonable rate of course completion, the primary purpose for developing an online course should be to provide students with effective instruction. The expectation that learning occurs must be communicated to students; not just through the instruction, but also through the administrative practices and policies that govern the course.

## REFERENCES

Ajzen, I. (1988). *Attitudes, personality, and behavior.* Chicago: Dorsey Press.

Amabile, T. (2001). Beyond talent: John Irving and the passionate craft of creativity. *American Psychologist, 56*(4), 333–336.

Anderson, L. W., & Bourke, S. F. (2000). *Assessing affective characteristics in the schools* (2nd ed.). Mahwah, NJ: Erlbaum.

Bandura, A. (2001). Social cognitive theory: An agentive perspective. *Annual Review of Psychology, 52*, 1–26.

Bates, A. W. (1994). Distance education, educational technology. In T. Husén & T. N. Postlethwaite (Eds.), *The international encyclopedia of education* (2nd ed., Vol. 3, pp. 1573–1580). Oxford, England: Elsevier Science.

Bereiter, C., & Scardamalia, M. (1993). *Surpassing ourselves: Inquiry into the nature and implications of expertise.* Chicago: Open Court.

Brentano, F. (1973). *Psychology from an empirical standpoint.* New York: Humanities Press.

Corno, L., & Kanfer, R. (1993). The role of volition in learning and performance. In L. Darling-Hammond (Ed.), *Review of research in education.* Washington, DC: American Educational Research Association.

Davies, R. (2002). *Exploring the meaning and function of learner intent for students taking online university courses.* Unpublished doctoral dissertation, Brigham Young University, Provo, UT.

Davies, R. (2003). Reflecting on learner intent. *Reflective Practice, 4*(3), 303–315.

Davies, R., & Mendenhall, R. (1998). *Evaluation comparison of online and classroom instruction for HEPE 129-fitness and lifestyle management course* (Evaluation project). Provo, UT: Brigham Young University, Department of Instructional Psychology and Technology. (ERIC Document Reproduction Service No. ED427752)

Eom, W., & Reiser, R. (2000). The effects of self-regulation and instructional control on performance and motivation in computer-based instruction. *International Journal of Instructional Media, 27*(3), 247–261.

Fishbein, M., & Ajzen, I. (1975). *Belief, attitude, intention, and behavior: An introduction to theory and research.* Reading, MA: Addison-Wesley.

Gagne, R. M., Briggs, L. J., & Wager, W. W., (1992). *Principles of instructional design* (4th ed.). New York: Harcourt Brace Jovanovich.

Gardner, H. (1993). *Frames of mind: The theory of multiple intelligences.* New York: Basic Books.

Gardner, H., & Boix-Mansilla, V. (1994). Teaching for understanding in the disciplines and beyond. *Teachers College Record, 96,* 198–218.

Gay, L. R. (1996). *Educational research: Competencies for analysis and application* (5th ed.). Englewood Cliffs, NJ: Prentice-Hall.

Gibbs, G. (1992). Improving the quality of student learning through course design. In R. Barnett (Ed.), *Learning to effect* (pp. 149–165). Buckingham, England: Social Research in Higher Education/Open University.

Gordon, J., & Zemke, R. (2000). The attack on ISD. *Training, 27,* 43–53.

Green, T. F. (1999). *Voices: The educational formation of conscience.* Notre Dame, IN: University of Notre Dame Press.

Heckhausen, H., & Kuhl, J. (1985). From wishes to action: The dead ends and short cuts on the long way to action. In M. Frese & J. Sabini (Eds.), *Goal-directed behavior: Psychological theory and research on action* (pp. 134–160; 367–395). Hillsdale, NJ: Erlbaum.

Jackson, D. (1994). *The exploration of a selection of conative constructs relevant to learning and performance* (Project 2.3). National Center for Research on Evaluation, Standards, and Student Testing, Los Angeles, CA. (ERIC Document Reproduction Service No. ED379300)

Jackson, D., & Snow, R. (1992). *Assessment of conative constructs for educational research and evaluation: A catalogue.* National Center for Research on Evaluation, Standards, and Student Testing, Los Angeles, CA. (ERIC Document Reproduction Service No. ED351388)

Keller, J. M. (1983). Motivational design of instruction. In C. M. Reigeltuth (Ed.), *Instructional design theories and models: An overview of their current status* (pp. 386–430). Hillsdale, NJ: Erlbaum.

Keller, J. M., & Suzuki, K. (1988). Use of ARCS motivational model in courseware design. In D. H. Jonassen (Ed.), *Instructional designs for microcomputer courseware* (pp. 401–434). Hillsdale, NJ: Erlbaum.

Kuhl, J. (1990, July). *Self-regulation: A new theory for old applications.* Paper presented as the keynote address at the XXII International Congress of Applied Psychology, Kyoto, Japan.

Kuhl, J., & Kazen-Saad, M. (1989). Volition and self-regulation: Memory mechanisms mediating the maintenance of intentions. In W. A. Hersberger (Ed.), *Volitional action* (pp. 387–407). Dordrect, The Netherlands: Nijhoff.

Mager, R., & Pipe, P. (1984). *Analyzing performance problems: Or you really oughta wanna* (2nd ed.). Belmont, CA: Pitman Management and Training.

Malle, B. F., & Knobe, J. (2001). Desire and intention. In B. F. Malle, L. J. Moses, & D. A. Baldwin (Eds.), *Intentions and intentionality* (pp. 45–67). Cambridge, MA: MIT Press.

Martinez, M. (1998). *Intentional learning and learning orientations.* Retrieved June 29, 2004, from Brigham Young University, Expert Learning Communities Research Program Web site: http://mse.byu.edu/projects/elc/ilsum.htm

McCarty, H., & Siccone, F. (2001). *Motivating your students: Before you can teach them, you have to reach them.* Boston: Allyn and Bacon.

Merrill, M. D. (1997). Instructional strategies that teach. *CBT Solutions,* November/December, 1–11.

Merrill, M. D. (2002). First principles of instruction. *Educational Technology Research & Development, 50*(3), 43–59.

Messick, S. J. (1979). Potential use of non-cognitive measurement in education. *Journal of Educational Psychology, 71,* 281–292.

Montessori, M. (1995). *The absorbent mind.* New York: Henry Holt.

Nelson, H., & Stoltermann, E. (2003). *The design way: Intentional change in an unpredictable world.* Englewood Cliffs, NJ: Educational Technology.

Osguthorpe, R. T. (2000, July). Teaching that lifts, learning that lasts. Paper presented at the Conference on Reflective Practice, Worcester, England.

Pervin, L. (1983). The stasis and flow of behavior: Toward a theory of goals. In M. Page (Ed.), *Personality: Current theory and research* (pp. 1–53). Lincoln: University of Nebraska Press.

Pratt, D. (1998). *Five perspectives on teaching in adult and higher education.* Melbourne, FL: Krieger.

Raven, J. (1992). A model of competence, motivation, and behaviors, and a paradigm for assessment. In H. Berlack (Ed.), *Toward a new science of educational testing and assessment* (pp. 81–97). Albany, NY: SUNY Press.

Reigeluth, C., & Beatty, B. (2003). Why children are left behind and what we can do about it. *Educational Technology, 43*(5), 24–32.

Renninger, K. A., Hidi, S., & Krapp, A. D. (1992). *The role of interest in learning and development.* Hillsdale, NJ: Erlbaum.

Richey, R. C., Fields, D. C., Foxon, M., Roberts, R. C., Spannaus, T., & Spector, J. M. (2001). *Instructional design competencies: The standards* (3rd ed.). Syracuse, NY: ERIC Clearinghouse on Information & Technology. (ERIC Document Reproduction Service No. ED453803)

Ryan, T. (1970). *Intentional behavior: An approach to human motivation.* New York: Ronald Press.

Rychlak, J. (1997). *In defense of human consciousness.* Washington, DC: American Psychological Association.

Sandberg, J., & Barnard, Y. (1997). Deep learning is difficult. *Instructional Science, 25,* 15–36.

Schiefele, U. (1991). Interest, learning, and motivation. *Educational Psychologist, 26,* 299–323.

Schunk, D. H., & Zimmerman, B. J. (1994). *Self-regulation of learning and performance issues and educational applications.* Hillsdale, NJ: Erlbaum.

Sierpinska, A. (1994). *Understanding in mathematics.* London: Falmer Press.

Snow, R., Corno, L., & Jackson, D. (1996). Individual differences in affective and conative functions. In D. C. Berliner & R. C. Calfee (Eds.), *Handbook of educational psychology* (pp. 243–310). New York: Macmillan.

Stokes, S. (2000). Preparing students to take online interactive courses. *The Internet and Higher Education, 2*(2–3), 161–169.

Torrance, E. P. (1970). *Encouraging creativity in the classroom.* Dubuque, IA: Wm. C. Brown.

Tyler, R. W. (1973). Assessing educational achievement in the affective domain. *Measurement in Education, 4*(3), 108.

U.S. Department of Education, Office of Postsecondary Education, Office of Policy, Planning and Innovation. (2003, July). *Second report to Congress on the Distance Education Demonstration Program.* Washington, DC: Author.

Warner, C. T. (2001). *Bonds that make us free: Healing our relationships coming to ourselves.* Salt Lake City, UT: Shadow Mountain.

Weiss, I., & Pasley, J (2004). What is high-quality instruction? *Educational Leadership, 61*(5), 24–28.

Weiss, R. (2000). Humanizing the online classroom: Principles of effective teaching in the online classroom. *New Directions for Teaching and Learning, 84,* 47–51.

Zimmerman, B. J., Bonner, S., & Kovach, R. (1996). *Developing self-regulated learners: Beyond achievement to self-efficacy.* Washington, DC: American Psychological Association.

Zimmerman, M. (1984). *An essay on human action.* New York: Peter Lang.

## CHAPTER 3

# AN EMERGING HYBRID MODEL FOR INTERACTIVE ONLINE LEARNING

**Martha Jeanne Yanes, Carmen M. Peña, and James B. Curts**
*University of Texas Pan American*

Principles of distance education recognize that effective online learning depends on the quality and quantity of opportunities for interactive learning. This chapter describes a trend that extends ideas from distance education about using Internet discussion technologies in face-to-face instructional settings with a hybrid model that integrates the use of online discussion. The theoretical basis for integrating online interactions in traditional instructional settings is presented along with examples from a study analyzing cognitive growth demonstrated in online student discussions in a teacher preparation course. Recommendations for planning and managing online discussions that merge face-to-face instruction with Web-based interaction are detailed.

### OVERVIEW

Student interaction in discussion is accepted as a desirable academic practice in university classrooms. The current trend toward constructivist

*Research on Enhancing the Interactivity of Online Learning*, pages 27–44

methods further emphasizes the importance of peer interaction and draws attention to the concept of social negotiation of meaning as an important factor in stimulating higher levels of thinking and in expanding learners' understanding. This concept has an instantly recognizable relevance in the context of developing habits of reflective thinking in teacher preparation programs. The use of Web-based discussion methods as used in distance education practice can provide new opportunities for peer interaction within traditional face-to-face (F2F) classes and can increase levels of student-student and student-teacher discourse.

## THEORETICAL FRAMEWORK

"The very process of generating dialogue, of having one's beliefs and ideas challenged, and of achieving equilibration, is necessary for provoking cognitive change" (Ehly & Topping, 1998, p. 36). The importance of dialogue and peer interaction is even more amplified when it is considered in the context of Vygotsky's understanding of sociocultural constructivism as a process for social negotiation of meaning.

> Vygotsky believed that an individual's immediate potential for cognitive growth is limited on the lower end by that which he or she can accomplish independently, and on the upper end by that which he or she can accomplish with the help of a more knowledgeable other such as a peer, tutor, or teacher. (Doolittle, 1997, p. 85)

The space for cognitive growth between the lower and upper ends is what Vygotsky referred to as the zone of proximal development (ZPD) (Doolittle, 1997). Within the ZPD, learners mutually benefit from social group processes, which create new means for learning and understanding through an exchange of ideas in reflective discussion. However, limited class time and the typical class trend of students acquiescing to the few most verbal participants (King, 2001) in F2F discussion invariably restrict reflective interaction by all students. According to Salomone (2004), the growing student diversity in areas of gender, race, ethnicity, and linguistic differences sometimes encumbers complete student participation in F2F discussion.

Such obstacles to student participation are of particular concern within contemporary teacher preparation programs that still call upon John Dewey's reflective thinking model to prepare teachers to be reflective practitioners. Peer interaction plays an important role in efforts to stimulate teachers' habits of reflective thinking, because peer feedback expands the individual's understanding of the teaching process. A reflective practitioner understands that improving one's teaching starts from within as a process of reflecting on one's own experiences (Canning, 1991; Cruikshank, 1987; Schon, 1983). Cooper (1999) extends ideas of the reflective process with the concept that the best way to learn about oneself as a teacher and directly influence the type of teacher one wants to be, is to reflect deeply, self-assess, and seek feedback from others. Reflective thinking contributes to the growth of higher order thinking skills, such as making inferences, synthesizing information, analyzing information, and evaluating information. Peer interaction, discussion of issues, and observations of classroom activity expand teachers' opportunity to learn about teaching practices.

The heightened awareness of learner interaction found in distance education research imparts approaches for enhancing student interaction. Based on Moore's (1989) delineation of the three levels of learner interaction (student-to-content, student-to-instructor, and student-to-student), there are several ways to improve student interaction (Moore & Kearsley, 1996). The use of both synchronous and asynchronous modes of communication within distance learning practice can enhance student interaction, because it provides a means for scaffolding on an individual level and within group process. According to Harrington (2002, p. 325), "computer conferencing activities can be uniquely structured to provide opportunities for communication that is educative." The use of asynchronous discussion boards in a traditional class allows students to participate more deeply because they "have had an active, multi-level learning experience that has given them a strong background in the subject...and [are] motivated to talk about it because they have personalized the material" (Creed, 1999, par. 6). Duffy, Dueber, & Hawley (1998) highlight the effectiveness of technology-based asynchronous applications in promoting reflective thought. The obvious difference between classroom and Web-based activity is that the asynchronous nature of Web-based discussion allows students to compose their thoughts, reflect, and review before making a contribution to the discussion. The delay time afforded by asynchronous computer-mediated discussion can encourage the participation of students who are reluctant to participate in traditional F2F classroom settings (Groeling, 1999).

Five major benefits emerge from research regarding the use of online discussion:

1. Online discussion fosters student interaction. Online discussion forums can increase the level of interactivity in the classroom. Discussion forums can be used to ask and answer questions, share experiences, provide support, give advice, reflect, and offer feedback. One consequence of the increased student interactivity is a greater sense of teamwork and collaboration (King, 2001).

2. Online discussion places learners in an active role. All students assume an active role, not just those who happen to be more extroverted (King, 2001). For an effective learning environment to exist, learners must be active participants. In an online discussion, everyone is accountable, because the instructor can easily determine who is and who is not responding; thus, students cannot simply remain silent as they often can and do in face-to-face classes. By virtue of the type of environment that online learning affords, students *must* be active learners.

3. Online discussion forums can enhance teacher-student relationships. Online discussion forums tend to democratize a classroom because they allow for divergent perspectives, balance power relations between teacher and students, give a voice to marginalized groups, and provide opportunities for thoughtful, reflective discourse that characterizes critical thinking. Also, in terms of practicality, they allow students to ask questions of the professor anytime and they allow the professor to respond at anytime. Online discussions forums also allow the professor and students to communicate privately as well as publicly. A result of the increased communication between professor and students is a greater feeling of connectedness (Romiszowski & Ravitz, 1997).

4. Online discussions encourage the use of higher order thinking skills. In terms of critical thinking skills, research demonstrates that online discussions allow students to improve their critiquing, questioning, and analyzing skills (Williams et al., 2001). Discussion forums also help students to make connections amongst related ideas and extend their thinking beyond the classroom (Williams et al., 2001).

5. The final benefit of online discussion forums is flexibility. There is the obvious flexibility of asynchronous discussions; that is, that they allow the professor and students to ask questions and respond to them at anytime. There is also the more subtle flexibility in terms of giving students more time to compose their answers before they post them, which often reflect a greater depth of thinking (Romiszowski & Ravitz, 1997).

Given the numerous benefits of online discussions and, specifically, the potential for cognitive growth that they offer, we decided to enact a study to track the level of students' cognitive growth and participation as a result of including online discussion activities in a traditional face-to-face class.

## METHOD

The study was conducted at the University of Texas Pan American to learn more about the value of online discussions in a F2F class during the summer semester of 2003, in a 4-week intensive teacher education graduate course on classroom assessment.

### Subjects

There were 32 participants in this study. The majority (80%) of the participants were female and of Hispanic origin (94%) and fully bilingual in English and Spanish. The subjects in this study had an average of nine years of teaching experience, and all were fully certified to teach in the state of Texas. A survey of students' technology backgrounds revealed that the majority had limited experience with technology and only 5% had participated in online discussion forums previously. All of the subjects were students in a graduate-level course on classroom assessment.

The course focused on assessment as a process of gathering information to make data-driven decisions to improve student learning. The course provided tools and practices designed to give teachers accurate information about the quality of student learning. WebCT was used as the communication platform for accessing course content, hypermedia presentations, group projects, and asynchronous discussion boards. The pedagogy entailed active, collaborative learning designed to promote student-instructor and student-student dialogue through the use of online discussions. Participation in the online discussions was required for all students and contributed to their overall grade for the course.

### Research Questions

Given that the purpose of this study was to track the cognitive progress of students as related to knowledge of a specific content area when using asynchronous discussion boards, we arrived at the following research questions as the focus of the study:

- How can cognitive progress be assessed using students' discussion postings?
- What was the change in cognitive level from the first to the last discussion posting?

## Analysis

A matrix was used to classify students' cognitive levels in online discussion postings and to document cognitive growth over time. The design of the matrix is presented in Table 3.1 and is based on an a priori set of categories adapted from Anderson and Krathwohl (2001).

**Table 3.1.   The Cognitive Progress Matrix**

| | *Cognitive Process Dimension* | | | | | |
|---|---|---|---|---|---|---|
| Knowledge Dimension | Know | Comprehend | Apply | Analyze | Synthesize | Evaluate |
| Factual | | | | | | |
| Conceptual | | | | | | |
| Procedural | | | | | | |
| Metacognitive | | | | | | |

The matrix represented in Table 3.1 was conceived as a chart of accounts to classify and document the progress of cognitive and knowledge assets of students' online discussions. It monitors the transition of students' basic declarative knowledge to more sophisticated knowledge structures that involve evaluation, critical analysis, and self-reflection. The idea is to analyze the verbs and noun phrases of selected discussion messages as follows:

1. Verbs are examined in the context of the Cognitive Process Dimension (Bloom's taxonomy: know, comprehend, apply, analyze, synthesize, and evaluate). It assumes that to know is more cognitively complex than to comprehend, and so on.

2. Noun phrases are classified in the Knowledge Dimension (factual, conceptual, procedural, and metacognitive). It is assumed that these four categories extend along a scale from concrete (factual) to abstract (metacognitive). Anderson and Krathwohl (2001) distinguish factual knowledge as "isolated bits of information" and conceptual knowledge as a more complex, organized knowledge that includes "mental models, schemas or implicit or explicit theories" (p. 28). Procedural knowledge is the familiarity of criteria of how to do something and when and where to use it. Metacognition is the awareness of and knowledge of one's own cognition.

One is aware that an online message will contain several verbs and noun phrases. Therefore, rules must be set up to guide how to code and classify a message into the matrix. One way of coding and classifying is to extract the verbs from the message and classify and count the frequency of occurrence.

The following is an example of one student excerpt (preassessment) responding to the first question of the course: Why do we assess students?

Message no. 13, Student no. 11
Date: Monday, July 7, 2003 12:14pm

The reason that I assess besides that it is required for us to do so, is basically to know what areas that need to be targeted so that the students may master those particular objectives or areas in which they are weak on. There are so many different ways to assess, but unfortunately with the TAKS test we have to limit the students to that, which I feel is not fair since all of us learn differently we must be given the opportunity to assess differently as well.

The noun phrase "there are so many different ways to assess" reveals the student's prior knowledge of the Texas Assessment of Knowledge and Skills (TAKS; Texas Education Agency, 2004), a state standardized test and its major drawback, that it limits the ways in which students can be assessed and does not consider multiple intelligences. This message contains some isolated bits of information and a rudimentary conceptualization of assessment. It also includes some concrete referents to important information about the TAKS and its limitations. This message can be classified as knowledge-factual (low cognitive scale in the upper left cell of the matrix).

Once a discussion message was classified, a numerical weight was assigned to allow further quantitative analysis. The cognitive process dimension was assigned a value from 1 to 6 because it is considered to grow in a linear fashion and the factual dimension was assigned a value from $e^0$ to $e^4$, because it is considered to grow exponentially. The sum of the row and column weights is shown in each cell in Table 3.2. As an example of the coding scheme used, a message classified as knowledge/metacognitive received a point value of 56 (1 for knowledge and 55 for metacognition). The scale point for the Cognitive Progress Matrix is shown in Table 3.2.

**Table 3.2.   Cognitive Level Weights in the Cognitive Progress Matrix.**

| Knowledge Dimension | *Cognitive Process Dimension* | | | | | |
|---|---|---|---|---|---|---|
| | Know (1) | Comprehend (2) | Apply (3) | Analyze (4) | Synthesize (5) | Evaluate (6) |
| Factual ($e^0$=1) | 2 | 3 | 4 | 5 | 6 | 7 |
| Conceptual ($e^1$=2.7) | 3.7 | 4.7 | 5.7 | 6.7 | 7.7 | 8.7 |
| Procedural ($e^3$=20) | 21 | 22 | 23 | 24 | 25 | 26 |
| Metacognitive ($e^4$=55) | 56 | 57 | 58 | 59 | 60 | 61 |

## RESULTS

The student data presented here correspond to the discussion question, Why do we assess students? For the purpose of this paper, Table 3.3 contains information on 5 subjects selected at random from a class population of 32. The table includes years of experience of each subject, gender, cognitive point value for the first posting in the discussion, and the cognitive point value for each of the students' last posting on a particular topic. Reliability coefficients (using Fisher's z transformation) were estimated for each student's message. Six coders classified the messages.

**Table 3.3.   Cognitive Progress Flow for a Random Sample of Students Answering the Message, Why Do We Assess Students?**

| Student ID | Gender | Years of classroom experience | Pre-assessment weight and reliability coefficient | Post-assessment weight and reliability coefficient |
|---|---|---|---|---|
| 11 | F | 14 | 2; 0.88 | 6.7; 0.81 |
| 24 | F | 8 | 3; 0.92 | 24; 0.95 |
| 17 | F | 10 | 4; 0.79 | 7.7; 0.80 |
| 9 | F | 12 | 3.7; 0.83 | 26; 0.69 |
| 12 | M | 6 | 3; 0.85 | 60; 0.71 |

The data in Table 3.3 revealed subjects' cognitive growth. There was a significant amount of cognitive growth at the end of the discussion. Due to the short length of the summer semester, the average time span between the beginning and end of a discussion was three days per topic. Nonetheless, there was still a high level of interaction as evidenced by the total of 1,088 postings for 8 topics. The 32 students averaged 4.25 postings per student. The data indicated that the use of discussion forums increased interactivity among participants, promoted and established a learning community beyond the classroom, and gave each student the opportunity to write and reflect on course topics.

Data also indicated that individuals with more years of teaching experience had a lower cognitive gain. In contrast, individuals with less teaching experience (e.g. Student 12) had a greater cognitive gain, supporting the premise that teachers can expand their understanding of teaching through peer interaction and scaffolding.

Finally, the data sample also showed that as postings became more complex in terms of cognitive level, the reliability coefficients tended to decrease (a reasonable reliability coefficient is greater than or equal to 0.80); the reliability coefficient was at or above the standard in all but two cases.

## RECOMMENDATIONS

To achieve the level of cognitive growth and interaction illustrated in this study, the authors followed a few practical guidelines for effectively planning and managing online discussions.

## Planning Online Discussions

Given the demonstrated pedagogical benefits of online discussion forums, it is important that educators learn how to plan and manage online discussions effectively. In planning online discussions there are several factors to be considered:

1. Types of questions
2. Purpose of questions
3. Number and pacing of questions
4. Asynchronous or synchronous discussions
5. The use of discussions

### Types of Questions

In composing discussion questions, it is important to consider the types of questions being asked and the extent to which they foster critical thinking skills. A useful guideline in developing questions is Bloom's taxonomy to ensure that the majority of questions are at the upper levels (Bloom, 1956). Generally, the level of question should progress from the lower to the upper levels of the taxonomy as students gain expertise (Boswell, 2002).

### Purpose of Questions

In planning online discussions, one should also consider the purpose of the questions. Discussion boards can be used to encourage students to reflect on readings, experiences, or video-based materials, and they can also be used to allow students to negotiate when working on group projects.

The effectiveness of discussion boards as a medium for reflecting on experiences was demonstrated in one study in which trainee teachers were sent out to schools to observe the teaching practices of cooperating teachers and to practice their own teaching skills (Khine & Lourdusamy, 2003). Students were then asked to share their experiences and observations of classroom management, discipline issues, teaching strategies, and any other significant events that occurred. Students were required to submit at least one posting on their personal experience and to reply to at least one other peer. In a survey, 90% of the teachers indicated that the online discussions were a valuable learning experience, because they allowed students to discuss their problems and share ideas (Khine & Lourdusamy, 2003).

### Number and Pacing of Questions

The number and pacing of questions also is an important consideration to prevent students from being overwhelmed. If a course meets once a week for three hours, faculty should consider how many questions could be discussed in that time frame given all of the other instructional activities involved. A reasonable requirement is one discussion per week (Slavit, 2002).

### Asynchronous Versus Synchronous Interactivity

Interactions can be synchronous or asynchronous. Synchronous interactions occur in real time and provide immediate feedback while asynchronous interactions provide delayed feedback. Each type of tool lends itself more easily to a different purpose. Research suggests that synchronous tools are better suited to social interaction (Im & Lee, 2004). In a study involving the use of online discussion forums, Im and Lee analyzed the interaction patterns of 40 preservice teachers. They found that the synchronous discussion forums were used more heavily to establish social bonds, while asynchronous discussions forums were used mostly for task-oriented activities.

There are several creative discussion techniques one can use to make both online and traditional face-to-face courses more interesting (Nader, 2002). One alternative to simply posting and answering questions is peer assessment. Students can submit their work to other students for comments based on an assessment rubric provided by the instructor. One benefit of peer assessment is that it can result in an increase in the quality of student writing because of the opportunities for writing afforded to students (Nader, 2002).

### Use of Discussions

Discussion boards can also be used to conduct virtual role-playing activities (Nader, 2002). Many students are intimidated at the thought of role-playing in front of a class; however, in an online class even the most reserved students are willing to engage in role-playing because the online forum provides a less threatening environment (Nader, 2002).

## Managing Online Discussions

### *Familiarize Students with Discussion Tools*

Because students may not know how to post to a discussion board, instructors should hold one face-to-face orientation session at the beginning of an online course, to teach students how to post to a discussion board. Following this orientation session, the instructor can give students a simple task such as introducing themselves online through the discussion board (Slavit, 2002).

### *Humanize the Environment*

For meaningful discourse to occur, the instructor must create a supportive and nonthreatening online environment (Nonis, Bronack, & Heaton, 2000). For example, students can be required to post a biography at the beginning of the semester (Poole, 2000). Instructors also can require students to include the name(s) of class members to whom they are responding in their messages to create a more personalized and unified atmosphere in the class (Poole, 2000).

### *Organize Discussion Topics*

Another key to managing online discussions effectively is to organize discussions into topics so that students can easily see what topics are being discussed (Driscoll, 1998). Organizing discussions into discrete topics allows students to quickly go to the correct discussion and post a response, and it also allows the instructor to grade postings more efficiently, as it prevents them from having to wade through a long list of messages (Driscoll, 1998).

### *Facilitate the Discussion*

Online discussions clearly have the potential to foster critical thinking and in-depth analysis, but this will not occur without the guidance of an effective moderator. It is the role of the moderator to teach and model critical thinking skills and in-depth thinking. Typically, in an online discussion there are a group of participants and one moderator. The role of the moderator is usually to start the discussion, keep it focused, and help participants reach a deeper level of analysis in their thinking. Shown below are questions a moderator can ask during an online discussion to extend and deepen participants' level of thinking and analysis (Berge, 1995):

- Clarification: What do you mean by that?
- Probe assumptions: What are you assuming?
- Probe reason: Give an example.
- Viewpoints: What would someone who disagrees say?
- Probe implications: What are you implying by your statement?

By responding to student postings with well-crafted questions, teachers can encourage students to engage in a deeper level of analysis (Knowlton & Knowlton, 2001).

Although instructors are responsible for shaping the general learning experience, and usually assume the responsibility of moderating online discussions, students, too, can moderate discussions. In fact, research indicates that students become more involved and responsible for their participation when a course is not driven entirely by the instructor (Cifuentes, Murphy, Segur, & Kodali, 1997). In one study, the instructor had each class member moderate the discussions for one week (Poole, 2000). Moderating assignments were made based on student interests and topic preferences. Prior to moderating a discussion, students were given an outline of their responsibilities as moderators. Upon completion of the course, several students commented that they appreciated their instructor's confidence in them. Clearly, allowing students to moderate not only creates a learner-centered environment, but also empowers students.

### Scaffold Discussions

Many times students may feel unprepared to participate in an online discussion. Instructors must ensure that students have the necessary background information needed to effectively participate in a discussion. Further, they should not only explain how to respond to a posting but should also model how to respond (Dewald, Scholz-Crane, Booth, & Levine, 2000; Ferdig & Roehler, 2004). Instructors need to model discursive practices; otherwise, students may simply reiterate information (Ferdig & Roehler, 2004).

In addition to modeling discursive practices, participants also need to be taught how to participate in an online discussion to take the conversation to a deeper level. Lucas (2002) demonstrated that by explicitly teaching participants how to participate in an online discussion, it is possible to significantly improve the quality of computer-mediated discussions. Each week, Lucas began a new discussion topic based on the material students were currently reading. He began each discussion with four or five posts consisting of questions, answers, or interest items. He then required students to post messages, and each time they posted a message they were required to (a) pose a question, (b) answer a question posed by someone else, or (c) provide an item of interest related to the topic being studied. Lucas reported 100 to 2,000 postings per week in a course of 20 students.

## Establish Guidelines for Discussions

### Netiquette

Prior to the use of online discussions, students need to be given a set of guidelines for online behavior (Fauske & Wade, 2004). Inappropriate or discourteous comments and personal attacks are less likely to occur when instructors specify rules of netiquette at the beginning of a class (Fauske & Wade, 2004). Several measures can be taken to ensure appropriate online communication:

1. Require that students use their names when posting to reduce incidences of flaming due to anonymity.
2. Make sure that students have met face-to-face prior to a discussion.
3. Allocate a certain percentage of credit to adhering to the rules of netiquette. Fauske and Wade (2004) reported a low occurrence of flaming and discourteous communication and attributed this to the fact that students were graded on how closely they followed the rules of netiquette.
4. Keep the discussion focused. It is recommended that instructors structure discussions around specific questions (Fauske & Wade, 2004).
5. Monitor discussions and intervene when a disruption occurs. Just as a professor would intervene when students engage in personal attacks in a classroom, he or she should also intervene when such attacks take place online (Fauske & Wade, 2004).

Although the lack of visual cues and the anonymity afforded by distance learning technologies can sometimes result in student conflict, the measures outlined here can significantly reduce the probability of conflicts occurring (Suler, 2002).

### Specify When Feedback Will Be Provided

Students need to be told when the instructor will provide feedback to online discussions to prevent them from developing unrealistic expectations (Driscoll, 1998).

### Format of Postings

Another guideline faculty must provide for their students concerns the format of the posting. Students may attempt, for example, to send their posting as an attachment instead of entering it directly in the body of the message. Providing a set of guidelines regarding the mechanics of posting ensures that all responses are easy to access and read (Driscoll, 1998).

*Specify Deadlines*

One key to managing a discussion effectively is to set deadlines for posting so that all students respond in the same time frame. A discussion cannot take place if students do not respond within a specific time frame (Driscoll, 1998).

*Specify Participation Requirements*

Prior to an online discussion, students should be given participation requirements. It is customary to have students post a reply to the instructor's posting and reply to at least one other classmate (Driscoll, 1998; Schrieber, 2002).

*Provide Feedback*

Following a discussion, instructors need to provide feedback regarding student participation. Postings should be graded based on pre-specified criteria such as clarity of expression, use of supporting evidence, and level of analysis (Driscoll, 1998). Further, the criteria being used to evaluate discussions also should be made available to students so that they can self-evaluate their own responses (Knowlton & Knowlton, 2001).

### *Specify* Different Roles of Students in a Discussion

When replying to another student, students should be made aware of the various roles they may assume in an online discussion. They may support another's viewpoint, take a different perspective, ask a question, provide information, or challenge a position. Students need to know that they can do much more than simply agree or disagree (Ferdig & Roehler, 2004).

## CONCLUSION

As this study demonstrates, online discussions can be used to promote students' cognitive growth. Further, this study also provides a mechanism for assessing and quantifying the level of cognitive growth. The study presented indicates that online discussion increases the level of student interaction in traditional instructional settings. Online tools such as discussion boards can be used in traditional face-to-face classes to enhance student interaction and to further the Vygotskian concept of social negotiation of meaning. Integrating the asynchronous format of typical distance learning discussion forums into traditional classroom procedures can afford students a beneficial delay time to carefully articulate their views, reflect, compare the views of others, and expand the meaning of the topic. This expanded opportunity for self-reflection is particularly valuable for teachers as a stimulus for reflective practice.

# REFERENCES

Anderson, L. W., & Krathwohl, D. R. (Eds.). (2001). *A taxonomy for learning, teaching, and assessing: A revision of Bloom's taxonomy of educational objectives.* New York: Longman.

Berge, Z. L. (1995). Facilitating computer conferencing: Recommendations from the field. *Educational Technology, 35*(1), 22–30.

Bloom, B. S., Englehart, M. D., Furst, E. J., Hill, W. H., & Krathwohl, D. R. (Eds.). (1956). *Taxonomy of educational objectives: The classification of educational goals. Handbook I: Cognitive domain.* New York: Longmans, Green.

Boswell, C. (2003, April). Well-planned online discussions promote critical thinking. *Online Classroom.* Retrieved April 15, 2004, from http://wilsontxt.hwwilson.com/pdfhtml/07445/AXEA3/USJ.htm

Canning, C. (1991). What teachers say about reflection. *Educational Leadership, 48,* 18–21.

Cifuentes, L., Murphy, K. L., Segur, R., & Kodali, S. (1997). Design considerations for computer conferences. *Journal of Research on Computing in Education, 30*(2), 177–201.

Cooper, J. M. (1999). The teacher as a decisionmaker. In J. M. Cooper (Ed.), *Classroom teaching skills* (6th ed., pp. 1–19). Boston: Hougton Mifflin.

Creed, T. (1999). A virtual communal space. *National Teaching and Learning Forum, 6*(5). Retrieved June 12, 2003, from http://employees.csbsju.edu/tcreed/vcs.html

Cruikshank, D. R. (1987). *Reflective teaching: The preparation of students of teaching.* Reston, VA: Association of Teacher Education.

Dewald, N., Scholz-Crane, A., Booth, A., & Levine, C. (2000). Information literacy at a distance: Instructional design issues. *Journal of Academic Librarianship, 26*(1), 33–44.

Doolittle, P. E. (1997). Vygotsky's zone of proximal development as theoretical foundation for cooperative learning. *Journal on Excellence in College Teaching, 8*(1), 83–103.

Driscoll, M. (1998). *Web-based training: Using technology to design adult learning experiences.* San Francisco: Jossey-Bass Pfeiffer.

Duffy, T., Dueber, B., & Hawley, C. (1998). Critical thinking in a distributed environment: A pedagogical base for the design of conferencing systems. In C. Bonk & K. King (Eds.), *Electronic collaborators: Learner-centered technologies for literacy, apprenticeship, and discourse* (pp. 25–78). Mahwah, NJ: Erlbaum.

Ehly, K., & Topping, K. (1998). *Peer-assisted learning.* Mahwah, NJ: Erlbaum.

Fauske, J., & Wade, E. (2004). Research to practice: Online conditions that foster democracy, community, and critical thinking in computer-mediated discussions. *Journal of Research on Technology in Education, 36*(2), 137–153.

Ferdig, R. E., & Roehler, L. R. (2004). Student uptake in electronic discussions: Examining online discourse in literacy preservice classrooms. *Journal of Research on Technology in Education, 36*(2), 119–136.

Groeling, T. (1999, September). Virtual discussion: Web-based discussion forums in political science. Paper presented at the national convention of the American Political Science Association, Atlanta, Georgia.

Harrington, H. L. (2002). Using computer conferencing to foster and assess prospective teacher's moral sensitivity. *Journal of Technology and Teacher Education, 10*(3), 323–342.

Im, Y., & Lee, O. (2004). Pedagogical implications of online discussion for pre-service teacher training. *Journal of Research on Technology in Education, 36*(2), 155–170.

Khine, M. S., & Lourdusamy, A. (2003). Blended learning approach in teacher education: Combining face-to-face instruction, multimedia viewing and online discussion. *British Journal of Educational Technology, 34*, 671–675.

King, K. P. (2001). Educators revitalize the classroom "bulletin board": A case study of the influence of online dialogue on face-to-face classes from an adult learning perspective. *Journal of Research on Computing in Education, 33*(4), 337–354.

Knowlton, D. S., & Knowlton, H. M. (2001). The context and content of online discussions: Making cyber-discussions viable for the secondary school curriculum. *American Secondary Education, 29*(4), 38–52.

Lucas, D. (2002). Structure encourages student participation in online discussions. *Online Classroom, 8*, 1.

Moore, M. (1989). Three types of interaction. *American Journal of Distance Education, 3*(2), 1–6.

Moore, M., & Kearsley, G. (1996). *Distance education: A systems view.* Belmont, CA: Wadsworth.

Nader, N. (2002). Online discussions? Text-based environment improves student writing. *Online Classroom, 8*, 9–10.

Nonis, A. S., Bronack, S. C., & Heaton, L. (2000). Web-based discussions: Building effective electronic communities for preservice technology education. *Journal of Technology and Teacher Education, 8*(1), 3–11.

Poole, D. M. (2000). Student participation in a discussion-oriented online course: A case study. *Journal of Research on Computing in Education, 33*(2), 162–177.

Romiszowski, A. J., & Ravitz, J. (1997). Computer-mediated communication. In C. R. Dilles & A. Romiszowski (Eds.), *Instructional developmental paradigms.* (pp. 745–768). Englewood Cliffs, NJ: Educational Technology Publications.

Salomone, R. (2004). The power of language in the classroom. *Thought & Action, 19*(2), 9–22.

Schon, D. A. (1983). *The reflective practitioner: How professionals think in action.* New York: Basic Books.

Schrieber, D. A. (2002, August 6). A non-constructivist approach to online discussions. *Online Classroom, 2.* Retrieved February 15, 2004, from http://wilsontxt.hwwilson.com/pdfhtml/07445/A5866/6S8.htm

Slavit, D. (2002). Expanding classroom discussion with an online medium. *Journal of Technology and Teacher Education, 10*(3), 407–422.

Suler, J. (2002). The basic psychological features of cyberspace. *The Psychology of Cyberspace.* Retrieved April 15, 2004, from http://www.rider.edu/suler/psycyber/basicfeat.html

Texas Education Agency, Student Assessment Division. (2004, May 27). Released TAKS™ tests: The use of TEA copyrighted materials. Retrieved February 15, 2004, from http://www.tea.state.tx.us/student.assessment/resources/release/taks/index.html

Vygotsky, L. S. (1978). *Mind in society: The development of higher psychological processes* (M. Cole, V. John-Steiner, S. Scribner & E. Souberman, Eds.). Cambridge, MA: Harvard University Press.

Williams, S. W., Watkinds, K., Daley, B., Courtenay, B., Davis, M., & Dymock, D. (2001). Facilitating cross-cultural online discussion groups: Implications for practice. *Distance Education, 22*(1), 151–167.

CHAPTER 4

# ASSESSMENT IN ONLINE LEARNING: ARE STUDENTS REALLY LEARNING?

**Jean Foster Herron and Vivian H. Wright**
*University of Alabama*

Online course offerings and enrollments have dramatically proliferated, especially since 2000. Such unbridled growth brings questions of student learning effectiveness and assessment, since many of the traditional assessment tools are not appropriate for the online environment. Interaction between faculty and students and students among other students remains key to learning, whether online or face-to-face (F2F). New assessment techniques may be used to gauge learning, some of which may have application in the F2F environment. Allowing assessment approaches to play a major role in the design of an online course may help answer issues regarding learning in the online environment as well as an F2F environment. The debates over online assessment have sparked review of all assessment techniques and generated innovative methods of assessment.

Online course offerings have dramatically proliferated in the last few years, likely driven by online enrollments, which grew from 1,344,000 students enrolled in 1997–1998 to 2,876,000 in 2000–2001 (Waits & Lewis, 2003), a growth of approximately 114% in a span of four years. According to *The Chronicle of Higher Education*, there was a "34% increase in the number

*Research on Enhancing the Interactivity of Online Learning*, pages 45–64

of users, from 47 million to 63 million from March, 2000 to September, 2002" (Pew Surveys, 2004, p. B29). Other sources report even more astounding numbers for courses offered and accompanying enrollments. For example, Johnson and Aragon (2003) report that during 1997–1998, "the use of asynchronous Internet-based technologies nearly tripled" (p. 31). The State University of New York (SUNY) posted phenomenal increases in a comparable time frame. SUNY reported "annual growth in courses, from eight [online courses] in 1995–96 to 1,000 in 1999–2000, and annual growth in enrollment, from 119 in 1995–1996 to over 10,000 in 1999–2000" (Fredericksen, Pickett, Shea, Pelz, & Swan, 2000, p. 8). And the growth in online activity does not stop there. The Student Learning Network (SLN) at SUNY expected to double its online enrollment each year, for the years 2000–2003 (Fredericksen et al., 2000). The Sloan Consortium reported that more than "1.6 million students took at least one online course during Fall 2002" (Allen & Seaman, 2003, p. 1) and "the number of students taking at least one online course is projected to increase by 19.8 percent over the one-year period from Fall 2002 to Fall 2003" (p. 1). It appears that these numbers will continue to grow.

Often in institutions of higher learning, change is not readily embraced, and rightly so in some cases. The aggregate faculty and administrators (often called "the Academy") in higher education institutions have the responsibility to monitor change that affects learning and to assess suggestions and implementations for change. Online learning has its skeptics in the Academy. The phenomenal growth and the new way of learning can be problematic for faculty as faculty roles shift from teacher-led learning to facilitated learning and more frequent interaction with individual students.

Assessing online learning is important. Learning effectiveness is at the core of education (Swan, 2003), but measuring learning is a difficult process in a traditional classroom, and potentially, even more so in a virtual classroom. For example, for students who are enrolled in an online course, nonverbal feedback that is received "through physical distance, eye contact, facial expression, and personal topics is not present for these individuals" (Johnson & Aragon, 2003, p. 41).

F2F classrooms may use survey instruments and tests to gauge learning, as well as assess daily attendance. Traditional means of assessment may shift to nontraditional means in an online course, such as examining participant engagement with the online course, interaction with course participants, and interaction with the instructor to determine attendance.

Since the student is the user of the online medium, what is the online student's assessment of his/her learning via this medium? Fredericksen et al. (2000) reported several indicators of perceived student learning.

Concluding from a quantitative study conducted at SUNY, these authors report, "Interaction with the teacher is the most significant contributor to perceived learning" (p. 24). Thurmond and Wambach (2004) agree, contending that interaction is the key factor and that there should be online interactions between "students and faculty, other students, and the course content" (Abstract section, par. 3). Swan (2003) writes that interaction is "central to the concepts of both learning and computer mediation" (p. 16). This is a move away from content- and teacher-centered methodology (Muirhead, 2002) to learner-centered methodology in which the faculty member is more of a facilitator (Gutierrez, as cited in Thurmond & Wambach, 2004). However, Swan also reports that research linking the interactions between instructor and student and their influence on learning effectiveness are inconclusive and are mostly grounded in the perceptions of learning held both by the student and the faculty member. If the quantity and quality of instruction interactions is linked to student learning (Swan, 2003), some suggest that online teachers should increase their virtual communication skills (Muirhead, 2002, Suggestions for Enhancing Online Interaction section, par. 1). Virtual communication skills may aid in interaction between and among students. Carr-Chellman and Duchastel (2000) noted that students in fact "learn as much from one another's experiences as they may from textbooks and provided information. This is particularly true for online courses which typically appeal to adult students actively engaged in full-time work" (p. 236).

At no other time in the history of higher education have there been so many inquiries into accountability for student learning, progress, and degree program viability. Funding for higher education has, in some states, been sharply reduced and any funding increase in the future may be linked to accountability. This climate of precise accountability for student learning creates severe constraints when a new learning format, such as online learning, is so rapidly growing in the number of students enrolled and the number of courses offered. Indeed, online learning may have additional appeal for both funding agencies and administrators, since it is a format that does not call for bricks and mortar for campuses and results in no physical maintenance. Another appeal is that online learning increases the access for students who do not reside on campus, allows students' work flexibility, and allows for adult students to spend more time with their families, all while advancing their education. The online format also reorders the importance of the role of the faculty member and the student.

In order to meet these calls for accountability and to demonstrate quality of product, assessment and demonstrated learning outcomes are probably the two most important features of online learning. Reeves (2000) contended that assessment of online learning is not to be conducted as it is or has been in a traditional classroom, and suggested that "traditional assessment measures are unlikely to reveal the complexities of the outcomes of student-centered online learning environments that are radically different from the dominant teacher-centered instructional paradigm" (p. 109). Reeves reported that traditional assessment has been based on knowledge recall and skills learned and applied in a few applications, written tests, and research papers. Robles and Braathen (2002) categorize this type of assessment as measuring "lower-level cognitive skills" (p. 41). According to Benson (2003), this type of assessment is at the lowest levels of Bloom's cognitive domain.

Reeves (2000) asserts that "alternative assessment" (p. 101) should be used in online formats. He proposes three approaches: (1) cognitive assessment, (2) performance assessment, and (3) portfolio assessment. Cognitive assessment relates to the development of critical thinking skills and more higher-ordered processing of information. Performance assessment is based on the student's application of the knowledge and skill learned to create a product that demonstrates learning (Haertel, as cited in Reeves, 2000). Performance assessment "measures learning in the psychomotor domain" (Zelif & Schultz, as cited in Benson, 2003, p. 70). Performance assessment is more complex and requires more synthesis of information than, for example, an objective paper and pencil test. Reeves's third alternative approach is portfolio assessment. A portfolio is a sample of work that grows over time with new products and learning activities being added as the student becomes more proficient at increasingly more difficult electronic tasks. It is not unusual to have students maintain and support a portfolio for a series of years as they progress through their program of college study.

While researchers have suggested that interactivity plays a large role in increasing student learning in an online course, what role does assessment of actual student learning play in future course offerings? We assert that assessment will guide the design of the course. Agreeing with this stance is Martin Oliver (2000) who reports that "the design of studies must be led by the aim of the evaluation, with ever greater levels of reflection and triangulation used to support studies" (p. 95). This chapter explores the literature in this important area and presents an overview of recommendations and implications to faculty (and future faculty) of online courses.

## METHODOLOGY

Because of its versatility, we used content analysis to identify online assessment themes or trends. Robson (1993) describes content analysis as "a refinement of ways that might be used by lay persons to describe and explain aspects of the world about them" (p. 275). Content analysis can be used to "identify the intentions, focus or communication trends of an individual, group or institution" (Writing@CSU, 2004, para. 1). Content analysis rose to importance in the early 1900s when investigations were being made into "yellow journalism" as quantitative research revealed that newsworthy items were being excluded and replaced with rumors, hearsay, and reports of corruption and scandals (Krippendorff, as cited in Robson, 1993). In our research, we were looking for trends regarding assessment in online courses. This topic has not been thoroughly addressed in the literature (Robles & Braathen, 2002).

In the search for documents regarding assessment, we used eleven different keyword descriptors:

- "online assessment"
- "online learning"
- "online student satisfaction"
- "online interaction"
- "online teaching and learning"
- "active learning"
- "online course evaluation"
- "quality online learning"
- "online instructional design"
- "alternative assessments"
- "traditional assessments"

These descriptors were used to search the Academic Search Elite database, the EBSCO publisher database, a research university's library catalogs, the Center for Applied Research in Educational Technology (CARET), online journals, texts, and conference presentations.

With the dynamic growth experienced in online offerings since 2000, we concentrated on publications beginning with that year through the current year of this research, 2004, identifying 47 potential resources. The themes that emerged regarding online assessment were categories of assessment, interaction, student perceptions of learning, self-assessment task performances, active learning, critical thinking, collaboration, and evidence of social presence.

One unexpected result of our searches was identification of the apparently rampant misconception regarding the often interchangeably used terms *assessment* and *evaluation*. According to Reeves (2000), assessment and evaluation are often used as though they were the same practice, but Zelif and Schultz report that "it is important to note the difference between assessment and evaluation" (as cited in Robles & Braathen, 2002, p. 42). Reeves describes assessment as "the activity of measuring student learning and other human characteristics such as aptitude and motivation, whereas evaluation is focused on judging the effectiveness and worth of educational programs and products" (p. 102). Some of the confusion may be due to the fact that the same data can be used for both purposes. For example, according to Reeves, a final grade in a course may be used to assess learning and be part of the grading process, yet the final grade may also be used to evaluate the course. Succinctly, Reeves suggests that "assessment" should be used when describing students and learning, while "evaluation" should be used for programs and products. Agreeing with Reeves, Robles and Braathen (2002) recommend that "online assessment should be viewed as a system for evaluating student academic achievement" (p. 39).

## CATEGORIES OF ASSESSMENT

Assessment can be categorized in several ways. One categorization method is to formulate the assessment approaches by purpose. According to Hanson, Millington, and Freewood, there are three categories: "1. diagnostic assessment; 2. formative assessment; and 3. summative assessment" (as cited in Benson, 2003, p. 70). Diagnostic assessment determines the student's skills for learning online and highlights potential learning problems. Formative assessment gives students information about their learning, describing what has taken place, but not adding to the overall assessment (Hanson, Millington, & Freewood, as cited in Benson, 2003). The purpose of formative assessment is to advance teaching and learning, not to give proof of acquired learning (Rovai, 2001). An example of summative assessment is using student evaluations of the instructor and the course, which does not contribute to student learning while they are taking the course (Zelif & Schultz, as cited in Robles & Braathen, 2002). Rovai (2000) equates summative assessment with assigning grades, a process that attempts to quantify the student's learning.

Others describe assessment as either direct or indirect and based on the student's understanding. Zelif and Schultz (as cited in Robles & Braathen, 2003) report that "assessing student work would be an indirect method of assessing student understanding of materials, while asking students if they understood the course content would be a direct method of assessing their understanding" (p. 41). However, a question that must be considered is whether we can be certain if students understand the materials when they say they do.

Another categorization of assessment methods is described as alternative and traditional assessment. Traditional assessment reports baseline cognitive skills and features the recall of facts and some comprehension (Zelif & Schultz, as cited in Robles & Braathen, 2002). According to Speck (2002), traditional assessment is the empty vessel and regurgitation method of measuring learning by answering test questions correctly and is at the baseline level of Bloom's cognitive domain (Robles & Braathen, 2002). True-or-false, fill-in-the-blanks, and multiple-choice tests are examples of traditional assessment. Traditional assessment is often found in the "traditional" F2F classroom, which may employ teacher-centered strategies.

Alternative assessment may include a number of approaches to gauge learning and is placed much higher on Bloom's scale. According to Benson (2003), "alternative assessment measures learning at the higher-order thinking of the cognitive domain (for example, application, analysis, synthesis, and evaluation), as well as learning that falls into the affective domain (for example, feelings, values, appreciation, enthusiasms, motivations, and attitudes)" (p. 70). Reeves (2000) refers to alternative assessment as "cognitive assessment" (p. 103) that seeks development of higher order thinking skills and includes some of the skills that help students "develop positive habits of mind such as commitment, motivation, and ethics, as well as higher order outcomes such as problem-solving, intellectual curiosity, and critical analysis" (p. 104). Included in this skill set are ideas about social learning and collaboration such as team activities, peer assessment, and self-evaluations (Benson, 2003, p. 70). These latter skills are more commonly provided by colleges and universities, in addition to knowledge about an academic discipline (Reeves, 2000). These skills are also more difficult to measure than is discipline knowledge and therefore may require a number of assessment tools, a tenet of alternative assessment.

Other categories of assessment are based on evident application of learning: performance assessment and portfolio development assessment. Performance assessment invites the use of another domain to assess learning: the psychomotor (Zelif & Schultz, as cited in Robles & Braathen, 2002). Performance assessment requires that the student display or "perform" the learning that has taken place. Reeves (2000) reported that "although it is not directly observable, deep conceptual knowledge can be inferred from students' performance on a range of cognitive assessments" (p. 107). Consequently, performance may be demonstrated in both the psychomotor and the cognitive domains.

Required components of performance assessment are that it (a) is focused on complex learning, (b) engages higher order thinking and problem-solving skills, (c) stimulates a wide range of active responses, (d) involves challenging tasks that require multiple steps, and (e) requires significant commitment of student time and effort (Linn, Baker, & Dunbar, as cited in Reeves, 2000, p. 108)

Another way to categorize assessment is to describe it as either traditional or authentic. Traditional assessment (described above) is more teacher-centered than is authentic assessment and relies on right or wrong answers to objective testing. Authentic assessment includes learning that is not just an acquisition of facts, but also provides the opportunity to use the information in a meaningful way, such as application to real life experiences (Rehak & Wise, n.d.). Authentic learning recognizes that students bring knowledge and experience to the classroom. Faculty and teachers should be capitalizing on that knowledge and experience and assist students in constructing their own knowledge base (Rehak & Wise, n.d.). (This valuing is a rich resource in the classroom and highlights the need to value students and their experiences in the classroom, whether F2F or online.) Among the examples of authentic learning are problem-based learning, project-based learning, performances, and portfolios.

No matter how the assessment categories are grouped, "the assessment process [of online courses] should be viewed as a system because there are many components to consider" (Robles & Braathen, 2002, p. 39). Hallmark components of assessment are "(1) measurement of the learning objectives, (2) self-assessments for students to measure their own achievement, and (3) interaction and feedback between and among instructors and students" (p. 40).

## ASSESSMENT TOOLS IDENTIFIED IN THE LITERATURE

### Interaction (Feedback)

Interaction was the almost universally named assessment tool for online learning. It is not just interaction between the student and the instructor, but interaction among other students in the course and interaction with the content of the course that are important as an assessment tool. Inarguably, interaction is the most important component of an online course and learning. No matter what the learning format, interaction is necessary for students to learn. Interaction has been defined as "the level of meaningful dialogue with the instructor, [and] in small groups among learners in the class" (Stein, 2004, p. 5). Wagner maintained that "interaction refers to reciprocal events involving at least two actors and/or objects and at least two actions in which the actors, objects and events mutually influence each other" (as cited in Swan, 2003, p. 16).

The design of the online course should include as many possibilities as are available for two interaction patterns: learner and faculty and learner and others in the course (Fredericksen et al., 2000). Dereshiwsky and Moan (2000) report that "students who are actively engaged in a timely series of relevant and interactive online activities are more likely to experience the maximal benefits of the instructional environment" (p. 9). Interaction between and among students is as critical as the interaction between a student and the instructor (Johnson & Aragon, 2003). Mende (as cited in

Sunal, Sunal, Odell, & Sundberg, 2003) reported a correlation between a student's level of participation in class postings and the likelihood that the student would produce a final product. This characteristic would allude to the likelihood of a student completing an online course. Lack of participation could be a danger signal that can be intercepted early. Swan (2003) adds a third type of interaction that is commingled with the other two, that is, learner and faculty and learner and other learners. This interaction occurs between the learner and the content.

> Broadly this interaction has to do with the learner's interaction with the course materials and so is primarily concerned with course design factors, but it plays out...across all the interactions. None of the interaction types operate in a stand alone manner. (Swan, 2003, p. 17)

All of these types of interaction interface with each other constantly during the online course. As Swan (2003) wrote, "Interaction among students, for example, is supported by instructor facilitation and support, and because it centers on content, can be seen as a variety of that type of interaction" (p. 16).

Interaction that includes feedback about performance should be completed immediately and should help learners understand and apply what they have learned. Students need to recognize the congruencies of what they have learned and what happens in their everyday lives (Robles & Braathen, 2002). Fredericksen et al. (2000) and Draves (as cited in Robles & Braathen, 2002) both argue convincingly that online courses encourage more interaction by all students than does a traditional classroom. In an online course, instead of just coming to class, the student must do something to make his or her presence known. One drawback to a traditional classroom that is remedied by an online classroom is that in a traditional classroom, when the instructor asks a question, usually the first student to answer the question is the only responder (Zelif & Schultz, as cited in Robles & Braathen, 2002).

Progressive disclosure of assignments supports student interaction with the content and the "construction" aspect of the learning procedure for online students (Dereshiwsky & Moan, 2000). Students quickly realize that almost daily interaction with the course Web site, and consequently the instructor and other students, is necessary in order to stay on task.

## Student Perceptions of Learning

Historically, student perceptions of what they have learned have been valued as an indicator of learning. According to Jones and Harmon (2003), student perceptions regarding whether the course was good or bad is a cornerstone of the course evaluation.

Fredericksen et al. (2000) surveyed the SUNY Learning Network participants in their asynchronous online courses. The researchers received replies from 1,406 students, for a 42% return rate. The results of this empirical study revealed that, statistically "interaction with the teacher is the most significant contributor to perceived learning in...online courses. Students who reported the highest levels of interaction with the teacher also reported the highest levels of perceived learning in the course" (p. 20). Fredericksen et al. also found that students, who were more active participants in their online courses than in their traditional classroom courses, reported "the highest levels of perceived learning" (p. 21). In the same study, interaction with classmates in an online environment was a "significant contributor to perceived learning in online courses as well. Students who reported the highest levels of interaction with classmates also reported the highest levels of perceived learning in the course" (p. 21).

Jiang and Ting's research results (2000) contradict the importance of interaction among students regarding perceived learning. However, their research results support the importance of interaction with the faculty. Jiang and Ting alleged that discussion played a role in the perceived learning of the student. Their "grade for discussion and requirements for discussion were significantly and positively correlated to students' perceived learning. It seems that students felt they had experienced better learning in courses, which emphasized online discussion" (p. 317). The researchers cautioned that interpretations of their findings were limited because of the small sample size (19 courses) and they encourage research using larger sample sizes.

Perceived learning is affected by the student's reasons for enrollment in an online course. Fredericksen et al. (2000) found that students taking courses because of convenience reported a higher degree of perceived learning than did students who were taking the online course because it was not being offered on campus.

Discussion plays a role in how much the student perceives she or he had learned. When posted discussions contributed more to a grade, the more satisfied the student, perception of learning increased, and the more students believed to have interacted with the faculty member and classmates (Fredericksen et al., 2000). In the same study, Fredericksen et al. found that gender affected the amount of perceived learning. According to the authors, "women reported higher levels of perceived learning than did men" (p. 24). Traditionally, males have dominated F2F traditional classrooms with their own conversations. In an online environment, gender may not be an issue and often, gender may not even be known.

Finally, student perceived learning could be considered as good an indicator of learning as any other measure. The student's perception may be the causal factor in undertaking coursework or other opportunities for learning in the future.

## Self-Assessment

Students should perform a personal self-assessment before enrolling in an online course and consistently after enrollment. This self-assessment should include honest personal observations about initiative, self-control, personal computer literacy, and the ability to accept the virtual environment of a course (Wade, 1999).

Self-assessment should be used to determine understanding of the course material. Feedback should be quickly provided for confirmation of learning. The capability for computer scoring makes immediate feedback possible (Robles & Braathen, 2002). Self-assessments can also be used to determine if a student is prepared to take an online exam. Practice exams or study guides are important in the role of self-assessment. For example, "a pre-test allows the instructor to have a form of measurement on which to base learning outcomes after the student has taken the post-test or the final exam" (Robles & Braathen, 2002, p. 45). Self-assessments also contribute to the student's involvement in his or her own learning.

Another use of self-assessment relates to modeling or having samples of assignments by which a student can determine the expectations of the instructor and the instructor can gauge a student's work and guide him or her in completing assignments. For example, one of the authors uses excellent products from the previous terms for resources. The resources are hyperlinked from the course syllabus and are accessible for students to use as a basis of comparison.

## Task/Performance Assessments

Task/performance assessment is a higher-order approach to assessment. Reeves (2000) suggested that this type of performance captures both cognitive and psychomotor domains. Reeves described performance assessment as spotlighting a student's use of the knowledge gained in the course in a murky, undefined context. In other words, only the general outline of what is expected is given to the student for a performance assessment. The way in which the student performs is in great part left up to him or her; thus, the activation of creativity.

## Portfolios

The development of portfolios may be considered to be a performance assessment by some, since it does exhibit learning; but it also depicts growth in learning since it is generally a work in progress. According to Knight (as cited in Reeves, 2002), portfolio assessment is "defined as any method by which a student's work is stored over time so that it can be reviewed in relationship to both process and product" (p. 108). For example, a student enrolls in a master's degree program in instructional technology. During the first course, the student is required to develop a Web page. During all subsequent courses in the program, the student adds to the site or continues to refine the site. Upon the completion of the program, the student has a portfolio that contains work samples from throughout the curriculum.

## Flyers and Newsletters

One of this chapter's authors uses the composition of a flyer and the creation of a newsletter for assessments. This approach is an embedded form of assessment. Both products require the use of technology requiring formatting, research, use of graphics, and synthesis of data. Higher order thinking skills are also required. In the case of the flyer, the students learn creativity and persuasion skills and the newsletter requires the student to be concise and discriminate among newsworthy items.

## Student-Led Conferences

Another innovative use of embedded assessment employed by one of this chapter's authors is a student-led conference that requires collaboration among the class members, researching with an assigned faculty member, preparation of an agenda, locating meeting room resources, developing promotional materials, advertising the conference, preparing invitations and, most importantly, presenting original research, either as a speaker, a roundtable discussion leader, or a poster presenter. A better understanding of conference logistics is part of the learning experience, as well as the experience of conducting research with a faculty member. Conference presentation is also practiced.

## Grades

Grades have traditionally been used to determine learning or understanding of material. Add to that the use of tests and quizzes to determine grades, and you have "instruments of the overall assessment plan" (Zelif & Schultz, as cited in Robles & Braathen, 2002, p. 42). Grade distribution does not tell an outsider what the student knows; that is, "grades cannot be used in isolation" (Wade, 1999, par. 8). Assessment should involve all of the domains; that is, cognitive, psychomotor, and affective, and be presented in a variety of ways.

For some instructors, course participation contributes to a grade. This is easily tallied in an online course using software that counts the number of times a student accesses the course Web site. Counters can also record the amount of time spent on the Web site or pages within the Web site. However, that is moderated by consideration of whether the student, and not a surrogate, is actually accessing the data.

## Writing

Writing, both online and in print, can be used as an example of student development and intellectual growth (Zelif & Schultz, as cited in Robles & Braathen, 2002). Writing responses to posted discussion questions in an asynchronous environment promotes thoughtful reflection for responses (Rovai, 2000; Shuey, 2002). The student is given time to formulate a response, framed to respond to either the instructor's discussion question or to another student's response. Viewing other students' writing in discussion responses also may serve as a model for the development of grammar and punctuation skills. Students may quickly evaluate their responses, thoughtfulness, and grammar and punctuation to the posted question in comparison to that of their classmates.

In some online courses, students may have to reconceptualize how to express their ideas in writing rather than in an oral discussion. There may be a side benefit for some students who have speech problems and are reluctant to participate in oral discussions (Canada, 2000).

Writing papers and using either the online attachment feature or a drop box may also be a form of assessment. The instructor may use the "track changes" or "insert" features (Benson, 2003) and permit the student to rewrite or correct. Peer review of writing may also be used in this manner. Group writing projects are especially efficient using the track changes feature.

## Active Learning

Active learning is critical to the success of an online course and "is more effective than passive learning" (Diamond, 1998, p. 156). Therefore, active learning should be included in an online course and some assessment of active learning should be present. Some examples of active online learning are "discovery learning, project-based learning, and cooperative learning...that involve considerable amounts of creativity, decision making, and problem solving" (Johnson & Aragon, 2003, p. 40). To facilitate this type of learning, the instructor should provide a variety of activities that are not centered on facts and are not "passive, top-down, vertical, lecture-oriented instruction" (Center for Instructional Technology, 2001, Active Learning section). Because this type of learning takes time to complete, persistent contemplation is required (Johnson & Aragon, 2003). This is characteristic of a higher order of learning as described in Bloom's taxonomy. Some of the activities associated with active learning are to "ask students to...locate essential content (fact-based); apply the content...synthesize the content; evaluate the content; reflect on findings, discuss, summarize"; and "using the discussion board, virtual classroom, or file sharing, present and discuss what has been learned" (Center for Instructional Technology, 2001, Generic Outline for Incorporating Active Learning Into On-line Environment section).

## Critical Thinking

Critical thinking skills can be promoted through online course interaction. Cognitive assessment reflects acquisition of critical thinking skills. Performance assessment may demonstrate critical thinking skills because integration of skills, data synthesis, task multisteps, and creativity are illustrated in a "performance." Problem-solving skills, collaboration, and real-life application are all examples of critical thinking skills.

Canada (2000) reported that online courses required students to write more and take a different approach to synthesizing knowledge. "In virtually every course, students at some time must make connections, interpret facts, and devise arguments through writing, usually by responding to essay exams or writing papers. But in an online course students have to write much more often" (p. 38). Swan (2003) praised online discussion as a positive contributor to critical thinking when reporting that "online discussion may be more supportive of experimentation, divergent thinking, exploring multiple perspectives, complex understanding and reflection than F2F discussion" (p. 13).

## Collaboration

Assessing online collaborative efforts can be accomplished via technology by providing opportunities for group work using software to communicate among group members. Because of the available tools, faculty can view the interaction among groups engaged in collaborative learning. Gray suggested "that group participation rubrics should include participation in group asynchronous discussion, participation in group synchronous discussion, group project grade, participation in drafting process, and participation in a peer preview of a draft" (Gray, as cited in Benson, 2003, p. 76). Benson (2003) has no reservations about the possibilities of learning from online groups, writing: "Individual and group projects can provide as high-level learning for online learners as they do for classroom learners" (p. 76).

## Social Presence

Students who feel comfortable and at ease with classmates and their instructor are engaged in the experience of social presence, and consequently may learn more (Yoon, as cited in Aragon, 2003). This level of comfort is necessary in both an online and a F2F environment. Some level of intimacy must be established in either format. The difficulty in promoting social presence in an online environment is attributed to the lack of F2F encounters with the instructor and the class members from which can be derived nonverbal cues and spoken cues (Swan, 2003). However, this can be overcome, and the online course instructor should take the lead role in creating relationships among and between students (Aragon, 2003). Creating social presence should not be an add-on to a course, but should be an integral part of the initial online course design (Aragon, 2003). Among Aragon's suggestions for creating social presence are a welcome page with audio and streaming video, if possible, and asking online students to create an information page about themselves, including a picture, brief bio, and e-mail addresses, and any other information they would like to share.

Class size may affect social presence. Aragon (2003) suggests that the maximum class size be set at 30, building in a dropout rate of approximately 17%. Because of the amount of interaction, the type of required assignments in an online course may also dictate enrollment caps; for example, fewer students if the course is more cumulative-assignment oriented or if there are less project-oriented tasks, which would permit more course enrollments.

Instructors who participate in discussion boards with their students add to social presence. When an instructor responds to students' posts by writing about student input, students feel valued and engage in the course more (Johnson, 2003).

The importance of a learning climate that reflects social presence cannot be overemphasized. Gunawardena and Zittle (as cited in Swan, 2003) report in two different studies that online students "rated the asynchronous discussion as highly interactive and social" (p. 15). Richardson and Swan adapted the Gunawardena and Zittle survey and found that "students' perceived learning, satisfaction with instructors, and perceptions of social presence were all highly correlated" (as cited in Swan, 2003, p. 15).

## THE FUTURE OF ONLINE ASSESSMENT

The debates over online assessment have fueled unexpected fallouts, as Northcote (2002) notes:

> One thing is certain—the increasing use of online assessment has not only renewed academic discussion of assessment design, it has also catalyzed the development of many innovative assessment examples across various course modes including online, distance, and on-campus courses. (p. 624)

Some writers conclude that online course delivery is contributing to the improvement of traditional classroom instruction. Sener (as cited in Sener & Humbert, 2003) reported that because online education has been held to a higher standard of scrutiny than classroom instruction, the resulting greater attention paid to evaluating online education, by using such measures as student satisfaction, has not only elevated the practice of online learning, but is starting to elevate the practice of traditional education, as well (p. 246).

Let us not be caught in the trap of being satisfied that online learning is only as good as traditional classroom teaching. Twigg (2001) asserts that would be a waste of online potential. The use of online learning tools has enormous potential to contribute to changing the way we teach and students learn.

It is incumbent upon the online educator to discover ways to show that student learning has taken place. Just one type of assessment will not suffice to measure all of the course objectives and anticipated outcomes (Zelif & Schultz, as cited in Robles & Braathen, 2002). There should be multiple types of assessment. This could be more equitable because of various learning styles.

Finally, Robles and Braathen (2002) view the questions regarding assessment as an opportunity. They write:

The opportunity for online education brings about new considerations in assessment. Online assessment is more than just testing and evaluation of students. By keeping in mind some basic tenets of assessment, online educators can adapt their assessment activities to provide useful feedback, accountability and opportunities to demonstrate quality. (p. 39)

## CONCLUSION

When considering the design of an online course, there should be accommodations for a variety of assessment possibilities. Assessment should drive the design of the course. Responding to research, both quantitative and qualitative, these assessment tools might include, but not be limited to, performance and authentic types of assessments, such as the use of portfolios, performances, and project-based learning, many of which rely upon interaction. As interaction appears to be the single greatest contributor to perceived learning by the student, it would seem that the online teacher should strive to increase virtual communication skills.

Through facilitated interactions between instructor and student, student and student, and student and content, the instructor can better create relationships in the online course, engage students in active learning, enhance students' critical thinking skills and ability to collaborate, and help establish a positive social presence experience. A key question for any instructor is, Are the students really learning in an online environment? Again, a multitude of assessments should drive the course design. Students' self-assessments may be encouraged through modeling efforts and self checks through reviewing past students' work. Portfolios may demonstrate student growth over time. Critical thinking and collaborative skills may be employed when addressing an issue through development of a performance or task such as a flyer, newsletter, or writing sample. We recommend the use of a variety of assessment tools that measure in all of the cognitive domains when designing an online course. One assessment is not enough. The growth of online courses and student enrollments will only continue to rise. Questions regarding online student assessment will continue to be asked. Longitudinal studies should be conducted to scientifically document the effectiveness or lack of effectiveness of online coursework on the retention of learning and the impact of online learning on students' other classroom experiences and learning. New instructional methodologies must be tested and proven not once, but several times to be not only as good as existing methodologies but also superior in promoting learning. Allowing assessment approaches to play a major role in the design of an online course may help answer questions regarding learning in the online environment as well as the F2F environment.

## REFERENCES

Allen, I. E., & Seaman, J. (2003, September). *Sizing the opportunity: The quality and extent of online education in the United States, 2002 and 2003.* Retrieved April 25, 2004, from the Sloan-C Web site: http://www.sloan-c.org/resources/sizing_opportunity.pdf

Aragon, S. R. (2003). Creating social presence in online environments. *New Directions for Adult and Continuing Education, 100,* 57–68.

Benson, A. (2003). Assessing participant learning in online environments. *New Direction for Adult and Continuing Education, 100,* 69–78.

Canada, M. (2000). Students as seekers in online courses. *New Directions for Teaching and Learning, 84,* 35–40.

Carr-Chellman, A., & Duchastel, P. (2000). The ideal online course [Electronic version]. *British Journal of Educational Technology, 31,* 229–245.

Center for Instructional Technology. (2001, December 3). *Active learning in on-line instruction.* Retrieved March 28, 2004, from http://ddls.jmu.edu/resources/activelearning.asp

Dereshiwsky, M., & Moan, E. (2000). Good connections: Strategies to maximize student engagement. *Education at a Distance, 14*(11), 1–11.

Diamond, R. (1998). Designing the learning experience. *Designing and assessing courses and curricula: A practical guide.* San Francisco: Jossey-Bass.

Fredericksen, E., Pickett, A., Shea, P., Pelz, W., & Swan, K. (2000, September). Student satisfaction and perceived learning with on-line courses: Principles and examples from the SUNY learning network. *Journal of Asynchronous Learning Networks, 4*(2), Article 1. Retrieved May 2, 2004, from http://www.aln.org/publications/jaln/v4n2/pdf/v4n2_fredericksen.pdf

Jiang, M., & Ting, E. (2000). A study of factors influencing students' perceived learning in a Web-based course environment. *International Journal of Educational Telecommunications, 6,* 317–331.

Johnson, J. (2003). *Distance education: The complete guide to design, delivery, and improvement.* New York: Teachers College Press.

Johnson, S., & Aragon, S. (2003). An instructional strategy framework for online learning environments. *New Directions for Adult and Continuing Education, 100,* 31–43.

Jones, M., & Harmon, S. (2003). What professors need to know about technology to assess on-line student learning. *New Directions for Teaching and Learning, 91,* 19–30.

Muirhead, B. (2002, July). Promoting online interaction in today's colleges and universities. *USDLA Journal, 19*(7). Retrieved January 30, 2004, from http://www.usdla.org/html/journal/JUL02_Issue/article04.html

Northcote, M. (2002). Online assessment: Friend, foe or fix? *British Journal of Educational Technology, 33,* 623–625.

Oliver, M. (2000). Evaluating online teaching and learning. *Information Services and Use, 20*(2/3), 83–102.

Pew Surveys. (2004, January 30). Instructional technology [Special section]. *The Chronicle of Higher Education,* B29.

Reeves, R. (2000). Alternative approaches for online learning environments in higher education. *Journal of Educational Computing Research, 23*(1), 101–111.

Rehak, J., & Wise, K. (n.d.). *Explicit examples of authentic learning.* Retrieved March 14, 2004, from http://tiger.coe.missouri.edu/~vlib/Kay.Janice's.stuff/Janice.Kay's.Page.html

Robles, M., & Braathen, S. (2002). Online assessment techniques. *The Delta Pi Epsilon Journal, 44*(1), 39–49.

Robson, C. (1993). *Real world research.* Malden, MA: Blackwell.

Rovai, A. (2000). Online and traditional assessments: What is the difference? *The Internet and Higher Education, 3,* 141–151.

Sener, J., & Humbert, J. (2003). Student satisfaction with online learning: An expanding universe. In J. Bourne & J. Moore (Eds.), *Elements of quality online education: Practice and direction* (pp. 245–259). Needham, MA: Sloan Center for Online Education.

Shuey, S. (2002). Assessing online learning in higher education. *Journal of Instruction Delivery System, 16*(2), 13–18.

Speck, B. (2002). Learning-teaching-assessment paradigms and the on-line classroom. *New Directions for Teaching and Learning, 91,* 5–18.

Stein, D. (2004, February). Student satisfaction depends on course structure. *Online Classroom, 1,* 5.

Sunal, D. W., Sunal, C. S., Odell, M., & Sundberg, C. W. (2003, Summer). Research-supported best practices for developing online learning. *Journal of Interactive Online Learning, 2*(1), Article 1. Retrieved May 29, 2004, from http://www.ncolr.org/jiol/archives/2003/summer/1/MS%2002029%20Sunal%20et%20al.pdf

Swan, K. (2003). Learning effectiveness: What the research tells us. In J. Bourne & J. Moore (Eds.), *Elements of quality online education; Practice and direction* (pp. 13–45). Needham, MA: Sloan Center for Online Education.

Thurmond, V., & Wambach, K. (2004, January). Understanding interactions in distance education: A review of the literature. *International Journal of Instructional Technology & Distance Learning, 1*(1), Article 2. Retrieved February 13, 2004, from http://itdl.org/journal/Jan_04/article02.htm

Twigg, C. (2001). *Innovations in online learning: Moving beyond no significant difference.* Paper presented at the Pew Learning and Technology Program 2001, Rensselaer Polytechnic Institute, Troy, NY. Retrieved March 21, 2004, from http://www.center.rpi.edu/PewSym/Mono4.html

Wade, W. (1999, October). What do students know and how do we know that they know it? *T.H.E. Journal, 27*(3). Retrieved May 2, 2004, from http://www.thejournal.com/magazine/vault/articleprintversion.cfm?aid=2291

Waits, T., & Lewis, L. (2003, July). *Distance education at degree-granting postsecondary institutions: 2000–2001.* Retrieved January 28, 2004, from http://nces.ed.gov/pubsearch/pubsinfo.asp?pubid=2003017

Writing@CSU. (2004). *Uses of content analysis.* Retrieved April 19, 2004, from http://writing.colostate.edu/references/research/content/com2a2.cfm

# CHAPTER 5

# AUTHENTIC ASSESSMENT THROUGH PROBLEM-BASED LEARNING IN THE ONLINE ENVIRONMENT

**Susan M. Powers, *Indiana State University***
**and**
**Lisa Dallas, *Eastern Illinois University***

Theory and research point to the relationship of problem-based learning (PBL) and authentic assessment to overall student learning. Translating these methodologies into the online learning environment can pose some potential challenges. A literature review reveals that PBL has a foundation within both computer-based instruction (CBI) and more traditional classroom instruction. Given the linkages between CBI and online learning, the presumption can be made that PBL can also find a home in Web-based instruction. Successful PBL scenarios within online instruction do need consideration of the desired learning outcomes, requisite technology skills, the support needed by both learners and instructors, as well as the time required to create effective online PBL. Despite these potential hurdles, excellent examples exist, among them simulations, gaming, and WebQuests.

*Research on Enhancing the Interactivity of Online Learning,* pages 65–78

The notion that students work harder when they understand how their learning connects with their culture, family, neighborhood, and personal concerns is an idea that has been around since John Dewey....It means that we [teachers] search for ways to help students translate the real dilemmas of their time...into the subject matter at hand. Passionate teaching can only be recognized, ultimately, in terms of students engaging in productive learning that connects with real-world problems and events. (Fried, 1995, p. 45)

## INTRODUCTION

Most individuals can recall that one passionate teacher in our academic lives who connected our learning to the real world and made us feel as though the work we were doing in the class had meaning and was relevant. However, our classrooms in the 21st century are not defined by desks, students in rows, blackboards, and a teacher up front. The word "cyber" defines many learning spaces. While the virtual, online classroom does not equate with tangible classroom elements, can an online class and instructor still resonate with the passion of teaching that connects real-world problems to learning? The challenge, therefore, is not only to bring the "passion" to the teaching, but also to use methods for assessing and evaluating students with this style of teaching and learning.

Assessment that addresses academic endeavors and efforts that have relevance beyond a classroom (physical or virtual) is considered to be authentic (Tanner, 2001). Authentic assessment works to create a learning environment that encourages students to transfer learning beyond the confines of the class. Authentic assessment requires the instructor to observe and evaluate student performance on tasks that reflect the real world or otherwise are intellectually worthy (Wiggins, 1990), rather than on tasks through which skill and knowledge can be inferred (i.e., examination or paper). Wiggins (1998) states that assessment becomes authentic when it is realistic, requires judgment and innovation, and asks the student to "do" (p. 22). Problem-based learning (PBL) is a tool for authentic assessment that can integrate the multiple facets of interdisciplinary learning, real-world experiences, and student motivation and engagement (Curtis, 2001). Educational technology has been shown to provide numerous opportunities for PBL. The challenge for educators is to conjoin the goals embedded within authentic assessment and potentials with PBL to the online, distance-learning environment.

This chapter strives to make the case for the role and potentiality of authentic assessment in the distance-learning environment by examining the literature related to PBL to demonstrate the potential and existing effectiveness of PBL in the online environment. An inverse pyramidic process was used to draw out the relevant research. First, it was important to examine the foundational premises of PBL. Even the most cursory analysis of the literature quickly reveals the foundational nature of Dewey to PBL. Next, much of what we know about designing effective instruction for the online learning environment comes from the literature on educational technology; therefore, it was determined to be important to continue building the case by learning from what the research has revealed about PBL in the area of computer-based instruction (CBI).

Research related to PBL and CBI covers many facets that range from implementation issues (e.g., learner control, design, learner characteristics) to research related to student achievement. Inasmuch as the World Wide Web that provides connective tissue and context for online learning emerged only in the early 1990s, it is important to draw upon related literature of similar learning environments. The literature in the area of CBI begins in the 1960s and a thorough presentation of that literature would be more encompassing than is needed here. Therefore, key journals in the field of instructional technology and seminal texts were used to examine the lessons that have been learned as to how PBL relates to CBI and its features that relate directly to online learning.

While the Web can be considered a relative newcomer, online, distance learning has quickly emerged in the literature as an area for empirical research with its own journals that are dedicated to research in the field. To explore the literature that discusses PBL in online learning, key peer-reviewed journals that are committed to research in distance education were examined across a five-year period and gleaned for relevant articles. Additionally, to ensure that discipline-specific studies were also captured, bibliographic databases were culled to find additional studies. Finally, to draw upon the literature related to pedagogical applications and implications of PBL and online learning, peer-reviewed journals devoted to issues of practice were examined. PBL does not ensure that authentic assessment practices are embraced and utilized. Rather, by understanding principles of PBL and their application to online learning, educators can elicit authentic performances and begin to create virtual learning environments where student achievement is based on authentic assessment.

## BACKGROUND OF PBL AND FOUNDATIONS IN TECHNOLOGY

"Thinking is objectively discoverable as that mode of serial responsive behavior to a problematic situation in which transition to the relatively settled and clear is effected" (Dewey, 1929/1988, p. 181). Although it could be considered that Socrates or Aristotle were the forefathers of PBL and the principles of constructed learning, in terms of modern education, the foundation of PBL can be found in the teachings of Dewey. PBL is not focused on memorization of facts and figures, but rather involves learners in deciding and managing their activities and course of action to synthesize and analyze information as a means to grow new knowledge and work towards a common goal to solve complex concepts (Solomon, 2003) and is aligned with brain research on learning (Erlauer, 2003, Wolfe, 2001). Support for this definition emerges from the work of Dewey (1938) when he theorized knowledge cannot be considered as something that is stagnant and constant, but rather exists as something that is an activity, a process of finding out.

The potentiality of PBL within a distance-learning environment is informed by research in the last several decades on effective PBL in a computer-mediated environment. CBI was introduced in the 1960s. Initial efforts at CBI focused upon programmed instruction; that is, instruction in which the software makes the learning decision and paths for the learner. Much of the research with CBI done to this point has been based upon the learning differences between programmed instruction and CBI in which learners have control, as well as upon what degree of learner control is most appropriate for different learning audiences (Williams, 1996). While there is evidence that learner control is not always the best choice for all learners (Lee, 2003), in the case of PBL, learner control in the CBI most parallels traditional delivery of PBL, and in turn mimics the hypertext, high learner control feature of online learning.

Technology can aid in the delivery of PBL by its very nature. Nuldén and Scheepers (1999) pose the possibility that the interactive, recursive nature of hypermedia allows learners to spend more meaningful and personally relevant time with the initial PBL scenario. Beyond just the presentation of the problem, CBI can also provide a support system for PBL and in turn make the process and learning environment more manageable for the instructor (Laffey, Tupper, Musser, & Wedman, 1998). Through interactive linking, data and document storage and retrieval, and multiple media for message delivery, CBI can provide support for PBL with scaffolding, coaching, and tools for planning, knowledge representation, communication/collaboration, and reflection.

Harada (2003) analyzed the literature to demonstrate that technology can, in fact, change the learning environment when integrated effectively into the educational environment. More specifically, technology can support discovery and creative construction by providing new options for knowledge representation *and* through the presentation of learning scenarios that are nonlinear and multisensory. Technology provides the ability to use simulations to drive problem-based inquiry that is process-oriented. Hypertext in CBI (and by extrapolation, online learning) is shown to be effective to "[help] students to integrate concepts, engage in problem-solving activities, and develop multifaceted mental representations and understandings" (Shapiro & Neiderhauser, 2004, p. 618).

## PBL IN DISTANCE ENVIRONMENTS

Distance learning, Web-based courses, and Internet classrooms all offer the opportunity for PBL and authentic assessment initiatives. Online learning does not lend itself well to structured test taking as a way to evaluate what the learner knows and understands (Alley & Jansak, 2001; McGrath, 2003c; Shuey, 2002). PBL focuses on a learner-centered approach as an educational goal and the online medium supports this type of learning (Murphy & Gazi, 2001; Wang, Poole, Harris, & Wangemann, 2001). Current research concerning PBL in the online environment is encouraging and shows positive learning outcomes (Erstad, 2002; Gibson, O'Reilly, & Hughes, 2002; Marchaim, 2001; McGrath, 2003c). Even more encouraging, these results have been found across diverse subject matter areas including science, theatre, marketing, English, health, history, and engineering education.

Lee and Tsai (2003) identified positive and higher levels of learning transfer as related to thinking styles among Internet PBL environments. Academic achievement and technology both support learning transfer. Lee and Tsai (2003) used the NetPBL tool and observed significant differences ($p < .05$, $p < .01$) in near transfer among the studied groups involved when Scheffe's analysis for posteriori comparisons was applied to the ANCOVA results. Using strength of association ($\omega^2 = .339$), the authors found that thinking styles influenced 33.9% of the total variation of near transfer. In addition to near transfer learning, cooperative learning involves foundations of PBL, due to its use of learner control of the learning environment and the involvement of collaboration with learning tasks.

A study completed by Singhanayok and Hooper (1998) observed a significant increase in knowledge construction through cooperative versus individual learning ($M = 11.60$, $SD = 4.35$ vs. $M = 9.34$, $SD = 3.57$) as determined by a comparison of posttest completion scores. Using the Tukey HSD analysis, results also showed cooperative learning delayed posttest scores higher ($M = 12.48$, $SD = 4.46$, $p = .0001$) than immediate posttests scores ($M = 10.72$, $SD = 4.22$). On the same analysis tool, individual learners scored significantly lower ($M = 9.33$, $SD = 3.64$, $p = .0004$) when compared to the cooperative learning group (Singhanayok & Hooper, 1998). Through a MANOVA analysis (Wilks's $\Lambda = .0458$; $F[10,80] = 3.83$, $p = .0003$), the authors attributed the increased and unusual higher delayed posttest score to higher time-on-task values and increased concept learning checks that occurred with the learners in the learner control and collaborative learning groups. This was followed by a univariate analysis of dependent measures for time on task ($F[2,44] = 11.85$, $p < .0001$) and concept learning tasks ($F[2,44] = 4.41$, $p = .018$). Elaboration (feedback provided) and/or categorical encoding (organism relationships tested) are possible explanations of the higher posttest scores observed for the cooperative-learning/learner control (Singhanayok & Hooper, 1998). Additionally, PBL success primarily depends on supportive technology and the prior work of the instructor before the class begins (Blumenfeld et al., 1991; Lee & Tsai, 2003; Singhanayok & Hooper, 1998).

## THE PEDAGOGY OF PBL IN ONLINE LEARNING

### Learning Outcome Goals

With the increased availability of inexpensive digital technology, students can begin to create original works as a way to express their knowledge and understanding of course objectives (Pellegrino & Altman, 1997). Instructors considering PBL in an online learning format need to evaluate the course content for projects that lend themselves to quality student learning outcomes. PBL projects contain two fundamental components: A challenging or driving question or issue that has meaning and value, and the resultant artifacts or products created and combined produce the final project as explained by the learner (McGrath, 2003a; Murphy & Gazi, 2001).

Once a topic is selected, the instructor needs to break it down into components to identify assessments and time frames of completion. Multiple, authentic assessments are necessary and need to allow enough time for learners to investigate, synthesize, and materialize an artifact before moving to their next step (Blumenfeld et al., 1991; Blumenfeld, Fishman, Krajckik, Marx, & Soloway, 2000; McGrath, 2003b; Murphy & Gazi, 2001). Characteristics of artifacts usually involve components of an observable and definable elements created by learners and ones that they can discuss and explain, such as a tangible object or model, audio or video creation, digital images, multimedia creation, and computer-aided instruction. Through the artifact, the instructor observes what students learned through the application of knowledge (Blumenfeld et al., 1991; Blumenfeld et al., 2000; Erstad, 2002; Murphy & Gazi, 2001). Likewise, the process of creating the artifact is where students learn the concepts they transfer to more permanent areas of memory (Erlauer, 2003; Gillani, 2003; Lee & Tsai, 2003; Wolfe, 2001) and where they have moved from being consumers of knowledge to creators of knowledge (Pellegrino & Altman, 1997).

## Skills and Necessary Technology

Both faculty and students will need to assess their cognitive and technological skill levels for PBL inclusion and success. Online learning encompasses computer literacy, technology literacy, and communication literacy. Computer literacy involves the hardware, software, and networking issues associated with online learning. Types of computer literacy elements include knowledge of an operating system (e.g., Windows, Mac, Linux), productivity software (e.g., word processing, slide show presentation, spreadsheet, database), Internet connectivity, and course management tools (e.g., WebCT, BlackBoard, TopClass). Technology literacy involves the various software programs and hardware devices that could potentially be used to both create and evaluate learner-generated artifacts. Examples of technology components might be a scanner, digital camera or video camera, CD±R/CD±RW, DVD±R/DVD±RW, Web camera, microphone, headphone, image manipulation and creation software (e.g., Paint, Photoshop, Flash, Fireworks, Freehand, Illustrator), and desktop publishing (e.g., Publisher, Quark, InDesign). Communication literacy involves the tools necessary to interact and track learners in online learning. Possible communication literacy tools might be a listserv, Web board, discussion board, chat, e-mail, and collaborative meeting software (e.g., WebEx). Each area of literacy offers opportunity and challenge for both the instructor and student when incorporated with online learning initiatives that include PBL.

## Support Issues

Faculty and institutions, which embrace authentic assessment as part of expected student outcomes, must be prepared to facilitate the resultant technological and pedagogical needs of students and faculty who operate in online learning environments.

### Faculty Support Issues

Faculty teaching in a distance-learning environment have several support issues. Ideally, local technology hardware and software support, network support, instructional support, and administrative support are available. Studies and articles have shown that the level of comprehensive support is directly related to instructor success with this type of learning (Cohen, 2001; Institute for Higher Education Policy, 2000; Mylott, 2003). Faculty support for PBL initiatives may involve interaction with educational technologists, consultants, and peers experienced with this type of learning. The instructional support specialist can assist the faculty member with topic identification, breakdown of clearly stated project requirements, and appropriate assessments. Since several assessments along a specific time line are required for PBL, the instructional specialist can help shape the scope and dimension of the project's assessments to ensure manageability for both the faculty and learner (Blumenfeld et al., 1991; Blumenfeld et al., 2000; Erstad, 2002; McGrath, 2003a; Murphy & Gazi, 2001).

Motivation is also a key to learner success. Careful project planning allows both the faculty and learner to visually and conceptually digest the necessary requirements. Faculty will need to develop examples of possible acceptable artifacts (Blumenfeld et al., 1991; Blumenfeld et al., 2000; Solomon, 2003). Another support mechanism for faculty is the identification and utilization of communities of practice relative to their subject area and PBL in the online environment. Communities of practice extend over a long period of time to allow members to grow and know each other and exist for encouragement and support (Lee & Tsai, 2003).

### Learner Support Issues

Students involved in online learning with a strong emphasis on PBL also need to have access to support beyond that which the instructor provides. Students should be able to expect help desk support, timely faculty feedback, and motivators throughout the learning experience. PBL environments can be overwhelming for learners when they are given freedom to plan their approach and at times plan their assessments. However, this freedom exists as a fragile balance between faculty direction and support with the student as an independent learner (Collison, Elbaum, Haavind, & Tinker, 2000; Meichenbaum & Biemiller, 1998). Either way, the faculty member needs to provide concrete guidelines, rubrics, and time frames for project phases to keep learners on track and motivated. Examples of what is permissible as an artifact for submission should be provided by the faculty member, to help students visualize expectations and relieve learner anxiety. Examples also help to relieve learner anxiety and to maintain motivation at each phase of the project.

Faculty need to be flexible, approachable, and timely with feedback for student inquiries. Faculty-generated resources and frequently asked questions (FAQ) information guides further aid students in their learning processes. The faculty will be facilitators in the PBL environment. Therefore, they are a primary support mechanism for learners. All of these practices follow good online teaching practice; however, they become paramount in online learning environments that use PBL initiatives.

Projects best suited for PBL, and in turn for online learning, involve the learner in the process of creating digital artifacts of information. As technology devices continue to decline in price and become more readily accessible, digital images, digital recordings of audio and video, as well as individual digital art creations are within the reach of most distance learners. Technology is inherent in online learning and lends itself nicely to PBL initiatives. Creativity is limited only by the faculty member, the learner, or both. Project success is dependent on faculty guidance and motivation (Blumenfeld et al., 2000; Erstad, 2002; Murphy & Gazi, 2001; Siegel, 2000).Creating Effective Projects for Online Learning

## Development Time

Prior planning is critical to successful PBL initiatives in distance learning environments (McGrath, 2003c; Solomon, 2003). The time factor is determined by topic, project scope, faculty, computer technology, and communication literacy. Individual faculty preparedness and capabilities will determine the window of development. PBL and online course development require substantial time commitment (Blumenfeld et al., 1991; Murphy & Gazi, 2001).

## Examples

Gillani (2003) presents a model for PBL in online environments that employ principles of constructivist theory to move the learner from reliance on others to self-reliance, much as Pellegrino and Altman (1997) describe the learner who moves to the role of knowledge creator in a technology-enriched environment. Some technology-enhanced PBL learning examples that exist or are compatible with online environments include WebQuests, gaming (Dede, Reigle, Squire, & Klopfer, 2004; Gredler, 2004), simulations (Gredler, 2004), and virtual learning scenarios (Canny, 2001; Mayer, Musser, & Remidez, 2001; McAllister, 2004). Murphy and Gazi (2001) used PBL activities for a graduate-level Web-based course for simulations, panel discussions, evaluations, role plays, and discussion. They found that successful PBL environments engaged students in authentic learning experiences, expected student collaboration, and used electronic communication tools to conduct collaboration. Yang and Huang (2003) designed a series of PBL activities for a Web-based historical curriculum using primary resources to promote discussion, interpretation, hypothesizing, triangulation, articulation, exploration, and summarization, similar to the concepts found in a WebQuest. They found the result to be an increase in student engagement to course topics. The following is presented as examples of different PBL learning scenarios that can be used in online learning environments. This list is by no means inclusive. Fortunately, online portals such as MERLOT (n.d.) provide links and descriptions to curriculum, lessons, simulations, and more tools for using PBL in higher education.

### WebQuests

A WebQuest is an inquiry project that uses the Web for not only presentation of the inquiry project but also as the basis for information retrieval (Dodge, n.d.). WebQuests have a structured format to encourage students to consider the information as outlined, rather than spend the time seeking the necessary information. Originally designed for the K–12 classroom, they are increasingly being developed for adult learners. WebQuests are process-oriented and are designed to not be an end point but to develop student skills to use real information sources to solve future problems (March, 2004). The problem solutions that a student team will develop can in turn be posted to the Web and therefore disseminated to others outside the classroom for comment and student feedback, increasing the authenticity of the assessment. Evaluation of student performance generally occurs from a rubric that targets specific processes and allows for student self-assessment and reflection as well. The end solution is not the goal as much as the process and efforts that were engaged to solve the problem. Well-designed WebQuests include an instructor's guide, as well as a recommended student evaluation rubric.

### Gaming

Virtual U represents one example of a gaming solution in PBL. Developed to put users in the role of a university president, the simulation forces the user to make decisions related to budget, hiring, athletics, infrastructure, and so forth, with every decision having an impact on other decisions (Foresight and Governance Project, 2002). Although it does not function as on online game, in which multiple players can play at one time, the software is used in graduate programs of higher education, including those offered at a distance, to aid in the understanding of the impact and complexity of decisions at the presidential level. Because of the complexity of Virtual U, the focus of student assessment would not be on the "correct" solution, because there is often not a correct solution in PBL and authentic assessment environments. Instead, rubrics are used to assess more authentically the degree to which students can justify their administrative decisions and acknowledge the outcomes of these decisions. However, gaming can be more than a project within a class. To capture student interest, increase motivation, and challenge students to engage in holistic PBL, Riegle (2003) has developed an online philosophy of education course that moves "players" through a series of "Tolkienesque" quests to solve problems that grow increasingly difficult, both in terms of education concept and in technology. Student grades are determined by the number of quests that are solved and whether the solution submitted adheres to pre-determined criteria. This example would be the farthest extreme of PBL in the online environment, inasmuch as it is the only learning strategy that students employ.

### Real-World PBL

Intelligence and espionage issues as PBL initiatives for business schools teaching online marketing courses are examples of the learning possibilities and real-world situations (Siegel, 2000). Students are required to create a competitive intelligence project, expanded competitive intelligence project, and an international marketing plan project in which students investigate the competitions' Web sites and other relevant materials for a particular business or industry (client). Students must interact with the client during each phase of each project to continually refine and develop the necessary components of each project. As a result, both client and student benefit from the final project. Students learn about the areas in which intelligence serves to enhance marketing strategies while also determining and weighing the ethics of the role of espionage as a way to gain competitive advantages (Siegel, 2000). Clients benefit from current analysis directly associated to their business and its competitors. In real-world PBL such as this example, effective authentic assessment is reached through a two-prong approach. Faculty have the opportunity to assess students according to predetermined standards and expectations. The authentic assessment occurs when the client is given the opportunity to provide feedback and assessment as to the usefulness of the business analysis or project.

## CONCLUSION

Returning to the original premise that PBL is an effective tool for authentic assessment, we need to understand why PBL learning and, therefore, authentic assessment, are important in an online learning environment. Authentic assessment is an effort to understand and assess in a meaningful way how learners perform when they must use their knowledge in meaningful, real-world tasks (Wiggins, 1990). In the 2000–2001 academic year, there were over 3 million enrollments in distance education courses (National Center for Educational Statistics, 2002). This number can only be expected to increase with time. We would be remiss to not consider methods that can be used to bring the most meaningful learning and assessment experiences to those students who choose or have to participate in online learning. Through initiating PBL learning experiences in the online learning environment, student learning can be more authentically assessed.

## REFERENCES

Alley, L. R., & Jansak, K. E. (2002). The ten keys to quality assurance and assessment in online learning. *Journal of Interactive Instruction Development, 13*(3), 3–23.

Blumenfeld, P. C., Fishman, B. J., Krajckik, J., Marx, R. W., & Soloway, E. (2000). Creating Usable Innovations in systemic reform: scaling up technology-embedded project-based science in urban schools. *Educational Psychologist, 35*(3), 149–164.

Blumenfeld, P. C., Soloway, E., Marx, R. W., Krajcik, J. S., Guzdial, M., & Palincsar, A. (1991). Motivating project-based learning: Sustaining the doing, supporting the learning. *Educational Psychologist, 26,* 369–398.

Canny, E. A. (2001). Virtual U: A simulation of university system management. *Information Technology, Learning, and Performance Journal, 19*(1), 55.

Cohen, D. E. (2001). The role of individual difference in the successful transition to online teaching. *Journal of Instruction Delivery Systems, 15*(3), 30–34.

Collison, G., Elbaum, B., Haavind, S., & Tinker, R. (2000). *Facilitating online learning: Effective strategies for moderators.* Madison, WI: Atwood.

Curtis, D. (2001). *Start with the pyramid.* Retrieved January 2, 2004, from http://www.glef.org/php/article.php?id=Art_884&key=037

Dede, C., Reigle, R., Squire, K., & Klopfer, E. (2004, February). *Video games and learning: The new big thing?* Paper presented at the annual meeting of the American Association for Colleges for Teacher Education, Chicago.

Dewey, J. (1938). *Logic: The theory of inquiry.* New York: Holt.

Dewey, J. (1988). *John Dewey: The later works, 1925–1953: Vol. 4. 1929: The quest for certainty* (J. A. Boydston, Ed.). Carbondale: Southern Illinois University Press. (Original work published 1929)

Dodge, B. (n.d.) *WebQuests.* Retrieved April 3, 2004, from http://webquest.org/

Erlauer, L. (2003). *The brain-compatible classroom: Using what we know about learning to improve teaching.* Alexandria, VA: Association for Supervision and Curriculum Development.

Erstad, O. (2002). Norwegian students using digital artifacts in project-based learning. *Journal of Computer Assisted Learning, 18,* 427–437.

Foresight and Governance Project, Woodrow Wilson International Center for Scholars (2002). *Serious games: Improving public policy through game-based learning and simulation* (Publication 2002–1). Retrieved April 3, 2004 from http://www.seriousgames.org/images/seriousarticle.pdf

Fried, R. L. (1995). *The passionate teacher.* Boston: Beacon Press.

Gibson, I. S., O'Reilly, C., & Hughes, M. (2002). Integration of ICT within a project-based learning environment. *European Journal of Engineering Education, 27*(1), 21–30.

Gillani, B. B. (2003). *Learning theories and the design of e-learning environments.* Lanham, MD: University Press of America.

Gredler, M. E. (2004). Games and simulations and their relationships to learning. In D. H. Jonassen (Ed.), *Handbook of research on educational communications and technology* (2nd ed., pp. 571–581). New York: Macmillan Library.

Harada, V. H. (2003). From instruction to construction. In M. A. Fitzgerald, M. Orey, & R. M. Branch (Eds.), *Educational media and technology yearbook 2003* (pp. 40–48). Littleton, CO: Libraries Unlimited.

Institute for Higher Education Policy. (2000). *Quality on the line—Benchmarks for success in Internet-based distance education.* Washington, DC: Author.

Laffey, J., Tupper, T., Musser, D., & Wedman, J. (1998). A computer-mediated support system for project-based learning. *ETR&D, 46*(1), 73, 86.

Lee, C. I., & Tsai, F. Y. (2003). Internet project-based learning environment: The effects of thinking styles on learning transfer. *Journal of Computer Assisted Learning, 20,* 31–39.

Lee, J. (2003). Do you want to be in control or not? In M. A. Fitzgerald, M. Orey, & R. M. Branch (Eds.), *Educational media and technology yearbook 2003* (pp. 49–63). New York: Macmillan Library.

March, T. (2004, May 13). *WebQuests for learning: Why WebQuests?, an introduction.* Retrieved May 13, 2004, from http://www.ozline.com/webquests/intro.html

Marchaim, U. (2001). High-school student research at Migal science institute in Israel. *Journal of Biological Education, 35*(4), 178–182.

Mayer, C., Musser, D., & Remidez, H. (2001). Description of a Web-driven, problem-based learning environment and study of the efficacy of implementation in educational leader preparation. In C. D. Maddux & D. L. Johnson (Eds.), *The Web in higher education: Assessing the impact and fulfilling the potential* (pp. 249–266). New York: Haworth Press.

McAllister, G. (2004, February). *Sim-school: Tag you're it.* Paper presented at the annual meeting of the American Association for Colleges for Teacher Education, Chicago.

McGrath, D. (2003a). Artifacts and understanding: What kinds of products should we consider having our students construct as a result of project-based learning (PBL)? What factors do we need to consider as we design project tasks? *Learning & Leading with Technology, 30*(5), 22–27.

McGrath, D. (2003b). Rubrics, portfolios, and tests, oh my! Assessing understanding in project-based learning. *Learning & Leading with Technology, 30*(8), 42–46.

McGrath, D. (2003c). We now join collaborative projects in progress; joining an existing online project not only makes getting started easier, but it can also serve as the model for designing your future projects. *Learning & Leading with Technology, 31*(6), 36–42.

Meichenbaum, D., & Biemiller, A. (1998). *Nurturing independent learners: Helping students take charge of their learning.* Cambridge, MA: Brookline Books.

MERLOT, Multimedia Educational Resource for Learning and Online Teaching. (n.d.). *Welcome to MERLOT.* Retrieved June 10, 2004, from http://www.merlot.org

Murphy, K., & Gazi, Y. (2001). Role plays, panel discussions and simulations: Project-based learning in a Web-based course. *Educational Media International, 38,* 261–270.

Mylott, D. (2003). Teaching and learning online: Challenges to the student and instructor. *Journal of Instruction Delivery Systems, 17*(3), 37–40.

National Center for Educational Statistics, U.S. Department of Education (2002). *Distance education at degree-granting postsecondary institutions, 2000–2001.*

Retrieved April 4, 2004, from http://nces.ed.gov/surveys/peqis/publica-tions/2003017/

Nuldén, U., & Scheepers, H. (1999). Interactive Multimedia and Problem-Based Learning: Experiencing Project Failure. *Journal of Educational Multimedia and Hypermedia, 8*(2), 189–215.

Pellegrino, J. W., & Altman, J. E. (1997). Information technology and teacher preparation: Some critical and illustrative solutions. *Peabody Journal of Education, 72*(1), 89–121.

Riegle, R. (2003). *EAF 228.* Retrieved April 3, 2004, from http://coe.ilstu.edu/rpriegle/eaf228/introduction.htm

Shapiro, L., & Niederhauser, D. (2004). Learning from hypertext. In D. H. Jonassen (Ed.), *Handbook of research on educational communications and technology* (2nd ed., pp. 605–620). New York: Macmillan Library.

Shuey, S. (2002). Assessing online learning in higher education. *Journal of Instruction Delivery Systems, 16*(2), 13–18.

Siegel, C. F. (2000). Introducing marketing students to business intelligence using project-based learning on the World Wide Web. *Journal of Marketing Education, 22*(2), 90–98.

Singhanayok, C., & Hooper, S. (1998). The effects of cooperative learning and learner control on students' achievement, option selections, and attitudes. *Educational Technology Research & Development, 46*(2), 17–33.

Solomon, G. (2003). Project-based learning: A primer. *Technology & Learning, 23*(6), 20–30.

Tanner, D. E. (2001). *Assessing academic achievement.* Boston: Allyn & Bacon.

Wang, M., Poole, M., Harris, B., & Wangemann, P. (2001). Promoting online collaborative learning experiences for teenagers. *Education Media International, 38,* 203–215.

Wiggins, G. (1990). The case for authentic assessment. *Practical Assessment, Research & Evaluation, 2*(2). Retrieved January 22, 2004, from http://PAREonline.net/getvn.asp?v=2&n=2

Wiggins, G. (1998). *Educative assessment: Designing assessments to inform and improve student performance.* San Francisco: Jossey-Bass.

Williams, M. D. (1996). Learner-control and instructional technologies. In D. H. Jonassen (Ed.), *Handbook of research for educational communications and technology* (pp. 957–983). New York: Simon & Schuster Macmillan.

Wolfe, P. (2001). *Brain matters: Translating research into classroom practice.* Alexandria, VA: Association for Supervision and Curriculum Development.

Yang, S. C., & Huang, L. J. (2003). Designing a Web-based historical curriculum to support student engagement. *Journal of Computer Assisted Learning, 19,* 249–253.

# CHAPTER 6

# COLLABORATING ON AN INTERACTIVE ONLINE STUDY GUIDE

**Catherine Collier**
*Roberts Wesleyan College*

This chapter discusses the impact of a shift in the major assignment of an online course from a traditional paper to an interactive study guide. The study involved 79 master's degree students, all of them K–12 teachers. Teacher reflections indicated that the interactive study guide assignment offered a richer learning experience and that the learning experiences will carry over to the K–12 classroom. Teachers gained in their writing and research abilities, responded with greater enthusiasm, and made use of more technology for reading, research, and writing than was the pattern in the past, often stretching their technical ability in their desire to succeed. The comparative study raises questions concerning the place of the traditional paper in online learning. Quantitative data concerning student use of technology for collaboration shows a marked increase in the use of real-time techniques (instant messaging, telephone, and face-to-face meetings). It is unclear what is behind this increase. Other uses of technology are consistent with that found in the research literature. The course experience suggests the following factors are important for success: preparation of students for collaboration, monitoring and active feedback, and planned reflection.

*Research on Enhancing the Interactivity of Online Learning,* pages 79–100
Copyright © 2006 by Information Age Publishing
All rights of reproduction in any form reserved.

The online graduate course Technology in Language Arts engages K–12 teachers in a variety of learning experiences that showcase innovative uses of technology to enhance reading and writing across the K–12 curriculum. From the beginning of the online class five years previous, the instructor has conducted research to understand the student experience and to improve the course, with particular attention to the major collaborative assignment. Scarafiotti (2003) discusses the merit of having faculty collect both quantitative and qualitative data for ongoing course improvement. The ongoing research associated with this course has led to modifications at regular intervals to ensure achievement of learning outcomes, student satisfaction, and instructor satisfaction (Collier & Morse, 1999, 2002; Yoder & Collier, 2003).

For the current study, the instructor modified the nature of the major assignment, shifting it from a traditional paper to more innovative use of technology. Teachers now were expected to collaborate in developing their own interactive, online learning activities. For the six semesters since the new assignment was introduced, research has focused on the following questions:

(a) Did changing the major assignment affect previous gains in writing and research skills?
(b) To what extent does the collaborative experience open teachers to further collaboration, more informed collaboration, and use of collaboration in their classrooms?
(c) Which aspects of the new assignment are teachers likely to carry into their classroom teaching experiences?

Additional attention was given to the concern of how the greater technical demands of the new assignment could be offset so that less technical teachers could still succeed.

This chapter discusses the new interactive assignment, the interactive study guide, and selectively reports the results of the research. Where appropriate, comparisons are made between experience with the traditional paper (Paper) and the new, interactive study guide (ISG). The chapter finishes with implications for other online courses and suggestions for further study.

## THEORETICAL BASIS FOR THE COLLABORATIVE, INTERACTIVE STUDY GUIDE

Four schools of thought informed the design of the new major assignment. First, the assignment is a collaborative undertaking; hence, the work of

Johnson and Johnson (1996) is an important underpinning, especially as more recently discussed in an online context by Curtis and Lawson (2001). Second, the English educator's perspective is important, particularly recent experience with multigenre (Moulton, 1999; Romano, 2000) and hypertext or hypermedia (Myers & Beach, 2001). Next, the WebQuest initiative of Dodge (Dodge, 1995) and the related Web Inquiry Project work of Molebash (Molebash, Dodge, Bell, Mason, & Irving, 2001) provide a basis for the interactive study guide as an inquiry-based, Web-oriented research activity. Finally, the design draws on Jonassen's conception of mindtools, particularly the application of multimedia for students to make meaning (Jonassen, Peck, Wilson, & Pfeiffer, 1998).

## COLLABORATION

The course was conceived as a network-based learning experience for teachers in a global classroom. Participants were never expected to meet face-to-face. Hence the power of the network for collaborative writing was an underlying design element. Early failure of collaborative assignments led to corrective action (Collier & Morse, 1999, 2002). Before introducing the new ISG assignment, the instructor tested the course design to ensure participants were well prepared for collaboration (Yoder & Collier, 2003). O'Regan's (2003) design considerations speak to several tenets of the current course design:

- Content is designed to make explicit the structure of the material and to facilitate the user's navigation through and awareness of location in that structure.
- Guidance is provided for appropriate, relevant, and constructive participation in discussion groups; responsibility is taken for moderation and facilitation of discussion groups.
- Posting processes are explicit with students receiving prompt and automatic acknowledgement when postings are received.
- Provision is made for class members to become known to each other as real people with their own idiosyncratic interests and characteristics. (p. 89)

## INTRODUCTION OF THE INTERACTIVE, ONLINE STUDY GUIDE ASSIGNMENT

While the redesigned course exhibited strength with regard to online collaboration, it had a weakness in the sense that the nature of the major collaborative assignment was a traditional paper. In its defense, the collaborative paper gave practice in the writing process and in the research process. Teachers generated questions of interest relevant to any topic within the scope of the course. Peer feedback contributed to the quality of the papers and the quality of the learning experience.

However, the instructor and others believed it was not enough, in the age of interactive hypermedia, to have participants use technology for text editing and to share their peer review through electronic communication. As "technoliteracy" theorists Lankshear and Snyder (2000) criticize, "literacy education continues to involve students learning and using 'old skills', but 'applying them in new ways' via new technology and new media" (p. 25). The nature of the major assignment needed a major redesign to showcase effective use of technology for reading and writing, preferably centered on the study of literature.

## MULTIGENRE PAPERS AND HYPERMEDIA

English educators beginning with Romano (2000) have had success at the K–12 level with multigenre papers. Allen and Swistak (2004) describe it this way: "A multigenre research paper involves students in conducting research and instead of writing a traditional research paper format, they write in a range of genres." (p. 224)

Moulton (1999) conducted a study with preservice teachers who were asked to prepare multigenre papers and then reflect on the experience. Teachers remarked on the high level of effort, enjoyed the research, preferred the creativity inherent in the exercise, and noted the benefit of writing for a genuine audience, rather than for academicians.

The multigenre paper is not necessarily hypermedia or even electronic. In a technology in language arts course, it was important that the major assignment incorporate technology in an effective manner for both research and writing and, ideally, for the exploration of literature and the generation of a guiding question for inquiry.

Myers and Beach (2001) regard hypertext as a rich opportunity for the exploration and creation of meaning around literature. They argue:

> technology tools allow readers to connect to the text a vast array of multimedia life experiences that become relevant through their response to the text. They may create their own hypertext versions of texts, including thematic/lexical annotations or intertextual links or path/trails to related texts, themes, topics, biographical information, or historical contexts. While much talk or writing about texts focuses simply on response to a text, hypermedia invites students to explain their textual experience within the larger cultural and ideological contexts that shape their interpretations. (p. 541)

Having teachers "create their own hypertext version of text" fits well with the goals of the course in this study. The instructor used the term "interactive study guide" to describe such a product. The product also shared characteristics of a WebQuest or Web Inquiry Project.

## WEBQUESTS AND WEB INQUIRY PROJECTS

WebQuest is defined as an "inquiry-oriented activity in which most of the information learners work with comes from the Web" (Dodge, 1995, par. 2). The WebQuest follows a template utilizing these building blocks: Introduction, Task, Process, Resources, Evaluation, and Conclusion. While the packaging has given many K–12 teachers an approachable way to integrate Internet resources in the curriculum, it is thought by some to be too prescriptive. The work of Molebash and colleagues (2001) has extended the popular notion of a WebQuest by de-emphasizing scaffolding and placing more emphasis on higher levels of inquiry. This work lends an important perspective to the research aspect of the new assignment.

## MINDTOOLS

The new interactive study guide assignment also draws from the mindtools perspective of Jonassen et al. (1998). Of its "useful roles for technology" (p. 13), the interactive, online study guide assignment focuses on "technology as information vehicles for exploring knowledge to support learning-by-constructing" (p. 13). That is, teachers use the Web to find information relevant to their question, fashion activities that engage K–12 students in interaction with these resources, and package the whole as an interactive study guide. While the teachers have freedom to design the guide in any way they choose, is it not surprising that a good number of the teachers who are familiar with WebQuests package their guide as a WebQuest with high-level thinking activities.

Stepping back from the content of the assignment and the packaging of the final product, it is important to look at the context for the activity. This collaborative, online experience also uses "technology as a social medium to support learning by conversing" (Jonassen et al., 1998, p. 13). Whether teachers choose to create a joint interactive, online study guide or merely collaborate through peer review, they are required to use technology to support their learning activity.

## INTERACTIVE STUDY GUIDE

The instructor decided to craft a new learning experience that incorporated technology in innovative ways, rather than simply require a multi-genre paper. The new assignment, an interactive study guide (ISG), was designed to give teachers experience with the use of technology for three related experiences: interactive reading of a piece of literature (in this case, Robert Hayden's poem "Runagate, Runagate"), advanced study of the social context of the poem and, finally, the challenge of developing their own online, interactive study guide related to some aspect of the poem.

The ISG writing assignment (the teacher's own study guide) was based on one of the National Education Technology Standards/Preparing Tomorrow's Teachers to Use Technology (NETS/PT3) exemplary lessons, "Weaving a Multimedia Approach to Literature" (International Society for Technology in Education, 2002). In this lesson, teachers are asked to construct a multimedia environment for the study of a piece of literature. The idea was expanded for use in the course to include interactive reading of the piece of literature.

As a basis for inquiry, when the teachers transition from the interactive reading exercises to the writing assignment, they are asked to focus on some aspect of the poem that interests them—its historical setting, its themes, its allusions, its parallels in modern history or current events, or even the science or math aspects of its subject. Some focus on the economics of slavery; some bridge to the Holocaust or to the Japanese internment in World War II; some explore the life of Harriet Tubman; others research the quilts that pointed the way to freedom for escaping slaves and devise lessons for their K–12 students to design secret-code quilts.

The topics vary a great deal, according to the interests of the teachers and their classroom curriculum. In all cases, as Jonassen et al. (1998) suggest, "meaning making is prompted by a problem, question, confusion, disagreement, or dissonance (a need or desire to know) and so involves personal ownership of that problem" (p. 5). Teachers then create an interactive, online study guide that explores their question or problem, integrating selected Web sites that support the research.

## EXPECTATION

It was hoped that the new ISG assignment, particularly its incorporation of reading and literature, would provide a richer learning experience than would a traditional paper. It remained to be seen how much of the new exercises would be carried over to the K–12 classroom for reading, research, writing, and possibly the use of literature tie-ins. However, given the popularity of WebQuests, teachers were expected to do well with the research aspect of the assignment and to create study guides that incorporated interactive use of selected Web sites for student research.

The research literature suggested that the teachers taking the class would enjoy and benefit from the hypermedia writing assignment (the creation of the study guide). Moulton's 1999 study with preservice teachers reported that the multigenre paper was a strong alternative to the traditional research paper. Grierson, Anson, and Baird (2002) had reported success with regard to researching, thinking, and writing when they used multigenre papers with sixth graders. Allen and Swistak (2004) expressed reservations at the outset but found that students exercised deeper and more critical thinking as they prepared their writing for genuine audiences. All reported greater enthusiasm, and none reported any deficits in the development of writing skills or research skills.

## RESEARCH DESIGN

The action research study reported here was informed by data from multiple sources, both quantitative and qualitative. The overarching goal of the study has been continual improvement of the course as a collaborative learning experience for K–12 teachers in the area of technology for the language arts curriculum. The course was first taught in 1998. Data reported here covers the most recent six semesters.

The course is fully online, and it is one of 11 courses in a master's program in technology in education. Almost without exception, students taking the class are K–12 teachers matriculated in the program as online students; one or two students each semester are members of a face-to-face cohort, who are taking the class online as a substitute for a face-to-face class with their cohort group.

## QUESTIONS

The questions of greatest interest in the current phase of the study focus on the changing nature of the major assignment, relative to the curriculum goals of the course and the students' collaborative experiences. Some findings are of interest to course designers who incorporate a research paper as a major assignment, and also to English educators. Other findings are of interest to online instructors and course designers who emphasize collaboration.

The research seeks to determine if changing the major assignment from a traditional paper to an online, interactive study guide has affected previous gains in writing and research skills. Teachers in previous semesters reported that engaging in a traditional research paper as a collaborative exercise brought modest gains in their ability to write a graduate-level paper, to research a topic using online and print resources, and to incorporate the writing process in their work (Yoder & Collier, 2003).

Second, the research asks to what extent the collaborative experience opens teachers to further collaboration, more informed collaboration, and use of collaboration in their classrooms. It is felt that collaboration is a vital skill for K–12 teachers and students (Johnson & Johnson, 1996; Curtis & Lawson, 2001). It is important that teachers undertaking the online, interactive study guide have a similarly successful collaborative experience, compared to teachers undertaking the traditional paper.

Third, since the new assignment incorporates a variety of interactive reading techniques as well as the preparation of an interactive study guide, the research asks which aspects of the new assignment teachers are likely to carry into their classroom teaching experiences. Finally, since teachers in past classes had not been asked to produce Web pages or even hypertext materials, the question is raised: Can the greater technical demands of the new assignment be offset so that less-technical teachers can still succeed?

## GROUPS: TRADITIONAL PAPER AND INTERACTIVE STUDY GUIDE

Teachers in the class were asked to prepare a traditional paper (the "Paper" group) or an interactive study guide (the "ISG" group) as the major assignment, depending on the section of the class in which they were enrolled. Over the six-semester period covered by this study, 30 teachers prepared a traditional paper, while 49 prepared an interactive study guide. Data indicated that the teachers in both groups (Paper and ISG) were comparable in their ability to do research and to write a paper at the point that they began their respective assignments. That is, a small number (less than 10%) in each group expressed apprehension about the assignment, indicated weak ability in writing or research skills, or both, at the outset. Most teachers in both groups self-assessed their ability to write a graduate-level paper as either "good" or "excellent." Those doing the traditional paper had slightly less experience doing joint projects and slightly less experience with the writing process before undertaking the assignment.

Teachers in both groups varied in their technical ability. A few teachers in each group self-assessed as "weak" their ability to attach files to e-mail messages and to save word processing documents in alternative formats (such as Rich Text Format) for exchange with a partner. The Paper group was not asked to assess their ability to prepare Web pages or to post HTML documents to the Web. The ISG group was asked, and fully half indicated they had "weak" ability or "no experience" in these areas of preparation.

## DATA SOURCES

Data for the study were gathered from surveys, e-mail messages, transcripts of peer review exchanges, rubric scores for Paper or ISG, and reflection papers. Both groups responded to two surveys. The first survey was sent to teachers as they began the major assignment, and teachers were asked to respond to the second survey as they completed the assignment. Presurvey questions addressed level of preparation, level of anxiety, criteria for selecting a collaborative partner, and plans for collaborating. Teachers in both groups had the following options for collaborating with a partner: They could elect to work on an individual product and simply use a partner for peer review, or teachers could engage with a partner in producing a joint paper or ISG. There was no stigma or advantage associated with either option.

Post-survey questions asked teachers to judge if the quality of the product was better, worse, or the same as previous efforts with regard to style, mechanics, and content. Teachers were also asked to judge the value of their partner's input to style, mechanics, and content. Teachers were asked to self-assess their ability to write a graduate quality paper and other skills, as a result of their work on the assignment. The post survey also asked teachers to indicate their sources of help, sources of information, technologies for communication with a partner, and technologies for editorial feedback (that is, peer review). Finally, the survey asked what criteria teachers would apply in choosing a partner after their experience and if they would elect to work jointly or individually on a similar assignment in the future.

Reflection papers provided insight into the teachers' experiences. Teachers were asked to assess the collaboration with their partner, as it was experienced. They were asked to comment on what they learned about themselves as researchers and writers. They were asked to evaluate the overall learning experience. Finally, they were asked how they could apply what they learned in their K–12 classrooms. These reflections were prepared as individual papers to be shared only with the instructor. They were free to criticize their partners and to critique the learning experience, whether positive or negative. The reflection paper was required and graded; its due date was several days following the due date of the paper or the ISG.Besides this quantitative data, a number of sources of qualitative data were used. The instructor archived all e-mail messages to and from the teachers. Teachers were required to send copies of their peer review sessions. These may have been e-mail exchanges between the teachers, summaries of phone conversations, copies of Word documents marked with track changes or other editing techniques, or logs of instant message conversations. The instructor spot-checked these exchanges, with particular attention to those teachers who had expressed anxiety about the assignment or concern about the responsiveness of a partner.

## FLOW OF INSTRUCTIONAL ACTIVITIES IN THE ISG ASSIGNMENT

It is helpful in reviewing the research findings to understand the flow of activities for the ISG group. This brief section describes the literature used in the assignment and the interactive reading exercises that provided the foundation for the interactive study guide. Those who recognize the title "Runagate, Runagate" know that Robert Hayden's poem recounts the heart-pounding experience of a runaway slave on the Underground Railroad. The poem was selected because it speaks to a universal theme and yet is rich in cultural and historical references that require further study for full understanding.

At the start of the interactive reading exercises, teachers are directed to an online copy of the poem. Teachers are asked to use the word processor for active reading—that is, taking notes and posing questions for themselves as they read the poem carefully. Following the first reading exercise, they are asked to journal their understanding of the action, the main characters, and the shifts in emphasis during the poem. Next, teachers use a technique called "read between the lines" (Strickland, Freeley, & Wepner, 1987), in which they wrestle with a phrase or allusion in the poem that has puzzled or intrigued them. Following these interactive reading activities, teachers use a brief, two-paragraph, interactive, online study guide, prepared by the instructor as a simple model, to explore the cultural and historical context of the poem. Embedded hyperlinks (a) lead them to audio narratives of former slaves describing their life in captivity, (b) show and tell them more about Frederick Douglass's escape from slavery, and (c) engage them in multimedia exploration of the Underground Railroad. Teachers are then asked to comment on how this exploration extends the experience of the poem.

Before shifting their attention to the written assignment, teachers are asked to summarize their understanding of the poem, to synthesize their experience with interactive reading, and to share their summary and synthesis with classmates through the class discussion board. Their unedited notes from the interactive reading exercises are submitted as e-mail attachments to the instructor. Teachers report that these experiences open their eyes to techniques they can use with their students for the study of literature. While teachers are also encouraged to read and respond to one another's postings, there is no evidence that they do so. This is an area for further investigation. Later versions of the assignment will push for deeper understanding through consideration of classmates' insights and approaches (Thorpe, 2000).

The rich experience of reading the poem and briefly studying its cultural context provides a foundation for teachers to create their own interactive learning experience related to the poem. Using Myers and Beach's (2001) terminology, teachers are now prepared to create their own hypertext version on some aspect of the poem, which is referred to here as an interactive study guide (ISG).

## RESEARCH FINDINGS

The quantitative data collected over six semesters gives a clear picture of the teachers' use of technology, their approach to collaboration, and their areas of greatest difficulty with the collaborative assignment. The teachers' reflective papers provided insight into their view of the literature tie-in and the likelihood that various activities in the ISG assignment will find their way into their K–12 classrooms.

The tone of the reflective papers for the group doing the traditional paper is best summarized as dutiful. One student reported:

> I learned that I can actually write a research paper and enjoy the process. I learned that persistence leads to satisfaction. I learned how to narrow my results by using Boolean searches and really improve the quality of my research by using this kind of search....I knew that the proper way to start a paper was to create an outline, but working with a partner really showed me the value of it.

In contrast, the tone of the same reflections by the ISG group is enthusiastic. Reflecting on the ISG assignment, one student summarized:

> Perhaps the most important thing I learned during this experience is that the research available on the Internet opens doors to thousands of creative avenues and ideas...if only a teacher wishes to explore them! I would like to take my experience with this project and remind teachers that they have the know-how to create exciting and innovative lessons.

Two teachers who collaborated on a study guide on the American internment of Japanese during World War II described their experience in this way:

> We found fabulous websites with virtual tours of internment camps, video and audio recording, and photographs. Resources such as these would be great to use with students because they would catch the attention of young readers, elicit interest in the topic, and provide stimuli for thought and conversation.

The sections that follow present the teachers' experience, with emphasis on each group's perceptions of the value of specific activities to them as K–12 teachers.

## Carryover to the Classroom for the Paper Group

Teachers who engaged in the traditional paper indicated in their reflections that they were likely to use collaboration with their own K–12 students. They understood the benefit of using peer feedback for writing assignments and the difficulties inherent in having children collaborate on a writing project. They were favorably disposed to using the writing process in their classrooms, even if they had not used a process approach to writing before the class. In the words of one teacher:

> I loved the way that all of the activities in this course included effective utilization of technology to enhance the writing process. Each assignment used the computer either for drafting, responding, revising, editing, or publishing....I have learned how technology empowers student writing and enhances the process in all subject areas

Many of these teachers also formed or reinforced an appreciation for the wealth of resources on the Web that can be used to enhance their curriculum. Since they had not engaged in interactive reading in preparation for the paper, they made no comment in this area.

## Carryover to the Classroom for the ISG Group

The ISG group had much to say about their intentions to use aspects of the collaborative, interactive assignment in their own classrooms. Their enthusiasm applied to the interactive reading techniques, the use of literature tie-ins, the development and use of interactive study guides, strategies for writing and project planning, enhancements to student research, and the use of collaboration both within the classroom and between classrooms.

### General Comments

The following quotation shows the breadth of the assignment's applicability to the classroom.

> The literature study guide definitely was a learning experience. I learned how to better collaborate with others, cooperate, analyze resources, peer edit and review, take constructive criticism, as well as how to mesh writing styles. When I read the last sentence, these are things that I want my students to learn how to do!

Teachers also recognized the importance of scaffolding in general: "The resources included in the professor's guidelines were valuable, and I want to include that idea for my students when I set up assignments."

### Interactive Reading

Teachers saw the value of the interactive reading techniques for understanding literature. For example, one student stated, "I learned a lot by doing the interactive reading....I think this would be a great way to help fourth graders understand poetry better." Some teachers saw that the techniques could be used for genres other than poetry. An elementary teacher observed:

> The idea of reading between the lines (or inferencing for my students) is a real tough one....With guided practice, they would become much more at ease with this process of understanding what the literature is really trying to get across to the audience. I think it will also help them become better writers, as they understand inferencing better.

Unfortunately, there was no evidence that the teachers would use the interactive reading techniques for other subject areas. This is in spite of the information given at the outset that a teacher in a previous class had researched the read-between-the-lines technique (Strickland et al., 1987) and found it to be effective with at-risk teachers relative to multiple subject areas (Seegers, 2001). This is an area for further study.

### Literature

Teachers in the class were not necessarily language arts teachers or even elementary teachers. For that reason, it was unclear how teachers would react to having to explore a poem in depth, particularly as the opening exercise in a major assignment. Fortunately, the teachers reacted well. One teacher expressed it this way:

> I had never had a poem as a jumping-off place for learning. I am so excited about this concept. It was an intriguing way to learn. I also want to find

poetry that lends itself to the thematic approach to study of math, science, social studies, art, and other areas.

Another teacher described the experience as follows.

I feel that taking a text and allowing students to delve deeper into an area of their own interest is incredibly valuable. This project gave me the opportunity to connect my interest in women's studies to the subject of slavery that is generally not overly interesting to me. This meant that I have gained a new interest and appreciation not only for the poem, but for the subject of the poem as well. I believe that this project could be very valuable in the classroom because it allows students to become hooked on new subjects through their own interests....This project is a good way to help kids become excited about literature.

Several teachers found the study poem itself (Robert Hayden's "Runagate, Runagate") to be relevant to their curriculum and planned to incorporate it into a unit. Two of these teachers, who worked together for their study guide, planned to continue their collaboration after the completion of the class. In their words, they were "planning to have our students e-mail each other and discuss this work and make connections to other literature that we will be reading about prejudice and intolerance."

### Study Guide

The study guide itself captured the interest of teachers as a vehicle for having their students engage in research using selected Web sites. The concept of the study guide as it was presented to the class was generic, and a variety of interactive examples were provided for teachers to consider. Many of the teachers were familiar with WebQuests and saw the connection with the interactive study guide. "I had created WebQuests. I began to see them in a new light. With the built-in sources of information, this becomes a powerful learning tool for students."

Teachers indicated they would use the interactive study guide approach in a variety of ways in their K–12 classrooms: "Various projects can be adapted to this format and I can use many 'stepping stones' to get students to create original thoughtful work. I can successfully and comfortably use technology to help create original projects in my classroom." The latter statement indicates a degree of confidence undertaking similar projects in the future. In fact, none of the teachers expressed frustration or a sense of failure with the technical demands of the assignment.

Teachers by and large saw the extensibility of the interactive study guide to other subjects and purposes. In the words of one:

I will probably put together additional interactive study guides for other subject areas. I think that students can find many ways to use interactive study
guides independently and in groups. As they answer the questions, they are
thinking critically and sharing with each other from their own perspectives. I
think that activities such as this help students to not only learn about the subject but also learn about themselves and others.

One pair jointly produced an interactive study guide that they both
planned to use in their respective elementary classrooms.

We both "oohed" and "aahed" as we found sites that fit the bill. The interactive sites were a lot of fun for us, so we knew they would be fun for our students. These sites also helped us design some built-in assessments. The
finished project is useful and fits our curriculum.

Their description suggests good instructional design practice—clear
learning outcomes, engaging tasks, high-quality resources, thoughtful
assessments, and solid links to the curriculum.

### Writing and Planning

Having been through the process of creating an interactive study guide,
the teachers had a realistic sense of the demands of the ISG and the importance to the whole of its component tasks. Several noted the importance of
planning a project with differentiation in mind, a hallmark of WebQuests
(Dodge, 1995). In their words:

I could handle doing a project such as this with my own students. I would
assign each student a responsibility and job title such as "Web Page
Designer"....As long as I structure the project and keep it in small steps, my
middle school students would benefit.

Teachers also seemed to understand the practical wisdom of requiring
and grading steps like peer feedback.

The only thing I would have done differently on this project would have been
to incorporate more peer-editing assignments. I think more than one peer-
editing session would have been helpful but oftentimes because it is not part
of the assignment or isn't graded some people may not do it.

### Research

It is gratifying that teachers perceived the central role of inquiry in the ISG
assignment. In the words of one student:

One of the important things that I am taking away from this experience is the
power of creating your own question to answer through research. I would let

my students have more say in the area of their research the next time we did a project.

This speaks to the distinction Molebash et al. (2001) make between the Web Inquiry Project and the WebQuest.

### Collaboration

Teachers also learned how challenging collaborative assignments can be, and they recognized the need to exercise care with collaboration, even within their self-contained classrooms: "I think that I could now design a more effective collaborative project with my students, knowing what challenges might come up during the course, and what techniques could be used to achieve a successful product."

### Summary

The current study shows that teachers who engaged in preparing an interactive study guide evidenced greater enthusiasm for the assignment, with no loss in the area of writing and research skills, compared to those writing a traditional paper. Reflection papers indicate the likelihood of carryover to the classroom for many aspects of the assignment: use of interactive reading, use of literature tie-ins, more informed use of collaboration with students, greater knowledge in preparing writing and research projects, increased attention to having K–12 students generate their own research questions, and classroom use of the interactive study guide.

Teachers who worked on the interactive study guide also had a more successful collaborative experience, although those data are not presented in this chapter in any detail. While careful preparation in both cases (Paper and ISG) led to successful collaboration, the ISG group was more likely to collaborate again with the same partner, and to do the project jointly next time. Several moved from individual to joint projects during the assignment. Many reported they would use their finished study guide as is in their classrooms, and a few reported that they planned to have their K–12 students collaborate with students in their partner's classroom at a distance. All of these outcomes are desirable for the field of teacher education, and they represent good use of technology for learning.

## USE OF TECHNOLOGY

Use of technology for the traditional paper and the interactive study guide is similar to that reported in the research literature, with one important distinction. Recently, Mayben, Nichols, and Wright (2003) reported that teacher educators involved in their study relied primarily on e-mail for communication. Sixty-six percent used the telephone, 22% used discussion boards, and 11% used instant messaging.

In the current study, every teacher who worked on the traditional paper used e-mail messages and attachments to communicate for peer review. Most teachers working on the ISG also used e-mail messages (96%) and attachments (92%). Sixty percent of the teachers developing the ISG made use of file transfer protocol (FTP) to post files to the Web for review. This is a high percentage, in light of the relative inexperience with FTP at the start of the activity. That is, at the outset, nearly half the teachers reported "novice" (38%) or "no experience" (10%) with Web page editing and "novice" (28%) or "no experience" (10%) with FTP.

Despite their level of technical preparation and the range of asynchronous options available to them, a surprising number of these online students chose real-time contact for their collaboration, in the same proportion for chat, telephone, and face-to-face meetings. In particular, more than 80% of teachers in the ISG group used real-time techniques for communication during the collaborative, interactive activity, with several of them making use of multiple synchronous technologies.

While the data provide a much more complete picture of technology use, the most salient information concerning technology use from this online class experience is the use of real-time techniques by distance education students engaged in a collaborative, interactive learning experience. The use of real-time technology for collaboration at a distance was markedly higher for the ISG group than the Paper group, and higher than that reported in the literature. Fifty-three percent of those collaborating on a traditional paper used real-time techniques. In contrast, 82% of the ISG group used real-time techniques. Four teachers used all three (instant messaging, telephone, and face-to-face encounters), 6 used two, and 30 (61%) used one real-time technique.

It is unclear why the use of real time nearly doubled for the interactive assignment. The instructor would like to think the teachers were more engaged or had a higher stake in creating a joint product for use in their respective classrooms. However, teachers in this technology in education program are introduced in an earlier class to instant messaging, including audio and video capabilities. The increased use may be more a function of their familiarity with the improvements in instant messaging and its pervasiveness in today's communication habits.

Those who design online classes and those who provide the technology infrastructure for online classes would benefit from knowing how and why students choose real-time communication for collaborative work. Would students make use of whiteboards and other shared-workspace technologies if they were available?

## DISCUSSION

The current study involves K–12 teachers, and it is grounded in language arts and the use of technology for student learning. What implications does the study have for online learning in general?

The increased use of real-time technology for collaboration at a distance is an interesting finding that transcends the particular subject matter and student makeup of the class. The course was designed for an asynchronous learning environment, as many online classes are. Students in such environments typically have e-mail and threaded discussion available as their primary means of communication, and most course materials are presented as HTML files through a Web browser or a course management system. Nevertheless, teachers in this class, when engaged in an interactive, collaborative assignment, sought out real-time means of communication: instant messaging, the telephone, and even face-to-face meetings.

### Real-Time Communication

This raises questions concerning the importance of synchronous communication for online collaboration, particularly for the development of an interactive product. When more than 80% of a group chooses synchronous communication, and some of those teachers choose several modes of synchronous communication, the matter bears further investigation. Is synchronous communication necessary or simply desirable for online collaboration? Are students satisfied with text-based instant messaging or do they need audio and video capabilities? Would they make use of shared workspaces, or is it sufficient to attach documents to an e-mail or post drafts of Web pages on a Web server?

### The Place of Traditional Papers

The study noted the greater effectiveness of an interactive study guide, compared to a traditional paper, for the goals of the technology in language arts course. Other researchers have found similar results among students, with regard to multigenre research papers (Moulton, 1999; Allen & Swistak, 2004). Does the traditional paper still have a place in online learning? If multigenre, multimedia, or hypermedia products are to replace the traditional paper, what standards apply?

What of the greater technical demands of this kind of assignment? At least for teachers in this class, the increased technical difficulty of the interactive study guide did not pose problems. Teachers had the option of producing the ISG as a Word document, which adequately incorporates images and hyperlinks. Nevertheless, many pushed themselves to learn new skills (Web page editing and FTP) to produce Web-based study guides.

## Learning from Others' Insights

One of the questions raised by the study relative to the internal goals of the course is how to further teachers' understanding of the value of interactive reading techniques across the curriculum. A consequence to that has implications for other online learning: As teachers construct knowledge in new areas, they can deepen their understanding through reflection on one another's insights. Mary Thorpe (2000) of the Open University addresses this critical issue in her article "Encouraging Students to Reflect as Part of the Assignment Process." Thorpe lays out a thoughtful, systematic approach to the matter that bears further study in online classes.

Thorpe's approach presumes tutor (instructor) feedback as a key element in the process. Could peer feedback relieve some of the burden on the instructor? How would online students need to be prepared for such feedback? Could this preparation happen in the time frame of a typical course, or is it something that needs to be fostered over an entire program of study? For instructors and program directors who are concerned about the depth of insight among their students, this is an important issue that bears further investigation.

## Preparation for Online Collaboration

The current study is the third phase in an ongoing action research study to better understand collaboration in an online context. The success of the activities reported here would not have been possible without careful preparation of teachers leading up to the collaborative assignment. Giving teachers the opportunity to know one another, involving them in a series of collaborations before the major assignment, teaching and testing component skills, having contingency plans for teachers who abdicate responsibility (or whose partners do so), and establishing an environment of trust are necessary underpinnings for successful online collaboration (Yoder & Collier, 2003).

As online collaborators make use of new technologies, including synchronous technologies and hypermedia technologies, in the development of interactive products, such as the interactive study guide in this class, are there new "component skills" required of students? Can these be addressed in the confines of a course? How can students with unlike skill sets collaborate so that all parties experience growth, success, and satisfaction in the learning experience?

## CONCLUSION

These questions and more grow out of interactive, online learning experiences, as students push the limits of the learning technology available to them. The changing use of technology in the content area of the course and the literature on teaching and learning online are two important areas for online instructors to watch as they continually improve their online courses. As discussed in this chapter, effective online teaching also involves understanding the students' experiences. Instructors need to look beyond the assessments they plan for their assignments and listen to the student voice. Careful monitoring, active feedback, and planned reflection are vital aspects of successful online teaching.

## REFERENCES

Allen, C. A., & Swistak, L. (2004). Multigenre research: The power of choice and interpretation. *Language Arts, 81,* 223–232.

Collier, C., & Morse, F. (1999, July). *The Internet ate my homework: Experiences with online collaborative writing.* Paper presented at Syllabus99, Santa Clara, CA.

Collier, C., & Morse, F. (2002, Summer). Requiring independent learners to collaborate: Redesign of an online course. *Journal of Interactive Online Learning, 1*(1). Retrieved April 19, 2004, from http://www.ncolr.org/journal/current/collier/1.html

Curtis, D. D., & Lawson, M. J. (2001, May). Exploring collaborative online learning. *Journal of Asynchronous Learning Networks, 5*(1), 21–34. Retrieved June 3, 2004, from http://www.aln.org/publications/jaln/v5n1/pdf/v5n1_curtis.pdf

Dodge, B. (1995, May). *Some thoughts about WebQuests.* Retrieved April 19, 2004, from http://webquest.sdsu.edu/about_webquests.html

Grierson, S. T., Anson, A., & Baird, J. (2002). Exploring the past through multigenre writing. *Language Arts, 80,* 51–59.

International Society for Technology in Education. (2002). Weaving a multimedia approach to literature. In *NETS for teachers: Preparing teachers to use technology* (pp. 178–182). Eugene, OR: Author.

Johnson, D. W., & Johnson, R. T. (1996). Cooperation and the use of technology. In D. H. Jonassen (Ed.), *Handbook of research for educational communication and technology* (pp. 1017–1044). New York: Simon and Schuster Macmillan.

Jonassen, D. H., Peck, K. L., Wilson, B. G., & Pfeiffer, W. S. (1998). *Learning with technology: A constructivist perspective.* Upper Saddle River, NJ: Prentice Hall.

Lankshear, C., & Snyder, I. (2000). *Teachers and technoliteracy.* Sydney, Australia: Allen and Unwin.

Mayben, R., Nichols, S., & Wright, V. H. (2003, Fall). Distance technologies in collaborative research: Analyzing the successes and barriers. *Journal of Interactive Online Learning*, 2(2). Retrieved May 30, 2004, from http://www.ncolr.org/jiol/archives/2003/fall/02/index.html

Molebash, P. E., Dodge, B., Bell, R. L., Mason, C. L., & Irving, K. E. (2001). *Promoting student inquiry: WebQuests to Web Inquiry Projects (WIPs)*. Retrieved April 19, 2004, from the San Diego State University EdWeb page: http://edweb.sdsu.edu/wip/WIP_Intro.htm

Moulton, M. R. (1999). The multigenre paper: Increasing interest, motivation, and functionality in research. *Journal of Adolescent and Adult Literacy, 42*, 528–539.

Myers, J., & Beach, R. (2001). Hypermedia authoring as critical literacy. *Journal of Adolescent and Adult Literacy, 44*, 538–546.

O'Regan, K. (2003, September). Emotion and e-learning. *Journal of the Asynchronous Learning Networks, 7*(3), 78–92. Retrieved June 3, 2004, from http://www.aln.org/publications/jaln/v7n3/pdf/v7n3_oregan.pdf

Romano, T. (2000). *Blending genre, altering style: Writing multigenre papers*. Portsmouth, NH: Boynton/Cook.

Scarafiotti, C. (2003). A three-prong strategic approach to successful distance learning delivery. *Journal of Asynchronous Learning Networks, 7*(2), 50–55. Retrieved June 3, 2004, from http://www.aln.org/publications/jaln/v7n2/pdf/v7n2_scarafiotti.pdf

Seegers, M. (2001). Special technological possibilities for students with special needs. *Learning and Leading with Technology, 29*(3), 32–34.

Strickland, D. S., Freeley, A. J., & Wepner, S. B. (1987). *Using computers in the teaching of reading*. New York: Columbia University Press.

Thorpe, M. (2000). Encouraging students to reflect as part of the assignment process: Student responses to tutor feedback. *Active Learning in Higher Education, 1*, 79–92.

Yoder, M. B., & Collier, C. (2003, November). Practical strategies for designing online collaboration and providing effective feedback. *Proceedings of the World Conference on E-Learning in Corporate, Government, Healthcare, & Higher Education (E-Learn), 2003*(1), 809–815. Abstract retrieved May 31, 2004, from http://dl.aace.org/13794

CHAPTER 7

# USING NARRATIVE STRATEGIES TO ENHANCE INTERACTIVITY ONLINE

Linda Lohr, *University of Northern Colorado*
Kathy Miller, *North Carolina State University*
and
Donald Winiecki, *Boise State University*

This chapter explores the use of narrative as an instructional strategy for enhancing interactivity in distance learning environments. The chapter describes research of three narrative strategies used during a completely distance course. Overall, students demonstrated the ability to write effective instructional narratives for all three assignments. While usability measures indicated that students found the strategies worthwhile and satisfactory, room for improvement in the design of these strategies was noted. As could be expected, interactivity increased with the complexity of the assignment and the requirement to work in groups. Suggestions for improving the design of narrative strategies from usability and interactivity perspectives conclude the study.

The effectiveness of many distance-learning environments today relies on facilitator and learner ability to communicate effectively with written text. Most chat rooms and discussion threads require that the learner type ideas, responses, and general information in text form. While many participants

*Research on Enhancing the Interactivity of Online Learning*, pages 101–126
Copyright © 2006 by Information Age Publishing

bemoan communication by text only, others think that requiring the learner to write is not necessarily a bad thing. The ability to communicate effectively in writing is one of the most important skills a person can possess. "Often the struggle of writing, linked as it is to the struggle of thinking and to the growth of a person's intellectual powers, awakens students to the real nature of learning" (Bean, 2001, p. xiii). Increasingly, the ability to write in a number of different formats is advocated. Expressive writing, for instance, with its roots in the language-across-the-curriculum movement, emphasizes individual voices and cultures in an effort to reverse alienating curriculum. "One of its main functions is to help the individual assimilate new ideas by creating personal contexts that link new, unfamiliar material to what one knows or has experienced" (Bean, 2001, p. 47).

Many distance learning writing activities require students to apply what they are learning to personal life experiences. As a result, students often share experiences in the form of stories from their lives. The effectiveness of this strategy is theoretically supported by a large body of literature suggesting that deeper learning is fostered when new knowledge is integrated into prior knowledge. Students telling a story that relates to a new concept are essentially integrating that concept into their memory.

Some learning theorists believe that a story structure of memory, or a schema arranged in story elements, provides a stronger support for memory. Because stories are deeply engrained in most people's experiences, we naturally have a schema or organizational structure set up to remember stories. Since we know that a story has a beginning, middle, and end, as well as conflict and character, we subconsciously attend to and remember those elements.

The promise of using story structures for teaching has been advocated by a number of researchers (Bruner, 2002; Coles, 1989; Egan, 1986; McEwan & Egan, 1995). Despite some skepticism of the story schema theory, the use of stories has intuitive appeal. Most teachers have experienced the rapt attention of students when a story is introduced to reinforce a concept. Teaching environments today, however, are less teacher-centered and more student-centered. Constructivist orientations promote students' learning from each other. This research explores student roles in story construction and how these stories facilitate instructional interaction in the online classroom.

## LITERATURE REVIEW

To date, research on the effects or affects of student-generated narrative for the instructional benefit of other students in an online environment have not been taken up by academic researchers. Teacher-generated narrative activities are more prevalent in the literature, and when teacher-generated narrative strategies are researched and published, they typically describe a face-to-face context, not a distance-learning format.

While this face-to-face literature base is somewhat removed from the purposes of this chapter, many insights are gained from general research relating to narrative teaching strategies. In this chapter, specific definitions of narrative, case study, and meaningful learning are articulated. Additionally, the rationale for the use of narrative, examples of narrative use in adult education, and a story model of writing provide a solid basis for exploring the topic.

## DEFINITIONS

Four terms important to this chapter include "narrative," "story," "case study," and "meaningful learning." Narrative refers to the "structure, knowledge, and skill required to construct a story" (Gudmundsdottir, 1995, p. 24). Story and narrative are considered similar in meaning; however, some (e.g., Chatman, 1978; Culler, 1975) distinguish between story and discourse elements of narrative. The story consists of characters, beginning, middle, and end sections, and plot. Discourse is the presentation of the story and relates to how the story is expressed as a written form, drama, or motion picture.

A case study is a narrative format that seeks to describe as completely as possible an event or issue. Unlike a story, a case study does not seek to explain or analyze a situation. The purpose of a case study is to provide a thorough description that others can use for analytic purposes (Goodson & Walker, 1995).

Several narrative strategies are described in this study because they are believed to foster meaningful learning. The assimilation of new information in ways that help the learner solve future problems is considered meaningful learning. Meaningful learning occurs as a result of the learner's cognitive activity, rather than exclusively behavioral (or observable) activity, while learning (Mayer, 2001).

## USE OF NARRATIVE STRATEGIES IN INSTRUCTION

Stories have long been part of informal and formal training for most subject areas, and are told and read from elementary school history and English to highly advanced law and medical school training programs. Case study methodology is frequently used in graduate education where students are required to "think outside the box" and to consider a variety of fuzzy or ill-defined facts or concepts prior to making decisions.

A significant body of research has established the important role of narrative in education (Bransford & Johnson 1972; Bruner, 1986). Human schemas are organized into story structures that allow the anticipation and interpretation of information. Children, as young as three-years old, recognize that stories have beginnings and endings. There is "at the simplest level a rhythm in stories. [Stories] set up an expectation at the beginning, this is elaborated or complicated in the middle, and is satisfied in the end" (Egan, 1986, p. 24). Aside from providing support for memory, narrative "serve[s] as an interpretive lens for reflecting the storied nature of human lives, for understanding the moral complexities of the human condition, and for enabling classrooms to expand their borders as interpretive communities." (Witherell, Tran, & Othus, 1995, p. 40).

## A STORY MODEL

Egan (1986) proposes a story model for instruction consisting of five elements:

1. identifying importance
2. finding binary opposites
3. organizing content into story form
4. concluding the story
5. evaluating what was learned.

For a story to instruct requires attention to these elements. First, the story topic must be germane to the instructional topic. Second, some type of conflict (or polar/binary opposites) must be present to generate interest and provide the framework for the story plot. Third, the story must be organized around the conflict. Fourth, the conflict must be resolved. And, finally, the student's learning experience must be evaluated. This five-part model is used because it is a flexible alternative to what Egan calls an "assembly line" approach to instructional stories that traditionally emphasize instructional objectives. The problem with this approach, from Egan's perspective, is that objectives are not a natural element in stories and that a conflict or polar/binary opposite is a more interesting place from which to begin and develop narrative.

With the theoretical promise of improved learning efficacy from the incorporation of activities in which learners are required to produce narratives, thus generating story lines that may be incorporated into schema, we designed a research project to assess existing theories regarding narratives in learning and to evaluate the impact of three different narrative activities in a distance education class.

## RESEARCH QUESTIONS

Student stories, originating from three activities in one online class, are analyzed for how well they support the accomplishment of instructional objectives and facilitate interactivity. Four research questions guided this study:

1. Do students employ Egan's five elements of story writing in each of their narrative assignments?
2. How did students address each of Egan's five elements?
3. Did students find the experience worthwhile in terms of effectiveness (instructional objectives achieved), efficiency (ease of writing the stories and interacting with other students), and appeal (student liking of writing and reading the stories, and of interacting with each other)?
4. How did students interact with other students during the three narrative experiences?

## METHODOLOGY

All of the data used in this chapter are taken from a semester-long graduate course delivered in a totally online course hosted by a mid-sized university in the northwestern United States. All courses offered by the department in which this course is offered are available to students either in traditional on-campus format or entirely online. Names and identifying characteristics in the text of data used here have been altered to protect the identity of the participants. The class from which these data were taken was populated with 19 students. Students in this class were distributed throughout the United States, including four time zones, during the semester in which these data were collected. There were 10 female students and 9 male students in this class. The average age of students at the time of this class was 38 years (ranging from 27 to 62 years of age). All of the students enrolled in this course were pursuing a Master of Science degree in instructional and performance technology. The course in which this research was conducted addressed the topic of delivery technology for instruction. The curriculum of this course emphasizes theory and research of delivery technologies and the application of this knowledge in instructional design. This course was delivered using a Lotus Notes database specially designed by a faculty member of the department in which this course was taught. Like most software programs designed for instructional delivery, this database includes features for (a) organizing activity in discrete topic areas or "discussions," (b) threading messages posted to a discussion in terms of time posted, (c) identifying the person who writes/posts a message and an optional subject title for each message, and (d) displaying the contents of the selected message itself (see Figure 7.1).

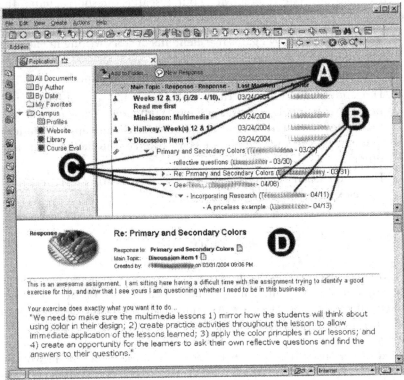

Figure 7.1.   Screenshot of dialog space.

During the first 8 weeks of the class, students enrolled in the class completed three narrative activities. The first activity took place during the first 2 orientation weeks of the course. Students were given a story starter exercise and were asked to work with one other individual to write a story ending to the story starter. The purpose of this activity was to have students work in smaller groups and to experience writing in a narrative, or creative story format. The second activity took place during the 3rd to 6th weeks. Students were asked to write a case study for a media selection model. Students were assigned to a particular medium (print, electronic performance support systems, teleconferencing, video, traditional computer-based training) and were asked to write a case study scenario that would require their fellow students to think through a number of decision points leading to the selection of their assigned media. The third activity took place during the seventh week, when students were asked to write imaginary dialogs between leading educational researchers (Richard Clark, Robert Kozma, Ruth Clark, Richard Mayer, and Diane Laurillard). The purpose of this activity was to help students articulate the key message of whichever researcher the student selected to write about. Students were asked to create a conversational topic that would require the student to think through the topic as they imagined the researcher would. During the eighth week, students were asked to analyze the three assignments from a learning theory perspective. Students were requested to share their impressions of the instructional value of the assignments, as well as how they would classify the assignments as behaviorist, cognitivist, constructivist, or a mixture of orientations. Data collection concluded with a Likert-scale survey of usability in effectiveness, efficiency, and appeal categories, with space for additional open-ended comments.

Survey instruments and student work examples on the three assignments, as well as their analysis of the assignments, were analyzed using descriptive and simplified discourse analytic techniques. Descriptive analysis was used to describe the Likert scale data measuring effectiveness, efficiency, and appeal. Simplified discourse analysis was used to identify the presence of story elements, the contents of the story, and student comments regarding the experience. Student entries for each assignment were transcribed. Transcriptions were coded into themes based upon predetermined (story elements, usability measures, interactivity) and evolving categories. Codes where assembled into themes and then analyzed for patterns and relationships between themes.

## FINDINGS

The results of data collection are presented in the order of the research questions stated above, beginning with a description of student ability to construct story according to Egan's (1986) five-part model, then describing the usability of the stories and ending with data on the impact of narrative (story starter, case study, and dialog) assignments on student interactivity (the frequency of student comments and responses to each other while completing these activities). Instructions for each of the narrative activities were posted in separate threads (see Figure 7.1). Students developed narratives in nested threads, set up according to group size. For the story starter, students worked in groups of two; for the case study, students worked in groups of two to four; and for the dialog activity, students worked alone.

## Student Employment of Egan's Five Story Writing Elements

A large majority of students addressed four of Egan's (1986) five elements of story for instructional purposes (see Table 7.1) in all three narrative activities. Two of Egan's five elements, topic and evaluation, were not addressed consistently by students. Slightly over half of the student groups related the story to an instructional topic in the story starter assignment, and all student groups failed to write an evaluation section to the narrative for the story starter assignment and the narrative.

**Table 7.1.   Percentage of Students Including Egan's (1986) Story Elements**

| Story Elements | Story Starter | Case Study | Narrative |
| --- | --- | --- | --- |
| 1. Topic | 5 groups or 55% | 7 groups or 100% | 15 students or 100% |
| 2. Polar Opposites | 8 groups or 88% | 7 groups or 100% | 14 students or 93% |
| 3. Organizing | 8 groups or 88% | 6 groups or 85% | 15 students or 100% |
| 4. Resolution | 8 groups or 88% | 7 groups or 100% | 15 students or 100% |
| 5. Evaluation | 0 groups or 0% | 7 groups or 100% | 0 students or 0% |
| n | 9 groups[a] | 7 groups[b] | 15 students[c] |

a. Students were assigned to groups consisting of 2 students.
b. Students were assigned to groups consisting of 2 to 3 students.
c. Students worked individually.

## How Students Addressed Each of Egan's Five Elements

Analysis of student writing of all three narrative assignments revealed three areas in which student groups displayed some difficulty in writing stories for instructional purposes (as defined by Egan, 1986). These areas included Egan's first (topic), third (story organization), and fifth (evaluation) elements. Student groups appeared to have few problems with Egan's second (polar/binary opposites) and fourth (conflict resolution).

## The Story Starter

### Topic

Topic themes for the story starter included American Society of Training and Development (ASTD), danger, science fiction, perceptions of reality, current culture, and humor. Five of the nine narratives centered on ASTD, one of the professional organizations associated with the students' degree program. Examples of ASTD entries include the following from Story A.

...it was not ASTD at her front door, but the enemy purporting to be ASTD.

Story B:

Due to ocular implants, which allowed her X-ray vision, that were given to her upon graduation of advanced ASTD training...

Topical themes of danger, science fiction, and real versus imaginary perceptions, contemporary culture, and humor are represented by these examples from Story C:

The sound was almost unearthly. She suddenly realized the unearthly noise was just two squirrels fighting over some popcorn.

Story D:

She turned her head to see 7 amoeba-looking aliens with huge black eyes.

Story E:

At this point, Leslie is unsure of her state of reality. She ponders, are the monsters real or is my family really here? She wonders if it really is her father who is at her side or a shadow of his former self.

Story F:

To maintain secret cover and yet communicate with ASTD operatives she used the usual procedure in Starbuck's. She would order another triple non-fat, sugar-free vanilla machiatto latte and settle down with her back to the wall.

Story G:

It was the teenage girls from the park! One was pointing to a large piece of paper with a picture of Brittany Spears on it....Handing Leslie a small hand mirror, the alien said "Oops! I did it again!"

### Binary Opposites or Conflict

Students focused story conflict around topical themes. Conflicts or binary opposites fell into categories of dangerous versus innocent (squirrels), good versus bad, ASTD special unit versus the bad guys, aliens/monsters versus humans, and dream versus reality.

### Story Organization

Students organized content into story form, marginally developing the story conflict by focusing information on the binary opposites or conflict themes. This development consisted of two to five paragraphs for story plot that moved the story line toward its resolution. From Story H:

> "You were a part of a highly covert operation with top level security on a plan with the highest importance," her father gently explained to her....."You had traveled to a different special dimension landing in a different lifetime than the one you knew....It was the past. In this world, you were working with the 'dark' side or the same people that are after you now."

From Story I:

> The blood curdling sound rang out again. This time it seemed as if [it] was coming from the bushes next to the fountain...the fountain where the old couple was hiding. Leslie was convinced that something more sinister than a squirrel fight was amiss. She decided to take a closer look.

From Story J:

> Just then, it dawned on Leslie what her dream meant. The horrible hairy mammal in her dream was an enlarged version of Marco! How could she not have seen it before?! Marco's mental capabilities extended far beyond discernment. It would be nothing for him to telepathically send her a vision in the night. She clutched her necklace and spoke into the hidden speaker! "Marco, I need your help!" she called. From behind the dumpster in the alley came the response. "Meow," which is to say, "Good morning, Leslie. I'm glad you finally called."

### Conflict Resolution

All of the stories submitted had a form of conflict resolution. In Story D, the protagonist (Leslie) was dreaming the conflict.

> Startled, and drenched with sweat, Leslie leaped out of bed. She realized she must have had a nightmare.

In Story E, Leslie had overdosed on LSD.

As the calming drugs administered to Leslie begin to wear off, she awakens in the hospital. This time she is cognizant of her reality. She recognizes her father at the side of the bed...calmly explain[ing] how she licked a stamp laced with LSD and was incoherent for three days.

Story F was part of a top-secret mission.

As the calming drugs administered to Leslie begin to wear off, she awakens in the hospital. This time she is cognizant of her reality. She recognizes her father at the side of the bed...calmly explain[ing] how she licked a stamp laced with LSD and was incoherent for three days.

Her thoughts were disturbed by the shrill ring of her ASTD pager. As she answered she realized that her life as Special Agent L had officially commenced.

Story G was part of a reality TV show.

Then she heard a raucous voice blast "CUT! That's a wrap!" She looked up and saw people started to close in on her. A camera crew, a director, and various stagehands were coming out of nowhere! Aghast, Leslie stormed over to the balding man who seemed to be in charge. "What are you doing?" she asked. "Thank you, young lady! You have just participated in the newest, hottest 'reality TV' yet! What did you think?" No words could express her horror adequately.

In Story H, Leslie took on a new identity.

A week later she came to a place called Nampa, Idaho, and changed her name to Linda. She wanted to make a new start and found a job teaching home economics at Nampa High School (home of the Bulldogs).

Some resolutions were purposefully vague, as in the following stories where the protagonist is described as waking up from a dream, but in the next sentence she is living the dream. From Story I:

Leslie rolled over in her bed to answer the phone. It was her father. "Hey Leslie, how's my girl today?" he asked. Leslie awoke, gained her senses, and replied, "Dad, I had the weirdest dream." "Really," he said, "How about meeting me for breakfast and we can talk about it?" "Sounds good," Leslie replied. "Great," her father said, "I'll meet you in 20 minutes." "Oh and Leslie, don't forget to bring your 9mm Uzi!"

From Story J:

"I know, I know it was just a dream." Leslie looks at the Viper key and whispers, "...or was it?"

## The Case Study

### Topic
All of the case studies focused on using an ASTD media selection model (reference). Each case study required students to solve an organizational problem using the appropriate media.

### Conflict and Story Organization
The case study conflict and story organization would more accurately be described as a problem-solving scenario, since the case study involved a workplace problem and a number of clues and resources necessary for solving the problem. Workplace problems included limited resources, management issues, audience/learner analysis, safety, and regulatory compliance.

In the following case study, the conflict is implementation problems with a new EPSS system.

> You have just been promoted to the corporate analyst position and are now responsible for...efficiencies with [a] new ERP (Enterprise Resource Planning) system....There is significant organizational pressure to get the [new ERP] information to the call center agents and keep them on the phones as the call duration is up due to the lack of experience with the new system....You implement this [distribution of information by ERP] process and find that not all employees are getting the information as you are seeing system errors.

Story organization includes clues to the solution, such as the following.

> You change the induction program and train the trainers to develop a comfort level with the EPSS in training by not answering a question until it has been looked up on the EPSS first. When you release the new hires onto the phones, there is some resistance from the existing employees as the new hires are performing at the same level as veterans. You observe the workings of both and see the new hires are making less mistakes and when in doubt are quickly accessing the EPSS for updates and how-to information and not their team leader. What is going on? Did you make the right choice with the existing employees?

*Conflict Resolution*

Case studies addressed conflict resolution by requiring students to resolve the conflict. The case study above concludes with these comments:

> What is going on? Did you make the right choice with the existing employees? Unsure of exactly what is going on, and as a professional in the HPT field you decide to analyze the situation.

*Reflective Question*

Using the ASTD's media selection book, specifically the business and delivery surveys, identify what scores this situation should generate and plot the results. Was the right medium selected?"

*Evaluation*

All case studies included an evaluation component. Case study writers included an answer key, which could be used by the reader to assess how well they solved the problem.

## The Dialog Activity

*Topic*

All of the student dialogs covered the media debate issue. This debate focuses on the role of media in learning.

*Conflict*

All but one of the dialogs were centered on the criticality of media's role in learning. Viewpoints expressed included media either playing an important but undiscovered role in learning versus media acting as a mere vehicle for learning only.

*Story Organization*

All dialogs were organized around conversations between different researchers. Richard Clark, Robert Kozma, Ruth Clark, Richard Mayer, and Diana Laurillard were characters in these conversations.

*Conflict Resolution*

Because the dialog activity centered on a popular debate in the discipline, conflict in the traditional sense was not resolved. Resolutions fell into one of two camps. Either the parties agreed to disagree, or the conversation ended, with the different sides of the debate maintaining their perspectives. This example from Dialog A illustrates the first outcome.

CLARK: Yes, as long as the instructional method is consistent; learning will occur in each situation. For example, let's say you have to shovel a sidewalk full of snow. You can use your hands, a shovel, a snow blower or a plow truck. Each way of removing the snow will give you the same results; some ways may be quicker, others may be more expensive.

KOZMA: I'll go for the plow truck! Anyway, I am not sure I agree that the type of media used does not influence learning. However, I will say that more research needs to occur.

From Dialog B:

KOZMA: Oh forget it, I guess we will never see eye to eye, why don't you just eat your croissant.

Different examples and analogies might have been used to illustrate the outcome that the underlying differences in opinion essentially remained the same. For example, from Dialog C:

UNCLE ROBERT K: So Ruth, when you mention instructional methods, you would agree that media and methods have an integral relationship, both being part of the instructional design?

AUNT RUTH: Absolutely! Instructional methods and media elements need to guide learners to effectively process and assimilate new knowledge and skills.

ME: So, what do you all recommend? How do I teach my daughter to drive?

UNCLE RICHARD C: Carefully! Remember, media are mere vehicles that deliver instruction. (Laughing).

### Evaluation

None of the case studies written included a learner evaluation component. Students were, however, asked to readdress the debate in the midterm examination. Fourteen of the 15 students received excellent midterm examination scores.

## STUDENT AND TEACHER ASSESSMENT OF USABILITY

Students were moderately positive about the effectiveness, efficiency, and appeal of the three narrative assignments. Overall the dialog activity received the most positive responses from students.

## The Story Starter

*Effectiveness*

More comments were made regarding the effectiveness of the story starter exercise than were made about efficiency or appeal. Student comments regarding effectiveness of the story starter exercise were based on how well the activity addressed the instructional objectives. The primary objectives that students identified for the activity included (1) to help the teachers and students remember each other in a novel way, (2) to serve as an icebreaker, and (3) to set the stage for future constructivist activities in the class.

Several students questioned whether the exercise effectively addressed objective 1 in helping either the students or the teacher to remember each other.

> I thought it was marginally successful. I feel like I got a good glimpse into others' personalities (e.g., who tends to be more serious, who is more light-hearted and humorous), but at the same time I didn't get a lot of the information I am accustomed to receiving—such as where people work, what their areas of expertise are, or the types of things they like to do.

As an icebreaker, 6 of the 16 students, such as the following student, indicated that the story starter was effective: "I think [it] was very effective in that it got people talking and working in groups." Comments of seven students indicated the story starter was an effective strategy for orienting the class to the constructivist nature of the course. One such student commented:

> I believe the objective of the exercise was to introduce us to the constructivist learning environment. The normal start up is "I post information about me" and the instructor says "welcome" and the interaction is student to instructor only. By creating a group task from the beginning, we had to get to know each other, how we would contribute, maybe our "mind" style, etc. Also, the instructor was out of the focus point, shifting our attention to working with each other.

*Efficiency*

Students made mostly negative comments regarding the ease of responding to the story starter activity. Two students mentioned not feeling comfortable with the approach. Three students mentioned the difficulty of following the story when it branched (a situation that occurred when students would add to the story at the same time, creating divergent paths or story plots.). As one student mentioning discomfort said,

> As I have stated before, I am having to explore concepts within a creative environment in which I do not feel comfortable. Answering questions that

prove my knowledge such as writing essays and papers surrounding a specific topic is an easier, less constructivist method that I like. Now whether I am any better at it or not, is another matter.

As another student put it:

[The activity] caused some confusion....The class often provided multiple responses for one thread, causing the story to twist. This forced the class to choose which thread they were going to contribute to.

## *Appeal*

Comments regarding the appeal of the story starter activity were mixed. Two people, such as the following, mentioned feeling energized by the environment.

From my take of the ID, it was a good energizer. We knew up front that this class would be more constructivist and we had to change our initial thinking pattern—well I did anyway.

Two students mentioned preferring the traditional approach, either because they were not comfortable with the novel approach, or because they wanted to know more about students in the traditional sense. One of them commented:

However, I don't feel that I really know my classmates because of what they wrote. I may recognize that some are more creative than others and identify some of their likes, but I don't know what they do professionally and their interests in the program. I actually prefer the "traditional" start-up week in which students express who they are, what they do, their interest in the program, etc. I like the info because then I feel "closer" to them.

## The Case Study

### *Effectiveness*

Survey data were moderately positive regarding the effectiveness of the case study. The mean student response to the statement, "I learned a lot," on a Likert scale from 1 (*strongly disagree*) to 5 (*strongly agree*), was 3.7. The most frequent comments regarding effectiveness of the case study, as in the following comment, mentioned the real-world nature of the experience.

The case study was a good way to bring "to life" the model selection process. We each had a hand in creating the case study by editing it to suit the model we selected. As we looked closer at the specifics of our model, we edited the scenario even further, again bringing a touch of reality to the model itself.

Two students remarked that they found the case study a less valuable experience than the online class discussion where students were required to compare and contrast two media selection models. One of them commented:

> I think I would have found it more beneficial to work on a matrix to compare the models or prepare a paper contrasting two in detail and looking at possible execution techniques.

### Efficiency

Student survey responses to the ease of taking part in the case study activity were somewhat neutral. The mean response to the statements, "Teamwork was easy" and "Directions were easy to follow," was 3.25 on a 5-point Likert scale.

Student comments related to the instructional ease of the case study focused mostly on the nature of teamwork experience. Both positive and negative comments were made. Positive comments were made regarding the varied work experiences of teammates and the convenience of students helping make assignment directions clearer. One such comment was, "I found working in a group helped me understand what the assignment was about." Management issues such as working in different time zones were expressed twice, as in the following comment.

> Although I enjoy preparing case studies, in a group situation I found it difficult. With different work approaches and time schedules, I felt that I lost a lot of valuable time on group management issues vs. studying and focusing on the models and their differences.

Two students remarked about the difficulty in working with people who tended to procrastinate. One stated:

> I am now fearful of what will happen when put into another group in this class. I have worked in small groups in practically every other class, and this is the only time that I was in jeopardy of not turning in a project.

As another said:

> This just tells me I will have to worry about waiting until the last minute waiting for others to do their part on the final project. I NEVER wait until the last minute, it's always better to get things done early and look them over. You never know what might come up.

### Appeal

Student responses in the appeal category were the highest, averaging 4 on a 5-point Likert scale. The mean response to the statement, "This activity should be used again," was 4.09. The mean response to the statement, "This activity was motivating," was 3.91. All comments related to appeal were made in the context of liking the case study assignment because it was "real world" or not liking the activity because of trouble working on teams or a preference for a different learning strategy (such as discussions around a matrix comparing two models).

## The Dialog Activity

### Effectiveness

A majority of students considered the dialog activity to have strong instructional merit. Meaningful learning was the theme addressed most frequently. Students mentioned:

- I felt that I really had to understand the points/views of Kozma and Clark to "speak for them."
- This activity required us to extrapolate on the different arguments in the articles by applying it to a narrative type scenario. Our creativity caused us to fill in the gaps and go beyond just the information contained in the articles.
- Diana Laurillard proposes that learning occurs in the conversational framework of the learner's cognitive processes. Regardless of the media used, when the learner can engage in a form of conversation, whether with the teacher, peers, or with oneself, the learning process can be activated, through constructivism. The creation of the dialog activity between Richard Clark, Ruth Clark, and Robert Kozma is an example of Laurillard's proposal.

### Efficiency

Few students mentioned that writing the dialog was difficult. Two students mentioned discomfort overall with the creative writing approach used in the class. One student mentioned adapting to the approach by the time the dialog activity was assigned (which was the last of the three creative writing exercises): "It was difficult at first. By the time we were at the narrative though I was much more comfortable. Kind of working through the discomfort at first!"

### Appeal

A strong majority of students stated liking the dialog activity and liking it the most. Five of the 11 comments regarding the positive appeal of the activity mentioned its constructivist orientation. As one student said:

By far the most constructivist of the above exercises is the narrative. Although I struggled to come up with something original, I enjoyed the fact that we could make it all up from our own experiences. There was a great deal of diversity among the narratives, including the Starbucks theme again. I felt the exercise was beneficial because I got to put my own spin on the debate, from a point of view that I understood.

## How Students Interacted During the Three Narrative Activities

Three types of data were collected related to student interactivity. Frequency of student interactions, Likert-scale responses to teamwork questions, and student suggestions related to improving teamwork experiences provide insight into how students interacted during the three narrative assignments.

### Frequency of Student Interactions
Students' levels of interactivity were measured by the number of online responses made to an entry by another student. Offline interactions were not counted. A majority of students did not use other means of communication during the activity. One group did, however, communicate frequently by phone during the case study activity, spending approximately 45 minutes on the phone together over the course of the case study assignment.

**Table 7.2.   Frequency of Student Interactions**

| Activity | Mean interactions | Range | |
|---|---|---|---|
| | | *Low* | *High* |
| Story Starter | 8 | 4 | 14 |
| Case Study | 10 | 8 | 15 |
| Dialog | 2.4 | 1 | 13 |

### Survey Responses Related to Interactivity
Two survey statements for the case study related to the interactive nature of the activities. The statement, "The teamwork experience was valuable," had a mean score of 3.09 on a 5-point Likert scale, from 1 *(strongly disagree)* to 5 *(strongly agree)*. The statement, "Teamwork was easy," had a mean score of 3.27.

*Student Suggestions for an Improved Team Experience*

Students were asked to make suggestions to improve the team experience for future class projects. The most frequently mentioned suggestions included the following:

(a)  establish a leader
(b)  get consensus on the project plan and deadlines
(c)  collect data on where people live (different time zones) and when and where they can be reached (phone numbers and e-mails)
(d)  include a catch-up day in the project plan
(e)  have a plan for dealing with team members that do not meet dead-lines or become unavailable
(f)  appoint one person as the master document keeper
(g)  allow time for revision
(h)  revisit the project plan

## ANALYSIS AND IMPLICATIONS

### Story Construction

As suggested by the literature, students who grow up in story-rich cultures tend to be story literate. A majority of students in this study employed all of the critical elements of story construction, with the exception of steps that Egan identified as applying specifically to instructional stories. Four of the 11 story starter activities did not relate to an instructional topic, and none of the case studies and dialog activities included an evaluation component. These missing story elements are not surprising as students were not directly instructed to address these elements. For the story starter activity, the topic was purposefully left vague, with the intent that students would have the freedom to write creatively. Including an evaluation component to the story made sense only for the case study, in which students were specifically instructed to include this component.

### Usability

Usability measures of the three strategies suggest that each activity had its strengths and weaknesses and that there was room for improvement in the design of each instructional activity. While the intent of the story starter was to break the ice, introduce the constructivist nature of the class, and to get to know classmates in a different way, its effectiveness in reaching these objectives is questionable. Several students mentioned not having a clear sense of who their classmates were. Perhaps the story themes, which took on creative, sometimes bizarre, and humorous twists actually obscured student personalities. Several students mentioned not feeling like they knew the other students, and that they preferred the more traditional introductions where students share occupations and interests. The open nature of the assignment was also troublesome to students who did not feel comfortable with creative writing or the novel approach. Requiring that students write about a class topic might be an approach that helps students connect the activity with course goals and feel more grounded in the context overall.

Some students criticized the nature of the case study activity itself. Writing a story took time to craft, and these students felt that an assignment that more directly addressed the content, such as a comparison/contrast of two or more media models, would be more beneficial for their learning style. The case study activity was praised for making the topic more like the real world. Not all students, however, were comfortable with this activity. Working within a team environment caused some distress. Individuals felt that working with other people caused issues that got in the way of learning. Managing different time zones and peers procrastinating took the focus off learning. While it was difficult to work with other people, the expertise of class members in this study was diverse. Student case studies were based on team member experiences, which varied in context (military, education, business, and industry) and problem type (change management, economic downturn, safety, regulatory compliance).

The dialog activity received the most positive student comments for all usability dimensions. Students found the activity effective in terms of learning. Interestingly, their comments were often made in the context of the constructivist nature of the activity. Meaningful learning, the ability to be able to "put themselves in the shoes" of the key researchers, and extrapolate ideas, were mentioned as positive instructional aspects of the activity. Only one student mentioned difficulty with writing the assignment, but attributed this more to his comfort level with creative writing than with the specific assignment.

## Interactivity

As might be expected, student interactivity (the number of responses students made in each of the threads; see Figure 7.1) was highest when students were required to work in groups. The story starter activity and the case study activity were the most interactive. The case study was slightly more interactive than the story starter. This could be expected due to the more instructional and challenging nature of the case study assignment. The interactivity on the dialog exercise was low. The mean score of 2.5

interactions included teacher comments, which were in most cases a simple confirmation that the student had done the assignment as expected. Though some students did mention other students' dialogs, the data are unclear as to how much students read through each other's scripts. Of interest is the high usability of the dialog activity. Although the interactivity was low, students found the dialog activity overall to be the most valuable and appealing assignment.

## Guidelines for the Design of Online Narrative Activities

Narrative activities appear to be a workable strategy for online environments and have the benefit of increasing interactivity and providing constructivist learning opportunities. Teamwork increases interactivity, yet the instructional value of teamwork interactivity is somewhat questionable, mostly due to student impressions that the added load of managing people's schedules and different work habits detracts from the educational experience.

The tools available for interaction in an online environment are likely to influence interaction to some degree. While one cannot safely consider that features of the technology used to deliver instruction will *cause* students to engage in particular ways, those features can provide contingencies that students may take up in modeling particular conversation patterns (Winiecki, 1999, 2003, 2004). That is, the ingenuity of the instructor and students to produce new ways of "doing conversation" in asynchronous settings is fundamental to the development and accomplishment of online conversations and instructional discourse.

The following guidelines for improved design of online narrative strategies are suggested to improve the effectiveness, efficiency, and appeal of the story starter, case study, and dialog narrative strategies.

## All Strategies

Egan's instructional story model provides a useful framework for story writing. Students might benefit from exposure to this model prior to narrative writing assignments in order to help them think through what they want to accomplish with their stories. Additionally, students might gain from specific instructions to consider their writing as not only an exercise for themselves but as instructionally relevant for other students in their class. Writing examples for each activity might reduce some of the initial confusion and discomfort for students not accustomed to learning in a constructivist setting.

Many students communicated discomfort with narrative strategies and mentioned this in the context of unease overall with constructivist approaches. Clarifying up front that an activity is likely to feel different than traditional teaching approaches might help students feel calmer. Additionally, both the teacher and the students need to expect some confusion with the narrative/constructivist activities, and welcome confusion and unease as a sign that students are being challenged to create meaning. The nature of constructivism is that students create their own meaning. As a teacher, one cannot know what that meaning will be; consequently, there is a period of time in a constructivist activity when the degree of unknown is fairly high. The teacher can help students, but only so much, since it is the job of the student to create their own sense of things. Informing students of this upfront might take out some of the initial panic that some students experience.

Modeling the effective use of conversational tools is one way to decrease student discomfort. Providing examples of good interactions, or simply pointing out good interactions, is one recommended strategy.

A story starter related to the course topic and continued throughout the course is one strategy for making the activity a better icebreaker and orientation to the class. Requiring students to include two or three things about themselves was suggested by one student in this study as a potentially better way of using the activity for acquaintance purposes.

Online environments introduce the possibility that students might add an extension to the story line at the same time, creating a branch in the story where the plot takes different and confusing directions. Procedures for handling this might be established. Perhaps students should be assigned a time period when they enter their section of the story.

The case study activity might be improved by helping students work in teams. Requiring teams to review teamwork guidelines (such as the ones shared in the Findings section of this chapter) and to clearly define their adoption of those and other guidelines would be beneficial. Clear instructions on how the case studies were designed would be accessible to the student. For example, students might view a flowchart showing major decision points that ideally take place when problem-solving a case. This flowchart would then be mapped to a sample study. A particular decision point on the flowchart would correspond with the case study text.

Methods to encourage student interaction with other student work might be increased. Asking students to compare and contrast different dialogs, name dialog themes, and identify new analogies and examples are all strategies to encourage student interaction with each other's work.

## CONCLUSION

Sixteen students in a completely distance course participated in three narrative activities in which they were required to add to a story starter, write a case study to help other students learn how to use a media selection model, and create a dialog between predominant educational technology researchers. Students, though not always comfortable with the creative nature of these activities, appeared to have the ability to compose stories. Egan (1986) suggests five components that make a story effective for instructional purposes: topic, conflict or binary opposites, organization, resolution, and evaluation. A majority of students in this study included these major story elements in their work, with the exception of writing about an instructional topic for the story starter exercise (which was not a requirement of the assignment), and including an evaluation component to the dialog activity (which were also not requirements of these activities).

Usability measures for the three narrative activities were moderately positive overall, but did suggest that design of the strategies could be improved to increase the instructional effectiveness, ease of performance, and appeal for students. Requiring students to focus their story starter activity on the course topic and to include information about their personalities and interests might improve the effectiveness of this strategy. Activities that are more difficult and involve teamwork require attention to administrative details, such as establishing leadership, setting realistic deadlines, and mitigating risk. Additionally, the instructor must provide the opportunity for students to develop into a functional team, working through the predictable stages of team building.

Students were most positive about the dialog experience, in part because they were able to work alone and did not need to depend on other students to get their work done. While this increased the usability of the assignment, interaction decreased and the opportunity to learn from each other was reduced. Requiring students to synthesize and analyze each other's work is suggested as one method of enhancing interactivity for individual assignments.

## REFERENCES

Bean, J. C. (2001). *Engaging ideas: The professor's guide to integrating writing, critical thinking, and active learning in the classroom.* San Francisco: Jossey-Bass.

Bransford, J. D., & Johnson, M. V. (1972). Contextual prerequisites for understanding: Some investigations of comprehension and recall. *Journal of Verbal Learning and Verbal Behavior, 11,* 717–726.

Bruner, J. (1986). *Actual minds, possible worlds.* Cambridge, MA: Harvard University Press.

Bruner, J. (2002). *Making stories: Law, literature, life.* Cambridge, MA: Harvard University Press.

Chatman, S. (1978). *Story and discourse: Narrative structure in fiction and film.* Ithaca, NY: Cornell University Press.

Coles, R. (1989). *The call of stories.* Boston: Houghton Mifflin.

Culler, J. (1975). *Structuralist poetics: Structuralism, linguistics, and the study of experience.* New York: Teachers College Press.

Egan, K. (1986). *Teaching as story telling: An alternative approach to teaching and curriculum in elementary school.* Chicago: University of Chicago Press.

Goodson, I., & Walker, R. (1995). Telling tales. In H. McEwan & K. Egan (Eds.), *Narrative in teaching, learning, and research* (pp. 184–194). New York: Teachers College Press.

Gudmundsdottir, S. (1995). The narrative nature of pedagogical content knowledge. In H. McEwan & K. Egan (Eds.) *Narrative in teaching, learning, and research* (pp. 24–38). New York: Teachers College Press.

Mayer, R. (2001). *Multimedia learning.* Cambridge, England: Cambridge University Press.

McEwan, H., & Egan, K. (1995). *Narrative in teaching, learning, and research.* New York: Teachers College Press.

Winiecki, D. J. (1999). Keeping the thread: Adapting conversational practice to help distance students and instructors manage discussions in an asynchronous learning network. *DEOSNEWS, 9*(2). Retrieved May 18, 2004, from http://www.ed.psu.edu/acsde/deos/deosnews/deosnews9_2.asp

Winiecki, D. J. (2003). Instructional discussions in online education: Practical and research-oriented perspectives. In M. Moore & R. Anderson (Eds.), *Handbook of distance education* (pp. 193–215). Mahwah, NJ: Erlbaum.

Winiecki, D. J. (2004). Reconstructing talk: Conversational patterns in the asynchronous classroom. Manuscript submitted for publication.

Witherell, C. S., Tran, H. T., & Othus, J. (1995). Narrative landscapes and the moral imagination. In H. McEwan & K. Egan (Eds.), *Narrative in teaching, learning, and research* (pp. 39–49). New York: Teachers College Press.

CHAPTER 8

# ENHANCING ELEMENTARY TEACHERS' UNDERSTANDING OF INQUIRY: TEACHING AND LEARNING USING ONLINE SCIENTIFIC DISCOURSE

Lea B. Accalogoun, *Empire State College*
and
Dennis W. Sunal and Sharon Nichols, *University of Alabama*

This study investigated the extent to which the use of online media to engage elementary practitioners in scientific discourse supports their learning to teach inquiry-based science. Twenty-eight elementary practitioners enrolled in a four-week graduate elementary science methods course were involved in the study. Teachers were given opportunities to experience inquiry-based activities, develop good explanations for their claims, and engage in online discourse for the negotiation of ideas concerning claims. As a result of their experience, participants' views of science inquiry learning and teaching significantly changed. This chapter describes challenges of using online resources to support the process of scientific argumentation and provides a model for application in teacher education and implications for further research.

*Research on Enhancing the Interactivity of Online Learning*, pages 127–148

The National Science Education Standards (National Research Council, 1996, 2000) frame inquiry as involving not only asking questions and engaging in experimentation, but also as peer critique and revision of ideas. However, for a decade, more emphasis has been placed on the experimental process, leaving little room for the practice of scientific discourse. Recently, researchers (Abell, Anderson, & Chezem, 2000) have stressed the importance of moving beyond the exploration and experiment stage of inquiry to include the argument process, a central element for the understanding of scientific knowledge construction (Newton, Driver, & Osborne, 1999; Smith & Anderson, 1999).

Previous studies indicate that online technology is an effective and promising tool that helps promote scientific discourse as "argument" (Bell & Linn, 2000), and as reflective practice (Avraamidou & Zembal-Saul, 2002; Loh et al., 1997). The online medium can be an archive of teachers' professional knowledge, assisting in storing teachers' exchange of ideas for further review and reflection. This study investigated the use of the online environment for enhancing elementary practitioners' understanding of scientific inquiry to support their teaching of science as inquiry in the classroom.

## REVIEW OF LITERATURE

Scientific discourse, a form of reasoning and argumentation, is central to the understanding of scientific knowledge construction. Previous studies have depicted scientific reasoning as involving the coordination of evidences and theories to form a coherent interpretation of knowledge claims (Kuhn, 1993; Lemke, 1993; Newton et al., 1999; Smith & Anderson, 1999). Claims are considered scientific knowledge when they conform to the norms of coherence, viability, and acceptance by the scientific community (Newton et al., 1999; Roth, Tobin, & Ritchie, 2001; Smith & Anderson, 1999). The process of acceptance results from rigorous scrutiny of claims and intensive argumentation (Smith & Anderson, 1999).

According to Roth et al. (2001), the process of argumentation is embedded with evidence and theories to help understand the extent to which knowledge claims are valid. If students are to think scientifically and value the nature of scientific inquiry, then teachers need to promote the practice of argumentation in their science instruction and engage students in the co-construction of knowledge (Abell et al., 2000; Newton et al., 1999). Because learning is an extremely social process, it is important that students be given opportunities for more involvement in scientific reasoning and argumentation (Kuhn, 1993; Lemke, 1993).

Also, elementary teachers' views of science inquiry are limited with regard to the role social discourse plays in the construction of scientific knowledge (Abell, Martini, & George, 2001; Abell & Smith, 1994). In their investigation, Abell et al. (2001) indicated that preservice elementary teachers did not perceive the importance of the role of communication and criticism in the development of scientific knowledge. Akerson, Abd-El-Khalick, and Lederman (2000) found that hands-on activities alone did not enhance elementary preservice teachers' views of the nature of science. Only activities that incorporated participants' involvement in rich discussion of their claims extended teachers' understanding of the nature of science. Without deep perceptions of the nature of science, teachers will have difficulty understanding how scientific knowledge is constructed and, therefore, difficulty in teaching science for understanding (Bianchini & Colburn, 2000; Eick, 2000).

Researchers have demonstrated that the online medium is a promising means for engaging learners in scientific reasoning and arguments (Bell & Linn, 2000; Land & Zembal-Saul, 2001) and in construction of science knowledge (Kanuka & Anderson, 1998). Further, some studies posit that online forums have the potential to develop learners' reflective practices (Haefner, Zembal-Saul, & Avraamidou, 2002) and collaborative learning (Bos, Krajcik, & Patrick, 1995; Hall, 1997). The purpose of this study was to investigate the extent to which the use of online media would promote elementary teachers' scientific discourse and their understanding of science inquiry. The overarching question that guided this study was, How does the use of online media to promote scientific discourse and to enhance elementary teachers' understanding of science inquiry support the teaching of science as inquiry in the classroom? The following are questions, which more specifically informed this central focus:

1. Do practicing elementary teachers' views of scientific inquiry and science inquiry teaching change as a result of their online experience?

2. To what extent does the online experience in scientific discourse affect teachers' development of argument and co-construction of scientific knowledge?

3. How does the online experience enable practicing elementary teachers to adopt the teaching of science as inquiry?

## RESEARCH DESIGN

A mixed design of quantitative methodology supported through qualitative data sources was used to inform this study. The course was offered during summer 2003 at a satellite campus of a major university in the southeastern United States. Study participants were selected using a convenient sample (Patton, 1990) from the university's summer graduate program. The sample included 28 of 31 elementary teachers enrolled in a four-week graduate elementary science methods course. Pseudonyms have been used to provide anonymity for all participants in this study. The authors shared responsibilities for teaching and research within the study; the first author, however, led all instructional activities related to online learning.

## DESCRIPTION OF COURSE ACTIVITIES

The course involved face-to-face meetings Mondays through Wednesdays, and online interactions Thursdays through Sundays. The face-to-face meetings provided opportunities for hands-on inquiries and reflective activities, and training for use of online argumentation tools. Teachers explored concepts of science and inquiry learning through hands-on activities. Learning focused on topics in earth science (phases of the moon) and physical science (density/buoyancy, sound, electricity, and change in matter with toothpaste). Curriculum materials were used from the Full Option Science System (FOSS) (Full Option Science System, 2004) and Great Explorations in Math and Science (GEMS) (Great Explorations in Math and Science, 2004) to support inquiry activities during class sessions. In accord with the National Science Education Standards and the Alabama Course of Study—Science (Alabama State Department of Education, 2001), participants learned about, and designed units, based on the learning cycle (Barman, 1990; Marek & Methven, 1991; Sunal & Sunal, 2003).

Participants worked in small groups of five to seven teachers representing grades K–1, 2–3, and 4–7. All class sessions generally followed the same routine. At the beginning of each week, participants were engaged in hands-on activities that served as springboards for science inquiry. After involvement in hands-on activities featuring electricity, each group designed inventions to extend their learning about science concepts and inquiry. Evidence and explanations developed by teachers about their inquiry experiences and products were reported online for claim development and online critiques.

The online session of the course occurred via the Alabama Virtual Campus (AVC) system Web site. The AVC system is a menu-driven course design that offers many tools including portfolio, discussion board, journal, and library applications. The purpose of the online resource was to guide participants in the development of good claims for scientific argumentation. The portfolio tool was organized as three entry sections: (a) original version of claims, (b) process of scientific argumentation, and (c) final version of claim (See Figure 8.1).

| Home |
I. Original Version of Claims |
| II. Process of scientific argumentation | IIa. Evidence | IIb. Conclusion | IIc. Warrant |
| IId. Backing |
| III. Final Version of Claims

Figure 8.1.    Structure of the scientific portfolio.

Upon completion of grade-level group inquiries in class, participants individually submitted explanations of their results in the first section of the portfolio, original version of claims, before engaging in the process of argument development. The second section of the portfolio, process of scientific argumentation, involved a series of sequential steps to guide participants in building convincing explanations. The structure of this second section was based on Toulmin's (1958) argument, which features four dimensions that contribute to an ideal explanation, including making *claims* based on *evidence* and supporting with *warrants* and *backing*. In the third part of the portfolio, the final version of claims, participants posted the overall summary statements from the whole process. This section helped understand how thoughtfully subjects developed their explanations. During the development of explanations, participants were encouraged to use the online library tool for their documentation. The library tool stored articles, documents, and relevant Web site links to assist participants in the development of their claims.

The discussion board tool engaged participants in interactions across groups (under the heading "All Groups"), as well as within groups (see Figure 8.2).

After refining their explanations, participants engaged in negotiation of ideas with partners within their group. At the end of the group discussion, presenters submitted their group's claim to other groups for critique. Participants were encouraged to express their thoughts and to actively participate in the discussion.

A journal tool assisted to follow participants in their growth in knowledge and change in conceptions. It displayed open-ended questions, which helped participants to stay focused during their weekly reflective writing before and after the use of the online media (Bennett, 1999).

Discussion Topics:

Messages

Topics | Sort as List | **Post**

❑ <u>**All Group 5(1, 3)**</u> by: <u>Lea Accalogoun</u> ✉ 7/6/2003 8:46:16 AM (words: )

❑ <u>**All Group 4(2, 5)**</u> by: <u>Lea Accalogoun</u> ✉ 7/6/2003 8:45:45 AM (words: )

❑ <u>**All Group 3(1, 4)**</u> by: <u>Lea Accalogoun</u> ✉ 7/6/2003 8:44:57 AM (words: )

❑ <u>**All Group 2(3, 5)**</u> by: <u>Lea Accalogoun</u> ✉ 7/6/2003 8:44:23 AM (words: )

❑ <u>**All Group 1(2, 4)**</u> by: <u>Lea Accalogoun</u> ✉ 7/6/2003 8:43:53 AM (words: )

❑ <u>**Group 5**</u> by: <u>Lea Accalogoun</u> ✉ 7/6/2003 8:39:51 AM (words: )

❑ <u>**Group 4**</u> by: <u>Lea Accalogoun</u> ✉ 7/6/2003 8:39:25 AM (words: )

❑ <u>**Group 3**</u> by: <u>Lea Accalogoun</u> ✉ 7/6/2003 8:39:05 AM (words: )

❑ <u>**Group 2**</u> by: <u>Lea Accalogoun</u> ✉ 7/6/2003 8:38:33 AM (words: )

❑ <u>**Group 1**</u> by: <u>Lea Accalogoun</u> ✉ 7/6/2003 8:37:41 AM (words: )

Figure 8.2.   Structure of the discussion board.

## COLLECTION OF DATA SOURCES

Multiple sources of qualitative data were gathered to enable multiple points of reference for analysis (Patton, 1990). Qualitative data included drawings and story writing, teachers' reflective writings, and interview transcripts. A Drawing and Story-Writing Instrument (DSWI) was developed to explore elementary teachers' images of science inquiry and the teaching of science as inquiry. For the DSWI, teachers sketched their image of science inquiry. Story writing engages participants in writing a story about teaching science inquiry in their classroom. Four teachers volunteered to participate in audio taped interviews during and after the course to provide contextual insights about their perspectives and practices.

Four data collection instruments were used: Beliefs About Scientific Inquiry and Science Inquiry Teaching Instrument (BASISITI), Science Teaching Efficacy Belief Instrument (STEBI-A), Learning Cycle Lesson Plan Rubric (LCLPR), and an online survey questionnaire. BASISITI was a modified version of the Beliefs About Science and School Science Questionnaire (Aldridge, Taylor, & Chen, 1997) used to assess elementary teachers' views of scientific inquiry and science inquiry teaching. Two-part scores are given for the BASISITI: scientific inquiry and science inquiry teaching. STEBI-A (Enochs & Riggs, 1990) was used to determine if there was an improvement in the level of teacher self-efficacy in teaching science. A modified learning cycle lesson plan rubric (Bland, Goldston, Sundberg, Sunal, & Sunal, 2003) was used to assess teachers' inquiry-based lesson plans. The online survey instrument developed by Kanuka and

Anderson (1998) was modified and used to assess participants' perceptions of the use of the online learning environment.

## DATA ANALYSIS

Qualitative analysis involved analytic induction (LeCompte & Preissle, 1993) to understand teachers' improvement in views about scientific inquiry and their desire to support inquiry-based learning in the classroom. Analytic induction was performed using Bell and Linn's (2000) coding scheme for argument characteristics, and reframed to fit the focus of this study (see Table 8.1).

**Table 8.1.    Modified Coding Scheme for Argument Characteristics Originally Framed by Bell & Linn (2000)**

| | |
|---|---|
| Type of Warrants | [1] Description—a retelling or summarization of the evidence |
| | [2] Single warrant—contains a scientific conjecture about the evidence |
| | [3] Multiple warrant—contains more than one scientific conjecture |
| | [0] Other—irrelevant evidence |
| Backings | [1] Cited other evidences, or |
| | [1] Cited experiments, or |
| | [1] Cited life situation |
| | [0] No citation |

The coding scheme was used to quantify types of explanations built during teachers' online arguments. Gunawardena, Lowe, and Anderson's (1997) model of analysis was performed to analyze transcripts of the online discussion and to identify and quantify patterns of interactions between and among participants during their online communications.

Descriptive statistics, correlation analysis methods, and paired $t$ tests were performed using the Microsoft Excel and the Statistical Product and Service Solutions (SPSS 11) software (Norusis, 2002). Upon the completion of the qualitative analysis, descriptive statistical analysis was done to determine the percentage of types of explanations built before and after the use of the online argument development. Types of knowledge construction produced during the online interaction of participants were quantified and group means calculated to examine the quality of interaction within and across groups that took place in the online environment.

Two separate paired $t$ tests were conducted on pre1test (given at the beginning of the control time period) and pre2test (given at the beginning of the experimental time period) and then pre2test and posttest, (given at the end of the experimental time period). The analysis involved two-part scores, scientific inquiry and science inquiry teaching, of the BASISITI survey to determine any differences in participants' beliefs about science inquiry and science inquiry teaching. The same analyses were repeated with STEBI-A scores to find out any difference in participants' self-efficacy in teaching science. In addition, a paired $t$ test was conducted to look for improvement in lesson plans. Correlation analysis was performed to identify any relationship between participants' improvement in beliefs and their planning of science inquiry-based learning cycle lesson.

## FINDINGS

Results of the study are represented under major topics in relation to the guiding questions of study. We begin with insights about teachers' views of science inquiry and science inquiry teaching since their understandings of inquiry were foundational to this investigation.

### Topic 1: Teachers' Views of Science Inquiry and Science Inquiry Teaching

During the early stage of the course and upon an introduction to the science inquiry concept, course participants were given two minutes to compose quick-write reflections. Analysis of written entries revealed that some teachers believed science inquiry is limited to asking questions and engaging in hands-on activities.

> I have learned that science inquiry is a hands-on activity. The purpose is to inspire students to ask questions about science. They need to "wonder" about things! (Sandra's in-class reflection, July 1, 2003)

Analysis of the scientific inquiry test scores of BASISITI survey using a paired $t$ test at an alpha level of 0.05 showed no significant difference in the mean comparison of the pre1test and pre2test scores ($t = -1.534$, $df = 18$, $p = .143$, $CI_{95}$). This indicated that there was no improvement in teachers' views of science inquiry during the first five days of the course involving only face-to-face activities. A significant difference was observed, however, in the mean comparisons of the pre2test and posttest ($t = -2.377$, $df = 17$, $p = .029$, $CI_{95}$). The mean score in the posttest was higher ($M = 65.33$, $SD = 7.96$) than in pre2test ($M = 61.28$, $SD = 8.24$). The results revealed that there was an improvement in teachers' views of science inquiry during the second part of the course, which involved the online experience. These outcomes are consistent with the findings of Akerson et al. (2000), who reported that activities that involve teachers in rich discussion about their science claims improve their understandings of the nature of science.

Analysis of teachers' views of scientific inquiry teaching scores using a paired $t$ test at an alpha level of 0.05 showed no significant difference in the mean comparison of the pre1test and pre2test scores ($t = 1.585$, $df = 18$, $p = .130$, $CI_{95}$). However, a significant difference was observed in the mean comparisons of the pre2test and posttest ($t = -2.505$, $df = 17$, $p = .023$, $CI_{95}$). The mean score in the posttest was higher ($M = 93.39$, $SD = 11.81$) than in pre2test ($M = 87.39$, $SD = 13.76$). The results indicated that there was no improvement in teachers' perceptions of science inquiry teaching during the first five days of the course, whereas during the remainder of the course, there was some improvement in teachers' views.

During the second phase of the course, online media were incorporated to help promote teachers' scientific discourse. After more involvement in inquiry hands-on activities and giving participants opportunities to practice scientific discourse, a fifth-grade teacher, interviewed one day before the end of the course, stated:

> I am glad to have this course. I learned a lot about science inquiry, especially its different stages. I appreciated the argument development process and believed it will be useful to kids in the classroom. Seeing and hearing the opinions of each other will help kids think logically, develop mature ideas, and understand each other. (Laura's interview transcript, July 22, 2003)

There was a tendency that as participants gained more understanding of scientific inquiry, they expressed greater willingness to implement it in the classroom.

Although participants showed improvement in their views about scientific inquiry upon completion of the course, most maintained a focus on hands-on-oriented activities. The post drawings showed 78% ($n = 18$) of the drawings depicted students asking questions and in small groups around tables or in outdoor activities. Twenty-two percent ($n = 5$) of drawings displayed science tools or classroom structure. None of the drawings included students presenting their results to the whole class or discussing the results of their investigation with their peers.

Contrary to the drawings of scientific inquiry, the findings of the story writings indicated some progress in their perception of science inquiry teaching. In the pre1test story writings, the majority of teachers described themselves as having direction-giving roles. There was a slight variation in the pre2test story writing, as 85% of teachers depicted themselves as less central figures, giving students more opportunities in finding ways to carry out their investigation. The remaining 15% told stories that also included students sharing their results with the whole class and engaging in the revision of ideas.

## Topic 2: Involvement of Elementary Teachers in Online Scientific Discourse

### *Improvement in Argument Development*

The findings indicated that participants benefited from the use of the online media. The results (see Figure 8.3) showed progress in participants' development of good explanations.

Further analysis of the portfolio transcripts revealed that participants improved in the types of explanations they developed. The results showed that during the second week of the course and before the use of the process of scientific argumentation, 81% ($n = 13$) of subjects made descriptive claims, which represented 62% of the total raw scores of explanations. This pointed out that the majority of the sample reported a summary of their evidence. Only 19% ($n = 3$) of the sample grounded their explanations in warrant (theoretical framework) supported with backing. This represented 38% of the total raw scores. After the use of the *argument development process,* only 31% ($n = 5$) of the sample presented just a description of their results. The descriptive claims represented 18% of the total raw scores, whereas the percentage of warrant and backing development increased to reach 82%.

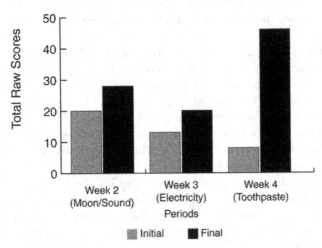

Figure 8.3.   Participants' progress in argument development.

The weekly comparison of the type of explanations developed at the initial and final phases showed an increased in the percentage of warrant and backing claims made at the final stages. The overall analysis indicated that before the use of the argument development section, participants made more descriptive claims (62%) than convincing explanations (38%). With the use of the online portfolio and at the end of the online experience, subjects shifted from descriptive claims (30%) to a more convincing form (70%), which include statements of scientific theory and examples to support their claims. Yet, final claims still needed some improvement. Illustrations of types of argument development are found in Table 8.2.

**Table 8.2.   Illustrations of Types of Explanations Built for Final Claims during the Online Experience**

| | |
|---|---|
| Descriptive claim | "We made a tanning bed using wires, 2 D batteries, a small motor for a fan, and a Christmas light bulb for the tanning bulb. We then used a paper towel tube and cut it to make the tanning bed. The idea was to keep the person tanning cool. The question we had after we were finished was if you could do the same thing but only use 1 battery." |
| Single warrant claim | "Our invention of the ceiling fan with light lead us to the following conclusion: In order for electricity to move through an object and make it work, the electrical current must make a complete circuit from a power source through the object and back again to the power source." |
| Multiple-warrant claim | "In our investigation we observed that the light lit only when the circuit was closed and conductive materials were used to complete the circuit." |
| Claim with backing | "Our toothpaste has an incredible taste and color. BACKING: Children are drawn to vibrant colors and minty taste is yummy! Warrant: Matter is made up of certain properties. PROVE CLAIM: Ask five children to test and give opinion on color and taste. Results: 4 out of 5 children liked the Hulk brand best." |

The weakness in the development of claims across conceptual topics might be related to many factors, including lack in science background, technology, and pedagogical issues. The unfamiliarity with the technology tools as well as the insufficient prior training of participants in argument development might affect their effective argument-building skills. Despite this weakness in their final claims, the use of the online portfolio demonstrated some progress in teachers' argument development skills.

### Patterns of Knowledge Construction Within and Across Groups

Categorization of types of knowledge construction produced during the online interaction of participants was done using Gunawardena et al.'s (1997) model of analysis. The number of each type of knowledge produced within each group per week was counted and group mean calculated. The findings indicated that there was little interaction for knowledge construction. The group mean of types of patterns of interactions is displayed in Table 8.3.

**Table 8.3.   Types of Patterns of Interaction Within Groups**

|  | Week 2 | Week 3 | Week 4 |
|---|---|---|---|
| Phase I: Sharing/Comparing of Information | | | |
| A. A statement of observation or opinion | 2.60 | 4.00 | 1.75 |
| B. A statement of agreement from one or more other participants | 1.20 | 1.40 | 0.50 |
| C. Corroborating examples provided by one or more participants | 0.80 | 0.00 | 0.00 |
| D. Asking and answering questions to clarify details of statements | 0.20 | 0.00 | 0.00 |
| E. Definition, description or identification of a problem | 0.00 | 0.00 | 0.00 |
| Phase II: Discovery of Dissonance and Inconsistency | | | |
| A. Identifying and stating areas of disagreement | 0.40 | 0.00 | 0.00 |
| B. Asking and answering questions to clarify disagreement | 0.00 | 0.00 | 0.00 |
| C. Restating participant's position and possibly advancing | 0.00 | 0.00 | 0.00 |
| Phase III: Negotiation of Meaning/Co-construction of Knowledge | 0.00 | 0.00 | 0.00 |
| Phase IV: Testing and Modification of Proposed Synthesis | 0.00 | 0.00 | 0.00 |
| Phase V: Agreement/Application of Newly Constructed Meaning | 0.00 | 0.00 | 0.00 |

Participants were more interested in sharing and supporting each other's opinions than engaging in dialogue that might lead to a negotiation or compromise. For example, in Group 2 during a discussion on factors affecting the pitch of the sound, one member posted:

The main objective of our experiment was concerned with length of an object and the number of vibrations observed. We found that the shorter an object is, the more vibrations are observed and the sound that results is higher and louder. When an object's length is increased, the number of vibrations decreases and the sound becomes lower and softer.

One of the group partners replied, "I agree, it was interesting to see how the length of the string changed the pitch. It was also interesting how the thin string sounded different than the rubber elastic." During the across-group discussion, one member from another group replied, "Our group thought that was interesting too. We also thought it was interesting how different materials created much different pitches." These interactions within and across groups showed statements of agreement, in which participants supported each other's ideas rather than involving in confrontation, for deeper understanding of the scientific concepts. These results are supported by previous studies (Gunawardena et al., 1997; Vrasidas & McIsaac, 1999). However, few interactions that led to clarification of positions and negotiation of meanings had been observed. An example of an all-group discussion demonstrates this type of interaction online:

CLARA. Lipstick stains are hard to remove and we found one toothpaste that cleaned more effectively than the other three leading brands.

DIANA. What brand of lipstick did you use? Was it a long-lasting type?

LAURA. How many toothpicks of soap did you have in the toothpaste that worked the best on removing the lipstick?

DORA. We used two toothpicks of soap for our toothpaste.

RONNY. How did you find that it cleans better?

CLARA. Two brands cleaned off the toothpaste, but left a sticky residue. One did not clean the toothpaste off at all and the one we chose cleaned off the lipstick and left a smooth, clean-feeling surface.

SYLVA. Did you all use different brands of lipstick or just different shades?

One member of Group 3 gave names of the lipstick brands that the group used to end the discussion. Even though this negotiation of meaning does not lead to the understanding of the concept of change in matter, it showed participants how evidence and "convincing" explanations are important for the validation of claims. The overall result indicated that participants within and across group were more involved in social interaction than in construction of new knowledge.

## Topic 3: Effect of the Online Scientific Discourse on Teachers' Enablement to Implement Inquiry-Based Science

Teacher self-efficacy is a determinant factor in understanding teachers' willingness to implement science inquiry teaching in the classroom. Because teachers' beliefs are consistent with their science teaching practices, STEBI-A (Enochs & Riggs, 1990) was used to determine whether or not there was an improvement in teachers' science teaching efficacy as a result of their experience online. Contrary to our expectation, the results of both paired $t$ tests showed no significant difference in STEBI-A scores of the first session ($t = .392$, $df = 18$, $p = .700$, $CI_{95}$) or the second session of the course ($t = .956$, $df = 18$, $p = .351$, $CI_{95}$). This revealed that despite teachers' claims of an increase in confidence to implement science inquiry in the classroom, there was statistically no significant improvement in their self-efficacy.

Many researchers have indicated that the views of teachers about the nature of science and how students learn science guide their classroom instruction (Brickhouse, 1990; Taylor, 1990). Accordingly, this study tried to understand to what degree teachers' improvement in views affected their planning of an inquiry-based learning cycle lesson. A pair of instructors assessed the lesson plans of teachers using the modified learning cycle rubric version (Bland et al., 2003). The estimated inter-rater reliability was .96. The results of the paired $t$ test at the .05 alpha level showed a significant difference in the mean scores of pre and post lesson plans ($t = -3.961$, $df = 27$, $p = .000$, $CI_{95}$). The mean score in the post lesson plan was higher ($M = 78.36$, $SD = 9.60$) than in the pre lesson plan ($M = 67.29$, $SD = 15.05$).

Pearson correlation analysis was used to examine whether there was relationship between teachers' improvement in beliefs about science inquiry and science inquiry teaching (BASISITI) and their improvement in inquiry-based learning cycle lesson planning. The results indicated a moderate correlation between teachers' beliefs about science inquiry and science inquiry teaching and their planning of inquiry-based lessons ($r = .553$; $N = 18$; $p = .017$). These results are supported by previous studies, which reported that there is a connection between science teachers' beliefs and their instructional practices (Brickhouse, 1990; Lederman, 1999; Taylor, 1990).

## DISCUSSION AND IMPLICATIONS

Several significant findings had emerged from the study. For the first question, the results revealed that elementary teachers had positively shifted in their perceptions of scientific inquiry and science inquiry teaching as a result of their online experience. The use of online media had a significant effect on their change in views ($p < .05$). However, teachers had maintained more traditional images of science inquiry in their drawings. Only a little enhancement was observed in their story writings. Some of the teachers' post writings mentioned students' reports of their work and comments, and revision of ideas.

The results of the second question of the study indicated that there was a progress in teachers' argument-building skills. Teachers had developed fewer descriptive claims upon the use of the argument development process in the online portfolio than they initially did. However, during their online interaction for negotiation of ideas, little construction of knowledge had occurred. Teachers preferred supporting each other's thoughts than being involved in confrontation of ideas. These findings are consistent with previous research, which pointed out that skepticism and confrontation were not welcomed in elementary teachers' culture (Spector & Strong, 2001). Thus, the use of online media has helped sharpen the argument development skills of participants to improve their understanding of science inquiry. However, elementary teachers valued more hands-on inquiry activities and face-to-face interactions rather than involving in scientific discourse in an online environment.

Many factors challenged elementary teachers' active involvement in argument building and construction of knowledge. These included the structure of the portfolio and discussion board, technical problems, technology ability of the teachers, time allocated for the online assignments, resistance of teachers, course structure, and background of the teachers.

## The Design of Portfolio and Discussion Board

The online survey results revealed that teachers found the technical part difficult. Many participants reported that the portfolio and the discussion board were too complex. One teacher expressed frustration: "Too complicated. Easier to just email or discuss in class" (Berth's comments of the online survey, July 23, 2003). This result was supported by a previous study (Vrasidas and McIsaac, 1999) that pointed out how the design of the medium can lead to less participation. Listening to participants helped set up an additional training time. Also, the portfolio was modified to a one-page template that included all the necessary steps for good argument building. For the within-group and across-group discussion, guidance and an in-class role-play helped facilitate participants' understanding of their online responsibilities.

## Technical Problems

During the online experience of teachers, many technology problems had emerged that added to participants' confusion.

> I am the reporter for my group....The discussion that I wrote on the AVC is not there anymore. I did do it though. (e-mail from Ava, July 11, 2003)

> I tried my best to post the assignment correctly. My posting is not under group 5 where it should be. It ended up at the top of the "Discussions" page. I am sorry. I have never used the AVC before and I am not sure of the correct procedures. (e-mail from Berth, July, 12, 2003)

## Technology Ability and Lack of Time for Online Assignments

Another challenging factor interfered in the quality of the online interaction. The lack of familiarity of teachers with technology tools caused fear and hesitancy.

> I wanted to let you know that I am having difficulty pulling up different segments of the online assignments. I took an online course in June and I had the same problem. I did not know what was causing the problem. (e-mail from Judy, July 14, 2003)

The time allocated for the online assignment as well as for the overall course influenced the quality of participants' online interaction. Many participants were disappointed by the short period of time given to make sense of how and why the AVC site was to be used in the course.

> The most difficult part is that it is too short for this type of experience. A course like this should be offered a full semester. We just started to be interested and already the class is over. (Interview with Mary, July 21, 2003)

This finding is supported by previous study (Vrasidas and McIsaac, 1999), which indicated that a course-heavy workload contributed to students' poor involvement in online discussion.

## Resistance of Elementary Teachers to the Online Experience

Despite the struggle to help better understand the use of online tools and assignments, some elementary practitioners were still resistant to the idea of online learning. One teacher admitted:

> I had trouble with participants waiting until the last minute to do their part. One person waited until 11:00 on Sunday night to do anything, and then I had already gone to bed. It was supposed to be finished on Sunday, but I had to answer her on Monday morning. I also didn't like it that people would not do anything (not even visit the site) then claim that they couldn't get it to work right when they tried. (Ava's comments of the online survey, July 23, 2003)

The unwillingness of some of the participants might be due to their perception of the online experience as not useful to their classroom teaching or unfit to their cultural practices.

> I do not see how online instruction will benefit a classroom teacher who wants to learn how to motivate his and her students. (Dora's comments of the online survey, July 23, 2003)

> We are more social people. They like to see each other's face when interacting. This is why online is so hard for them. (Interview with Mary, July 21, 2003)

## The Course Design

The structure of the course led some participants to claim that they found the online interaction unnecessary. They preferred interacting face-to-face in class than online.

> We have been working together and seeking results together in class so don't know why again discussing online. What new thing should be proved online? (Interview with Diana, July 22, 2003)

This finding is supported by Vrasidas and McIsaac (1999), who reported that when combining face-to-face and online meetings, students considered online meetings as a rest rather than an opportunity to involve in meaningful construction of knowledge.

## CONCLUSION

There is potential for online media to promote scientific discourse as a means to improve elementary teachers' understanding of scientific knowledge construction and to support their teaching of science as inquiry in the classroom. However, these elementary teachers preferred to see their growth in science inquiry through experiences in inquiry hands-on activities in face-to-face meetings than involving in scientific discourse in an online environment. This study provides insights about the challenges of helping elementary teachers to engage in science inquiry beyond the initial stages of question posing, data collection and analysis, and conclusion—they need to also engage in sharing results, peer review, and revision of outcomes. While the study also describes challenges using online resources to support teacher learning about inquiry as a process of scientific argumentation, the results offer useful suggestions for the design of online portfolios and teacher-training activities involving online interactions. Well-designed portfolio and discussion board as well as prior training in technology may boost teachers' positive attitudes toward the use of the online environment. Accordingly, an implication of this study is that improving elementary practitioners' online understanding of science inquiry and scientific discourse may be possible through extended training and technology support.

## REFERENCES

Abell, S. K., Anderson, G., & Chezem, J. (2000). Science as argument and explanation: Inquiring into concepts of sound in third grade. In J. Minstrell & E. van Zee (Eds.), *Inquiry into inquiry learning and teaching in science* (pp. 65–79). Washington, DC: American Association for the Advancement of Science.

Abell, S. K., Martini, M., & George, M. (2001). That's what scientists have to do: Preservice elementary teachers' conceptions of the nature of science during a moon investigation. *International Journal of Science Education, 23*, 1095–1109.

Abell, S. K., & Smith, D. (1994). What is science? Preservice elementary teachers' conceptions of the nature of science. *International Journal of Science Education, 16*, 475–487.

Aldridge, J., Taylor, P., & Chen, C. (1997, April). *Development, validation and use of the beliefs about science and school science questionnaire (BASSSQ).* Paper presented at the annual conference of the National Association of Research in Science Teaching, Oak Brook, IL.

Akerson, V., Abd-El-Khalick, F., & Lederman, N. (2000). Influence of a reflective explicit activity-based approach on elementary teachers' conceptions of the nature of science. *Journal of Research in Science Teaching, 37*, 295–317.

Alabama Department of Education. (2001). *Alabama Course of Study: Science.* Montgomery, AL: Author.

Avraamidou, L., & Zembal-Saul, C. (2002, January). *Using a Web-based task to make prospective elementary teachers' personal theorizing about science teaching explicit.* Paper presented at the annual international conference of the Association for the Education of Teachers in Science, Charlotte, NC.

Barman, C. (1990). *An expanded view of the learning cycle: New ideas about an effective teaching strategy.* Arlington, VA: Council for Elementary Science International, National Science Teachers Association.

Bell, P., & Linn, M. C. (2000). Scientific arguments as learning artifacts: Designing for learning from the Web with KIE. *International Journal of Science Education, 22,* 797–817.

Bennett, L. (1999). In response...Designing an online journal. *T.H.E. Journal, 26*(7), 52–56.

Bianchini, J. A., & Colburn, A. (2000). Teaching the nature of science through inquiry to prospective elementary teachers: A tale of two researchers. *Journal of Research in Science Teaching, 37,* 177–209.

Bland, J., Goldston, M. J., Sundberg, C. W., Sunal, D. W., & Sunal, C. S. (2003). Learning cycle lesson plan rubric: Version 3. Tuscaloosa: University of Alabama, Alabama Science Teaching and Learning Center.

Bos, N., Krajcik, J., & Patrick, H. (1995). Telecommunications for teachers: Supporting reflection and collaboration. *Journal of Computers in Mathematics and Science Teaching, 14*(1/2), 187–202.

Brickhouse, N. (1990). Teachers' beliefs about the nature of science and their relationship to classroom practice. *Journal of Teacher Education, 41(3),* 53–62.

Eick, C. J. (2000). Inquiry, nature of science, and evolution: The need for a more complex pedagogical content knowledge in science teaching. *Journal of Science Education, 4*(3), 1–14.

Enochs, L. G., & Riggs, I. M. (1990). Further development of an elementary science teaching efficacy belief instrument: A preservice elementary scale. *School Science and Mathematics, 90,* 695–706.

Full Option Science System (FOSS). (2004). *Full option science system.* Berkeley, CA: University of California, Lawrence Hall of Science.

Great Explorations in Science and Mathematics (GEMS). (2004). *Great explorations in science and mathematics.* Berkeley, CA: University of California, Lawrence Hall of Science.

Gunawardena, C. N., Lowe, C. A., & Anderson, T. (1997). Analysis of a global online debate and the development of an interaction analysis model for examining social construction of knowledge in computer conferencing. *Journal of Educational Computing Research, 17,* 397–431.

Haefner, L. A., Zembal-Saul, C., & Avraamidou, L. (2002, April). *Supporting prospective elementary teachers in developing scientific explanations using "Progress Portfolio."* Paper presented at the annual meeting of the National Association for Research in Science Teaching, New Orleans, LA.

Hall, D. (1997). Computer mediated communication in post-compulsory teacher education. *Open Learning, 12*(3), 54–57.

Kuhn, D. (1993). Science as argument: Implications for teaching and learning scientific thinking. *Science Education, 77,* 319–337.

Kanuka, H., & Anderson, T. (1998). Online social interchange, discord, and knowledge construction. *Journal of Distance Education, 13*(1), 57–74.

Land, S., & Zembal-Saul, C. (2001, April). *Scaffolding reflection and the revision of explanation during project-based learning: An investigation using progress portfolio.* Paper presented at the annual meeting of the American Educational Research Association, Seattle, WA.

LeCompte, M. D., & Preissle, J. (1993). *Ethnography and qualitative design in educational research.* San Diego, CA: Academic Press.

Lederman, N. G. (1999). Teachers' understanding of the nature of science and classroom practice: Factors that facilitate or impede the relationship. *Journal of Research in Science Teaching, 36,* 916–929.

Lemke, J. L. (1993). *Talking science: Language, learning, and values.* Norwood, NJ: Ablex.

Loh, B., Radinsky, J., Reiser, B., Gomez, L., Edelson, D., & Russell, E. (1997, June). *The progress portfolio: Promoting reflective inquiry in complex investigation environments.* Paper presented at the 2nd international conference on Computer Support for Collaborative Learning, Toronto, Ontario, Canada.

Marek, E. A., & Methven, S. B. (1991). Effect of the learning cycle upon student and classroom teacher performance. *Journal of Research in Science Teaching, 28,* 41–53.

National Research Council. (1996). *National Science Education Standards.* Washington, DC: National Academy Press.

National Research Council. (2000). *Inquiry and the National Science Education Standards: A guide for teaching and learning.* Washington, DC: National Academy Press.

Newton, P., Driver, R., & Osborne, J. (1999). The place of argumentation in the pedagogy of school science. *International Journal of Science Education, 21,* 553–576.

Norusis, M. J. (2002). *SPSS 11: Guide to data analysis.* Chicago: Prentice Hall.

Patton, M. Q. (1990). *Qualitative evaluation and research methods* (2nd ed.). London: Sage.

Roth, W. M., Tobin, K., & Ritchie, S. (2001). *Re/constructing elementary science.* New York: Peter Lang.

Smith, D. C., & Anderson, C. W. (1999). Appropriating scientific practices and discourses with future elementary science. *Journal of Research in Science Teaching, 36,* 755–776.

Spector, B. S., & Strong, P. N. (2001). The culture of traditional preservice elementary science methods students compared to the culture of science: A dilemma for teacher educators. *Journal of Elementary Science Education, 13(1),* 1–20.

Sunal, D. W., & Sunal, C. S. (2003). *Science in the elementary and middle school.* Upper Saddle River, NJ: Merrill Prentice Hall.

Taylor, P. C. (1990, April). *The influence of teacher beliefs on constructivist teaching practices.* Paper presented at the annual meeting of the American Educational Research Association, Boston, MA.

Toulmin, S. (1958). The layout of arguments. In S. Toulmin (Ed.), *The use of argument* (pp. 94–145). Cambridge, England: Cambridge University Press.

Vrasidas, C., & McIsaac, M. S. (1999). Factors influencing interaction in an online course. *American Journal of Distance Education, 13(3),* 22–35.

## AUTHOR NOTE

This work was in part supported by the National Center for Online Learning Research (NCOLR), a program administered by the University of Idaho and the University of Alabama and funded through the United States Department of Education, Fund for the Improvement of Postsecondary Education (FIPSE), although the views expressed here are the authors' only.

# CHAPTER 9

# COLLABORATIVE LEARNING ENVIRONMENTS ACROSS THE INTERNET

**Michael J. Berson,** *University of South Florida*
**Cheryl Mason Bolick,** *University of North Carolina at Chapel Hill*
**Scott M. Waring,** *University of South Florida St. Petersburg*
**and**
**Shelli A. Whitworth,** *University of South Florida*

Telecollaboration is a form of collaborative education that permits students and instructors to make scholarly and personal connections across distance. These collaborations facilitate learning through an online classroom or via teleconferencing by sharing in-class activities, findings, perspectives, and perceptions between instructors and students. The case study presented in this chapter documents the experiences of two university social studies education classes as they collaborate through videoconferencing. The findings from this case are translated into guidelines for the application of telecollaborative education with implications for teaching and learning in K–12 or higher education.

*Research on Enhancing the Interactivity of Online Learning,* pages 149–174
Copyright © 2006 by Information Age Publishing
All rights of reproduction in any form reserved.

## OVERVIEW

A new type of social studies classroom is under development. This classroom has four walls, yet one of the walls is shared with a classroom in a geographically disparate location. This "virtual wall," however, is a mirror image of a second room, reflecting a class in another location a thousand miles away. The two classes and two instructors are linked via a videoconferencing system and an electronic white board. A collaboration forms between the instructors and students, and the essence of social studies teaching and learning is enhanced by expanding the "walls" and broadening the perspectives captured in course discussions.

This chapter presents the process of telecollaboration with examples and tips to guide implementation. The illustrations of collaborative learning environments include two preservice teacher education classrooms following the 2000 presidential election and discussing an online activity featuring a representative example of a middle school class using digital resources to explore the relevance of the Bill of Rights. The chapter also provides a review of Web sites that support collaborative projects in K–12 classrooms.

## REVIEW OF THE LITERATURE

### Collaborative Education

Collaborative education is a method pioneered within a group of partnering teacher education programs, the Coalition for Innovation in Teacher Education, which is developing groundbreaking applications of technology by engaging in interuniversity initiatives (Center for Technology in Teacher Education, 2004). Collaborative education links two classes at geographically separate locations, but differs in a number of respects from superficially similar distance education courses (Karran, Berson, & Mason, 2001). A distance education course typically consists of a single instructor linked to multiple students with the goal of increased educational efficiency. The technology in a distance education course is employed as a delivery system. In contrast, a collaborative education course consists of two instructors and two classes of roughly comparable size. Instead of the one-to-many instructor-student relationship found in a distance education course, a collaborative education course supports a several-to-several relationship. The goal of a collaborative education course is to enhance the instruction with added depth and richness. There are a number of potential educational benefits associated with collaborative teaching (Dawson, Mason, & Molebash, 2000):

- Each instructor has an interested collaborator invested in the course content who can be used as a sounding board for discussion and feedback about the course.
- Innovative ideas are disseminated between the collaborating partners.
- Resources and materials can be shared across classes.
- Classes increase in diversity, with a broader range of perspectives, experiences, and backgrounds represented.
- The geographic separation of the classes encourages electronic discussion throughout the week in between course meetings.
- Modeling collaborative education methods for future K–12 teachers increases the likelihood that they will employ similar instructional strategies in their own classes.
- Students learn to use technology tools in context, which allows them to engage in professional dialogue with colleagues from other teacher education programs.

While at different universities, each professor gains a colleague who has similar interests and who is thinking deeply about the same scholarly issues. The students in the class also gain partners in learning and expand their exposure to other educational traditions. Students are often surprised, for example, that approaches to teacher education can differ greatly from institution to institution. Students also gain exposure to technologies that may make the walls of their future K–12 classrooms more permeable to innovation.

## Telecollaborative Education

The introduction of technology to the classroom has created many new educational experiences for students. By using the Internet and in-class technology, teachers can access a multitude of online resources and lesson plans and incorporate multimedia learning activities. Internet-based activities for students are becoming more abundant and include Web sites specializing in projects that engage participants from one classroom with learners at a distant site (Whitworth & Berson, 2003). This process, known as telecollaboration, is not merely a modern version of pen pals. It can include student or class e-mails, but also facilitates the evolution of an online classroom that shares in-class activities, findings, and perspectives. However, evidence of telecollaboration taking place in K–12 classrooms is sparse across the literature (Harris, 2002; Whitworth & Berson, 2003). Curriculum-based, as well as curriculum-enhancing, sites are available to assist teachers and instructors on both telecollaborative and collaborative education.

Telecollaboration can offer a variety of educational experiences for students in levels K–12. Harris (1999) highlights how telecollaboration can benefit global education. It can expose students to "differing opinions, perspectives, beliefs, experiences, and thinking processes; allow students to compare, contrast, and/or combine similar information collected in dissimilar locations; and provide a platform where students can communicate with a real audience using text and imagery" (Harris, 2001, p. 434). It also offers students and teachers opportunities to enhance computer skills, computer/e-mailing use, and etiquette.

## METHOD

Participants in this study included 29 students enrolled in two separate university courses. Seven of the participants were enrolled in Teaching Elementary Social Studies, a required course for fourth-year elementary education majors at the University of South Florida (USF). The remaining 22 participants, at the University of Virginia (UVA), were enrolled in Field Project in Social Studies Education, a required course for fifth-year education majors who were enrolled in a combined bachelor's/master's five-year program. Instructor observations derived from the development and implementation of the course activities served as complimentary data sources for this collaborative qualitative inquiry. In an ethnographic design, data sources were documented in writing by each instructor, as well as documented on videotape for future review. Content analysis of the documents was used to organize the qualitative data collected. Content analysis involves reviewing the artifacts of the research to select common themes and trends in the data. One may also note similarities and differences in the implementation process between instructors and sites. The primary goal of content analysis is to condense the amount of qualitative data into a list of variables that can be examined for correlations. The research team began with text (qualitative data), made formal hypotheses as to the nature of the text's content, performed systematic coding and analysis, and finally interpreted the results in conjunction with findings from the literature review, thus allowing for the triangulation of data sources.

Based on qualitative analysis of observation data and a review of existing standards for collaborative learning environments, a framework of critical components was documented. The combined data was unitized, a process whereby common units of information are identified. The units were then categorized by identifying commonalties and relevant content among and within the instructor's observations. Analysis of the data revealed the following five emerging themes, which were developed both a priori and a posteriori by the instructors: technical features, instructional planning, effective videoconferencing teaching, instructional strategies, and video-conferencing protocol.

## RESULTS

The following case study documents the experiences of two university-level social studies education classes. One course is located at the University of Virginia, while the other is located at the University of South Florida. The two classes linked via videoconferencing to discuss topics within the class and topics pertaining to the 2000 presidential election. The classes also participated in examining an online teaching activity that features the efforts of a first-year social studies teacher to incorporate technology into her social studies instruction. Other topics addressed in the context of the interactive exchange between the classes included the use of online primary sources and Internet safety.

### Case Study: Social Studies Teacher Education Classes

The photos in Figure 9.1 depict two social studies teacher education classes that are comparing and contrasting impressions of the final days of the 2000 presidential campaign. There are distinct differences in the composition of the two classes. The University of Virginia class is composed of traditional university students—with a majority of Caucasian females, in their early 20s. The Florida class includes a number of students of Hispanic heritage, and several individuals who are in their mid- to late-20s. Many of the students in the University of South Florida class commute, while the Virginia students are full-time students who live on or near campus. The course instructors used the differences in the classes to incorporate multiple perspectives in the social studies methods course through the *collaborative education* form of instruction.

The campaign advertisements in Virginia are predominantly regional, addressing state and local elections. In contrast, the national race is the focus in Florida. The presidential candidates have made multiple appearances, and the Florida class has been exposed to ubiquitous presidential campaign advertisements that have blanketed the state. The class members discuss the implications. The Republican candidate is all but assured of Virginia's electoral votes, while Florida appears to be in a dead heat—hence the national attention and focus. Collaboration between the classes offers a multitude of discussions that may not otherwise be addressed in a classroom that focuses only on related media coverage from its state. This collaboration allows students to examine and expand perceptions and perspectives that are an essential element of effective social studies teaching and learning.

Figure 9.1.   A Collaborative Education Classroom at the University of South Florida connected to a Collaborative Education Classroom at the University of Virginia.

The two classes also examined an online activity that details the daily successes and struggles of a first-year teacher attempting to integrate technology into her middle school social studies class (Center for Technology and Teacher Education, 2004). This Web-based example provided the springboard for discussion among the students at the two universities for three different class sessions. The activity was authored by a team of in-service teachers, teacher educators, and doctoral students with expertise in social studies education. Their goal was to create opportunities for students to analyze and reflect upon real-world classroom issues (Merseth, 1996). Educational technology faculty members and doctoral students worked with the activity team to transform the representative example into a Web-based, multimedia format that includes images, audio and video files, and pop-up text windows.

The online activity features a representative example of a first-year social studies teacher, Julia, who is struggling to design a meaningful Internet-based project that will not only introduce her eighth-grade students to the Bill of Rights, but will also encourage them to investigate the continuing significance of these essential freedoms. The teacher, Julia, is faced with numerous technology issues, from teaching her students how to categorize bookmarks to dealing with the school network shutting down. Julia is also confronted with many issues related to pedagogy, such as assessment, grouping of students, and classroom discipline.

## Excerpts from Online Activity: An Introduction

Social studies teachers often struggle to develop activities that teach the Bill of Rights in a meaningful way. Too often, we find teachers requiring their students to memorize these 10 amendments, rather than prompting their students to examine the influence of these rights through both a historical and modern-day lens. The teacher in this activity, Julia, is faced with this same dilemma.

You will meet Julia during the beginning months of her first year of teaching. Julia has tried to design a lesson that will not only introduce her middle school students to the Bill of Rights, but will also encourage them to investigate the continuing significance of these essential freedoms. The project she has developed takes advantage of the computer technology in her school to allow her students to learn in a way that was not possible before the advent of the Internet. As you work through each scene you will experience the problems and successes that Julia faces as a middle school social studies teacher.

The Project Calendar (see Figure 9.2) integrates activities for both Julia's class and the preservice teacher courses. It illustrates how the online activity (noted above) is incorporated into the preservice teacher course topics, discussions, and assignments.

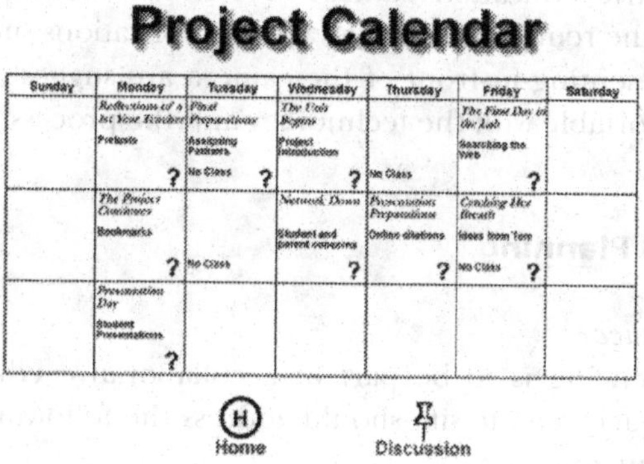

Figure 9.2.   The Project Calendar.

## Application to Practice

The case study presented in this chapter affords the authors valuable information on the challenges and rewards of collaborative education. Knowledge gained from this case has been integrated with the literature base to provide tips for implementation. Findings from this case study yielded the following guidelines: technical features or effects of videoconferencing on teaching and learning; instructional planning; effective videoconferencing; keeping the sessions interesting; instructional strategies; and videoconferencing protocol. Additionally, a review of Web sites that support collaborative projects in K–12 classrooms is provided.

## Technical Features

Collaborative education permits students and faculty to make scholarly and personal connections across distance. Using videoconferencing technology, two or more people at different locations can see and hear each other at the same time, and even share documents and computer applications for collaboration. Once the necessary hardware and software are in place (see UVa Information Technology and Communication, 2004), placing a video call is as simple as placing a telephone call or connecting to the Internet. Following a connection, a partnering classroom is visible in color video.

Planning is a critical component of videoconferencing technology and teaching. Once participants are familiar with the equipment, it is recommended that potential users observe other faculty members as they conduct collaborative education courses or sessions. Subsequently practice connecting to the remote site, using various applications such as the whiteboard, and presenting in front of the camera are suggested until participants are comfortable with the technology and the process.

## Instructional Planning

### Months in Advance

If videoconferencing is to be part of a collaborative education course, instructors at each remote site should address the following issues several months in advance:

- Number of participants: Between 6–12 students per site is a manageable size; no more than 20 students to allow for effective interaction.
- A detailed teaching/learning agenda for the class, including primary facilitation responsibilities.
- Room arrangement: Are there any special student needs?
- Schedule: Account for time difference, institutional holidays, exam schedules.
- Course credit: Is it the same for both sites?

- Assessment: Are both sets of students being assessed in the same way? For example, if at one site, 35% of a student's grade is based on participation in the videoconference class while participation only counts 10% at the other site, students may not be equally motivated to participate in discussion. Expectations and assessment methods must be clearly explained to students.
- Supplementary activities, such as asynchronous communication via newsgroups or threaded discussion.
- Differences in equipment that may affect learning process (e.g., Mac vs. PCs, access to technology, etc.).

### A Few Weeks in Advance

Final preparations a few weeks prior to the class sessions are intended to facilitate optimum learning outcomes through collaborative education. Suggestions for effective implementation include the following:

- Practice for the introductory class connection with the remote site. This trial session should include an evaluation of presentation techniques, visual and audio quality, and camera positions.
- Establish a protocol to be used in conducting class, particularly with regard to speaking. (Should students raise hands? Will there be a central microphone or place to stand when speaking?)
- Notify students of videoconferencing component and expectations and supplying any preliminary materials, such as classroom protocol for collaborative education sessions.
- Prepare visuals or other learning aids.
- Provide each instructor a list of students at the remote site in order to learn names.

### For the First Class

The first collaborative class session is important for establishing a sense of community among the participants and a class routine which is conducive to reciprocal interaction.

- Introduce students to the room, equipment, and the protocol for participating in a videoconference. Ask them to introduce themselves on camera. Demonstrate how the equipment works and let students practice on camera, writing on the whiteboard, and so forth.
- Distribute information, if needed, for asynchronous communication via e-mail, newsgroups, or threaded discussions. Demonstrate such tasks as how to log on, and supply supporting instructions for later reference.

## Effective Videoconferencing Teaching

Collaborative education can be further enhanced by attending to strategies that effectively utilize the technology to engage students. The following guidelines can promote quality integration of technology and instruction.

### Video Quality

- Place the camera directly above or below the video screen. Since students will naturally look at the video image of the other site, having the camera in line with the screen will ensure that the groups are looking at each other while interacting.
- Because compressed video uses a narrower bandwidth (typically 128 to 384 kbps) than the broadcast quality video seen on television, rapid movements may produce a blurred effect when viewed from the remote site. To compensate, try to avoid rapid movements, like sudden or dramatic gestures and avoid swaying, rocking, or pacing.
- Wear solid-colored clothing in dark or neutral colors. White can appear unnaturally bright, and patterns can create a "dancing" effect that is disorienting for viewers.
- Avoid wearing dangling jewelry or bright reflective surfaces.

### Audio Quality

- Users will probably notice a delay between talking at one site and a response from the remote site. This delay is just long enough for participants to talk over each other. Remind students to pause when they expect a response from the remote site.
- Change the speed of speaking to emphasize content and maintain interest. Use pauses to allow for questions and to add emphasis within statements.
- Enunciate clearly and speak at the lowest pitch level that is comfortable for the speaker.
- A full-duplex conference telephone is a good backup to have in the room. If the network audio has "technical difficulties" or should there be another problem, a speaker phone provides a channel between the sites while the problem is fixed.
- Cue students when their attention should be directed toward a certain screen or speaker.

### Keeping the Session Interesting

- Include the participants in the conference within the first five minutes. Use roll call to establish verbal contact or ask a compelling question that taps their affective domain.

- To encourage interactivity, remember the rule: No more than 10 to 15 minutes of instructor talk without some learner-centered response. This will shift the responsibility of learning back in the learner's hands. Devote 30 to 65% of each hour to student activity.
- For group work, select individuals at each site to participate on inter-site teams.
- When responding to questions, (a) look into the camera and answer, (b) ask the student who posed the question a couple of searching questions or invite contributions from others, and (c) try to maintain a discussion between sites whenever possible.

## Instructional Strategies

In terms of planning and classroom presentation, collaborative education generally requires more time than traditional education. Instructional effectiveness is maximized by establishing and communicating an agenda for each videoconferencing session. Other suggestions for optimizing instruction include:

- Provide copies of visual information to all students so that they can devote their full attention to the presentation and discussion.
- Develop channels for reinforcement, repetition, and remediation. Telephone access, office hours, and e-mail communication should be available and fully explained to students.
- Use case studies and "real life" examples to lend relevance and a personal touch to discussion topics.
- Complement lectures with discussion, debate, role-playing, and student presentations (no more than five minutes!).
- Integrate newsgroups or threaded discussions for enhanced learning and feedback.
- Maintain frequent contact with the collaborating teacher to review learning progress, student participation, and course effectiveness.

## Videoconferencing Protocol

Videoconferencing is most effective when a few basic protocols are used:

- At the start of each session, each site should confirm that the remote participants can be seen and heard clearly. Should technical difficulties surface, the other site should be notified immediately, even if it means interrupting a speaker.

- If class size permits, an informal roll call should open the session. It is used to initiate interaction between students from the remote site and the originating site.
- A location banner and name cards can be very helpful, especially during multipoint videoconferences of three or more.
- In advance of the session, the instructors should decide the means of acknowledging someone who wishes to speak (i.e., raising hands) and explain the procedure to the classes.
- Students should be referred to by name and encouraged to address others by name.
- Participants should introduce themselves before speaking and be sure that they are visible on camera. If speakers are to come to a certain spot or to a microphone, these expectations should be explained and upheld.
- Participation should be equally divided whenever possible, allowing students from each site to speak or ask questions.
- Students should refrain from talking to one another during a videoconference, especially while another speaker is on camera. It's important for students to remain engaged and attentive even when they don't have the floor.
- Because of an audio delay between sites, speakers should pause and wait for a response from the remote site to avoid "talking over" one another.

## DISCUSSION

The USF/UVA collaboration is an exemplar of a dynamic model of instruction. In this initiative, the professors apply creative and fluid teaching strategies, and model for the students the diffusion and implementation of emerging technology into instructional practices. Formative evaluations of this model have suggested guidelines for mobilizing and coordinating the transfer of technology innovation across instructional settings; however, the transfer of collaborative education into K–12 teaching will require ongoing shifts in instructional approaches. Enriching the learning process and overcoming the constraint of a single classroom setting necessitates innovation in blending collaborative opportunities with technological tools to expand access to resources and ideas.

While the Internet2 and the necessary equipment may not yet be readily accessible to educators, current uses of Web sites as a forum for telecollaboration proves to be feasible for educators of any classroom. Accessing Web site activities works well whether there is only one computer available with projection for an entire class, several computer stations for students to work in pairs or groups, or an entire computer lab that allows each student to work individually. Appendix A offers a review of Web sites that can be used to incorporate technology-based lessons into instruction. Some of the sites offer direct guidance in telecollaborative strategies; others provide excellent examples of the medium. A benefit of many telecollaborative Web sites is that educators can choose from a list of opportunities for their classroom or can participate in the development process by contributing ideas created by their students, thereby expanding the knowledge base for other educators.

As initiatives in the area of telecollaborative instruction via Internet2 continue to evolve, further work is needed in order to field-test instructional applications with local public schools, to contribute to materials development, and to introduce digital resource-based instructional materials to preservice teachers. The impact of these innovations needs intensive investigation, including an examination of preservice teachers' acquisition of desired knowledge and skills. Prototypes for assessing implementation are lacking, and the interrelationship between technology integration and collaborative interaction is a complex and little-understood dynamic. As systematic inquiry develops in this field of research, information about the role of social studies faculty members as pacesetters and potential change agents in the area of technological innovation also is needed. Using leading-edge technology such as Internet2, educators have an exciting opportunity to transform classrooms into collaborative and expansive learning environments where professional skills promote reflective practices (Karran et al., 2001, p. 153).

## CONCLUSION

Collaborative education can enhance the course with added depth and richness. The possibilities for collaboration topics are endless. The Internet offers a variety of support and resources for collaboration; however, as with any new curriculum or curriculum kits, it requires planning and adjusting along the way. Collaborations facilitate global education through an online classroom that shares in-class activities, findings, perspectives, and perceptions between the instructors and students. It is also an opportunity for instructors to gain a partner to share ideas.

Collaborative education within teacher education courses may increase the likelihood that new teachers will incorporate collaborative projects within their own classes. While collaborative learning is in its early phases, as educational institutions become more equipped with technology across the country, collaborations will be more common among colleges and universities, and public schools. The increased incorporation of technology-based activities are a reflection of the impact of technology on our daily lives and society at large and efforts should be made to capture the benefits of the educational opportunities that collaborative education can bring to students and instructors.

## REFERENCES

Center for Technology and Teacher Education. (2004). *Social studies meets technology: Reflections of a first year teacher.* Retrieved March 24, 2004, from http://www.teacherlink.org/content/social/casestudy/reflections/

Center for Technology in Teacher Education. (2004). *Content areas: Social studies.* Retrieved September 9, 2004, from http://www.teacherlink.org/content/social/

Co-nect. (2003). *With miles to go before I sleep...Our journey on the underground railroad.* Retrieved March 15, 2004, from http://exchange.co-nect.net/Teleprojects/project/?pid=3

Dawson, K., Mason, C. L., & Molebash, P. (2000, July). Results of a telecollaborative activity involving geographically disparate preservice teachers. *International Forum of Educational Technology & Society, 3*(3). Retrieved September 9, 2004 from http://ifets.ieee.org/periodical/vol_3_2000/f05.html

EPals Classroom Exchange. (1996). *EPals.com Classroom Exchange.* Retrieved March 15, 2004, from http://www.epals.com

Global SchoolNet. (2004). *The global school house.* Retrieved March 15, 2004, from http://www.gsn.org

Harris, J. (1999). First steps to telecollaboration. *Learning & Leading with Technology, 27*(3), 54–57. Retrieved March 15, 2004, from http://virtual-architecture.wm.edu

Harris, J. (2001). Teachers as telecollaborative project designers: A curriculum-based approach. *Contemporary Issues in Technology and Teacher Education (CITE Journal), 1*(3), 429–442. Available: http://www.citejournal.org/vol1/iss3/seminal/article1.htm

Harris, J. (2002). Wherefore art thou, telecollaboration? *Learning & Leading with Technology, 29*(6), 54–58.

International Education and Resource Network. (n.d.). *iEARN.* Retrieved March 15, 2004, from http://www.iearn.org

JASON Foundation for Education. (2001). *Welcome to JASON.* Retrieved March 15, 2004, from http://www.jasonproject.org

Karran, S. W., Berson, M. J., & Mason, C. L. (2001). Enhancing social science education through tele-collaborative teaching and learning. *Social Education, 65*(3), 151–154.

Merseth, K. K. (1996). Cases and case methods in teacher education. In J. Sikula, T. Buttery, & E. Guyton (Eds.), *Handbook of research on teacher education: A project of the Association of Teacher Educators* (pp. 722–744). New York: Macmillan Library Reference.

MidLink Magazine. (1994). *MidLink Magazine: The digital magazine by students, for students from 8 to 18.* Retrieved March 15, 2004, from http://longwood.cs.ucf.edu/~MidLink/

Mighty Media, Inc. (2002). *IECC.* Retrieved March 15, 2004, from http://www.iecc.org

United Nations Cyber School Bus. (2002). *Human rights in action.* Retrieved March 15, 2004, from http://www.un.org/Pubs/CyberSchoolBus/humanrights/index.html

UVa Information Technology and Communication. (2004). *Videoconferencing at UVa.* Retrieved September 4, 2004, from http://www.itc.virginia.edu/netsys/videoconf/home.html

Whitworth, S. A., & Berson, M. J. (2003). Computer technology in the social studies: An examination of the effectiveness literature (1996–2001). *Contemporary Issues in Technology and Teacher Education, 2*(4), Article 1. Retrieved March 24, 2004, from http://www.citejournal.org/vol2/iss4/socialstudies/article1.cfm

## APPENDIX A

## Reviewed Web Sites for Collaborative Teaching and Education

Incorporating activities from the following sites requires Internet connections with connection speeds that maximize students' time on task. However, computers or computer labs that experience slow downloads result in loss of student interest and detract from student confidence in completing particular activities. Educators may wish to search these Web sites from the school's computers to see if there are considerable download delays. Educators concerned about resources should consider following issues with the technology expert(s) at their school: (a) Will the Internet connections support fast downloads on Web sites that may be heavy in graphic images? (b) Will the Internet connections experience slow download during particular times of the day? (c) Are there additional computers on campus that use the same server that could decrease download time at particular times of the day?

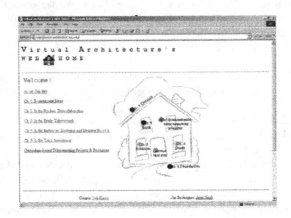

*Virtual Architecture: Designing and Directing Curriculum-Based Telecomputing*
http://virtual-architecture.wm.edu
Judi Harris, Pavey Family Chair in Educational Technology
Address: School of Education, College of William and Mary, P.O. Box 8795,
Williamsburg, VA 23187–8795
E-mail: judi.harris@wm.edu

Virtual Architecture is a site designed by Judi Harris, Ph.D., Pavey Chair in
Educational Technology at the College of William and Mary.

The site began in 1998 and has been continually updated to include
new readings written by Harris and new links to educational resources
including lessons and ongoing projects. The Web site follows a book format, where users follow the links as book chapters in understanding telecollaboration and the various ways to incorporate technology-based
projects into the classroom. The chapters address many topics, including
terminology, current trends in telecollaboration, and strategies for selecting activities for students. After reviewing all that this site has to offer, educators will have the foundational knowledge to move on to additional sites.

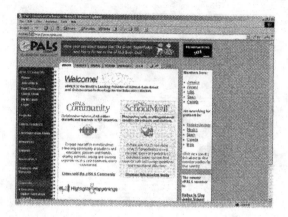

*EPals Classroom Exchange*
http://www.epals.com
Address: 353 Dalhousie Street, 3rd Floor, Ottawa, Ontario, Canada K1N 7G1
Phone: (613) 562–9847
Fax: (613) 562–4768

EPals was created in 1996 to help educators locate other classrooms with which their students can share information through the use of technology. The site assists educators in establishing e-mail exchanges between their class and others around the United States and the world relating to a particular topic or project. The site offers free e-mail service to those who do not currently have e-mail accounts. Educators can use one account and send group e-mail messages as correspondence to other classes or allow students to set up their own free e-mail exchange. Alternatively, educators may choose to participate in one of the ongoing "Class to Class Projects," such as the online book club, class flag creation project, or the weather watch program, where students compile information about their region's weather and share it with other students around the world. There are multiple options for integrating EPals into the classroom experience, such as monitoring other class activities, expanding projects to include U.S. or global participation, and posting a new project idea to the site. One might even correspond with his or her new EPals and arrange specific time frames or days of the week for replies. Teachers can locate a listing of other same-subject classes from around the world and a description of how they wish to correspond with other students on the subject. When joining, users will need to submit a profile and brief description of their class, its activities, and information they wish to share or hear about from other classes. The site can ultimately serve the class however the teacher prefers.

*JASON Foundation for Education*
http://www.jasonproject.org
Address: 11 Second Avenue, Needham Heights, MA 02494–2808
Phone: 781–444–8858
Fax: 781–444–8313

Sales & product related questions: 888–527–6600 or info@jason.org
The JASON Project was founded in 1989 by Dr. Robert Ballard, explorer, oceanographer and discoverer of the wreck of the RMS *Titanic*. The program offers an opportunity for students to follow and participate in a year-long scientific expedition, including a variety of interdisciplinary learning experiences, and offers teacher training, support, and opportunities to earn CEU credits. The program provides supplemental educational activities to enhance earth science, geography, and environmental programs for students in grades 4 to 9. The JASON Project is tailored to meet the national curriculum standards for science and geography and offers detailed information on how the program meets each state's standards.

Each fall the JASON Project begins a new scientific expedition. Students follow and participate in the expedition through the "kick-off video," in class lessons, video lessons, interactive Internet activities and broadcasts from the expedition site, or a combination of all three. Live broadcasts allow students to interact directly with the scientists and researchers of the expedition. Additionally, some classes travel to interactive network sites within their region to meet other students tracking the expedition and to participate in live sessions, which are transmitted via satellite to classroom participants.

To get started, it is recommended that teachers visit the site and click on "How to Participate" and "Frequently Asked Questions" on the left side column. Users should explore "The Teacher Center" link and click on

"Expeditions" to find out about this year's JASON Project or about past projects to get an idea of the types of expeditions students may encounter. The JASON Project also offers a variety of teacher training opportunities and has a toll-free telephone line to respond to questions. JASON Project material costs vary depending on the level of classroom involvement, and it is suggested that users follow the "How to Participate" link to find JASON projects in their area.

*The Global School House*
http://www.gsn.org
Global SchoolNet
Address: 132 N. El Camino Real, Ste. 395, Encinitas, CA 92024
Phone: 760–635–0001 or 619–475–4852
Fax: 760–635–0003
E-mail: helper@globalschoolnet.org

Global SchoolNet was founded in the early 1980s by two San Diego teachers who believed that the Internet could significantly impact learning. Global SchoolNet's goal is to increase student achievement by providing education resources that connect school and home with technology. Global SchoolNet serves grades K–college and is a completely free interactive service. Based in California, Global SchoolNet participants come from around the world. Not only does Global SchoolNet offer interactive online learning activities, it offers a large variety of free resources for teachers and schools, including free Internet sites for school and individual classrooms including ongoing telecollaborative projects, traditional and Internet-based lesson plans, searchable by subject, printable worksheets for grades K–8 reading/language arts and mathematics, and a collection of classroom thematic units, including "lesson plans, discussion questions, and assessment strategies." Additionally, the site offers a certificate maker, Web trip designer, and flash card maker for mathematics. First-time visitors should click on "Classroom Conferencing" and follow the links for the type of project that interests them and also look into the "Collaborative Learning Center" section of the site. A free membership is available and allows access to the wealth of online resources.

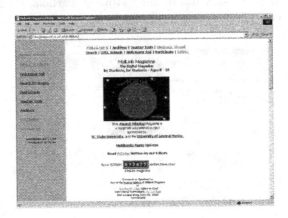

*MindLink Magazine*
http://longwood.cs.ucf.edu/~MidLink/
Address: SAS inSchool, SAS Campus Drive, Cary, NC 27513
Phone: 919–531–2869

MidLink Magazine is an online journal by and for students ages 8 through 18. The journal is sponsored by North Carolina State University and the University of Central Florida, but teachers and students from all over the world read and contribute to the journal. Examples of the stories reported on the Web pages of MidLink include student book reports, haiku poetry exchange between American and Japanese students, student dreams shared in the spirit of Dr. Martin Luther King Millennium Time Capsules, fairy tales, and hurricane reports from around the world.

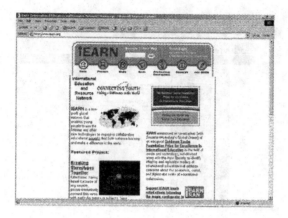

*iEARN*
http://www.iearn.org
International Education and Resource Network (iEARN)
Address: 475 Riverside Drive, Suite 540, New York, NY 10115
Phone: 212–870–2693

iEARN, Inc., is a not-for-profit corporation with its purpose aimed at assisting youth to engage in collaborative telecommunications projects that
make meaningful contributions to the health and welfare of people and
the planet. This site facilitates educational and development projects with
an approach that encourages students to collaborate with other students
from over 80 nations throughout the world. They give children the opportunity to create a project related to an issue affecting them or work with
pre-created projects and resolve them with help from other children by
interacting through this Web site. iEARN is attempting to make the world a
better place by having students work with others across the globe in a
worthwhile learning experience. They have created many great lessons for
the classroom teacher, which involve ongoing projects based on important
global situations. The iEARN site has many opportunities to interact with
others throughout the world and includes news sources to keep one up-to-
date on real-world issues.

*Intercultural E-Mail Classroom Connections (IECC)*
http://www.iecc.org

In 1993, three instructors designed the IECC Web site when they had difficulty in finding e-mail partners for a project on which they were working. They created an electronic mailing list specifically aimed at helping teachers "connect" with their colleagues in other countries for classroom e-mail exchanges. Currently, there are over 8,329 subscribers from 82 countries involved in the IECC project. They have created several separate sections within this Web site aimed at differing grade levels, and they included a section in which teachers can collaborate and assist each other on e-mail-based classroom projects. The IECC site has been designed so that a teacher can easily post a request for a partner classroom or search through the requests that others have posted as well as specify grade level, cultural, language, time frame, and class size parameters.

*UN Cyber School Bus: Human Rights*
http://www.un.org/Pubs/CyberSchoolBus/humanrights/index.html
Address: United Nations Headquarters, Room S-931B, New York, NY 10017
E-mail: cyberschoolbus@un.org

The United Nations Human Rights module was created in 1998 in conjunction with the 50th anniversary of the Universal Declaration of Human Rights. The project was designed to help students understand the idea of human rights, gain a sense of themselves as people with dignity and hence with rights, and finally encourage them to act. The main goal of this site is to foster students' desire and knowledge to defend and promote human rights in their own communities, neighborhoods, and communities. The teachers compile the stories of how this is happening with their students and submit them to be included in a global atlas of student actions that will be published on the Internet. The students are given the opportunity to understand their human rights in general and in particular the Universal Declaration through lessons mapped out in this Web site. The project aims to demonstrate that young people around the world are active in and concerned about their world, that the notion of rights has relevance everywhere in the world, and that young students can, indeed, make a difference.

*With Miles to Go Before I Sleep...*
Our Journey on the Underground Railroad
http://exchange.co-nect.net/Teleprojects/project/?pid=3
E-mail: edwyer@co-nect.net or imorris@co-nect.net

The Web site has the ability to magically transform the child from a student in a classroom into a fugitive slave in 1850, just after the Fugitive Slave Law was enacted, on his or her way from Ripley, Ohio to Canada with a small group of other runaway slaves. The student is assigned a new identity, of an actual slave during this time period. They are given their new name and identity and encouraged to think, act, and write as they might have in this situation. Together, with the other members in the group, they must decide how they are to reach freedom using the Internet and other sources and are encouraged to be as realistic and accurate as possible. They must choose routes, figure out which cities they will pass through, examine census specifics for that town, check weather conditions for that day, figure out how many miles they will travel each day, calculate travel times, as well as many other realistic decisions that must be made in an attempt to escape the life of a slave in the 1850s. Each student is to record the progress of each day in a journal that they must keep for the whole journey. The students are also confronted with realistic issues and problems that unexpectedly arise, and, as a group, they must figure out how to resolve them. There are links to many of the resources found here that are needed to make the important decisions to survive their trek. This site is designed to get the child to understand the complexity of a journey such as the one taken by many of the runaway slaves at this time in U.S. history. The unit was designed to last 15 days with teaching standards kept in mind when the lessons were created. This is a spectacular unit that could be used with a variety of age levels in several different areas of focus.

## APPENDIX B

## Additional Readings and Resources

Armstrong, S. (1995). *Telecommunications in the classroom* (2nd ed.). Eugene, OR: International Society for Technology in Education and Computer Learning Foundation.

Baugh, I., & Baugh, J. (1997). Global classrooms: E-mail learning communities. *Learning & Leading with Technology, 25*(3), 38–41.

Bradsher, M. (1995a). Making friends in the global village: Tips on international collaborations. *Learning & Leading with Technology, 23*(6), 48–51.

Bradsher, M. (1995b). Networking with kids around the world. *Educational Leadership, 53*(2), 42.

Brush, T. (1998). Using CMC to bring real-world experiences into the classroom: The electronic "pen-pal" project. In Z. L. Berge & M. Collins (Eds.), *Wired together: The online classroom in K–12* (pp. 101–109). Cresskill, NJ: Hampton Press.

Copen, P. (1995). Connecting classrooms through telecommunications. *Educational Leadership, 53*(2), 44–47.

Dawson, K., & Harris, J. (1999). Reaching out: Telecollaboration and social studies. *Social Studies and the Young Learner, 12*(1), 1–4.

Dyrli, O. E. (1996). Energizing the classroom with curriculum through telecommunications. *Technology & Learning, 16*(4), 65–70.

Dyrli, O. E., & Kinnaman, D. E. (1996). Connecting with the world through successful telecommunications projects. *Technology & Learning, 16*(6), 57–62.

Fabos, B., & Young, M. D. (1999). Telecommunication in the classroom: Rhetoric versus reality. *Review of Educational Research, 20,* 179–206.

Farley, R. P. (1999). A tale of two schools. *Educational Leadership, 56*(5), 39–42.

Fetterman, D. M. (1996). Videoconferencing online: Enhancing communication over the Internet. *Educational Researcher, 25*(4), 23.

Harris, J. (1998a). Activity structures for curriculum-based telecollaboration. *Learning & Leading With Technology, 26*(1), 6–15.

Harris, J. (1998b). Curriculum-based telecollaboration: Using activity structures to design student projects. *Learning & Leading with Technology, 26*(1), 6.

Harris, J. (1999). "I know what we're doing but how do we do it?"—Action sequences for curriculum-based telecomputing. *Learning & Leading with Technology, 26*(6), 42–44.

Harris, J. (2000). Taboo topic no longer: Why telecollaborative projects sometimes fail. *Learning & Leading with Technology, 27*(5), 58–61.

Hiltz, S. R. (1990). Collaborative learning: The virtual classroom approach. *T.H.E. Journal, 17*(10), 59–65.

Insinnia, E., & Cleery S. (1998). *Educators take charge—Teaching in the Internet revolution.* Eugene, OR: International Society for Technology in Education.

Karran, S. W., Berson, M. J., & Mason, C. L. (2001). Enhancing social science education through tele-collaborative teaching and learning. *Social Education, 65*(3), 151–154.

Kirk, R. H., Guenther, J., Loguidice, T., & Nkemnji, J. (2003). The long journey: Multicultural understanding through technology. *Delta Kappa Gamma Bulletin, 69*(2), 30–33.

Krannin, A., & Ehman, L. (1999). Help! I'm lost in Cyberspace! *Social Education, 63*(3), 152–156.

Mason, C. L., & Dawson, K. (2000). *Collaborative Education: Implications for Teacher Education* (Unpublished white paper). Reston, VA: National Technology Leadership Retreat.

Molebash, P., & Fisher, D. (2003). Teaching and learning literacy with technology. *Reading Improvement, 40*(2), 63ñ70.

National Educational Technology Standards (NETS). (1998). *National educational technology standards for students.* Eugene, OR: International Society for Technology in Education.

Riel, M. (1995). Cross-classroom collaboration in global learning circles. In S. L. Star (Ed.), *The cultures of computing* (pp. 219–242). Sociological Review Monograph. Oxford: Blackwell.

Roberts, N., Blakeslee, G., Brown, M., & Lenk, C. (1990). *Integrating telecommunications into education.* Englewood Cliffs, NJ: Prentice Hall.

Rubisch, J. C. (2000). Not the same old story—Long distance collaboration to increase interpersonal understanding. *T.H.E Journal, 28*(3), 60.

Smith, S. (2003). Online videoconferencing: An application to teacher education. *Journal of Special Education Technology, 18*(3), 62–64.

Szente, J. (2003). Teleconferencing across borders: Promoting literacy—and more—in the elementary grades *Childhood Education, 79*(5), 299–306.

Thomas, L., Clift, R. T., & Sugimoto, T. (1996). Telecommunication, student teaching, and methods instruction: An exploratory investigation. *Journal of Teacher Education, 47*(3), 165–174.

Trentin, G. (1997). Logical communication structures for network-based education and tele-teaching. *Educational Technology, 37*(4), 19–25.

U.S. Department of Education, Office of the Secretary. (2004). *Office of Educational Technology: Grants.* Retrieved September 11, 2004, from http://www.ed.gov/about/offices/list/os/technology/edgrants.html

Weston, N. (1997). Distant voices, shared lives: Students creating the global learning community. *Educational Horizons, 75*(4) 165–171.

Wresch, W. (1994). The challenges of creating networked connections among teachers and students. In C. L. Selfe & S. Hilligoss (Eds.), *Literacy and computers* (pp. 186–191). New York: Modern Language Association of America.

# CHAPTER 10

# PROBLEM-SOLVING AND COPING STRATEGIES USED IN AN ONLINE LEARNING ENVIRONMENT

**Cheryl White Sundberg, Dennis W. Sunal, Allison Mays,**
*University of Alabama*
**and**
**Michael R. L. Odell,** *University of Idaho*

The purpose of the case study involved research on the types of coping strategies used by students in an online learning environment modeling effective science teaching using the Internet. Two questions guided our research: (1) What strategies did students use to effectively converse online, and (2) why are these strategies important to effective learning? The research methodology involved qualitative analysis of artifacts including e-mail dialogue, telephone interviews, and facilitator field notes. Typical problem-solving and coping strategies included meeting face-to-face, using the telephone, posting humorous messages, venting online, and sending e-mail to the instructors instead of using the discussion board. In contrast, students who either dropped the course or dropped out of the discussion posted messages that reflected complete frustration. The researchers concluded that the students who were able to utilize problem-solving and coping strategies were more successful in completion of course activities and in achievement.

*Research on Enhancing the Interactivity of Online Learning,* pages 175–196
Copyright © 2006 by Information Age Publishing

Future research should focus on dialogue typology indicating student failure to address concerns noted in the literature of high rates of failure in online learning environments.

## OVERVIEW

What are effective problem-solving and coping strategies used in an online course and why are the strategies important to effective online learning? With increased emphasis on meeting the needs of nontraditional students and limited budgets, online learning has been viewed as a viable alternative to on-campus classes. However, there are barriers to effective online learning. In a review of current research on online learning, the literature revealed several themes. One important theme involved technical problems associated with online learning environments and their effects on learning achievement (Sunal, Sunal, Odell, & Sundberg, 2003). Administrators and instructors have voiced concern over the low completion rates of students in online courses compared to traditional face-to-face courses (Carr, 2000; Koory, 2003). In contrast, Thomas (2004) reported a completion rate of at least 89% through the use of a mentor system. In particular, students noted "clarification of materials and processes" and "encouragement" were important to course completion. However, there has been a lack of research in the type of effective strategies that are used by students to survive in an online learning environment. The focus of this study centered on the typology of messages posted by students who are no longer able to cope with online course learning, who otherwise would be successful in a traditional class. Increasingly, the availability and effective use of technology impacts success and, thus, research into dialogue indicators of distress are important for providing needed assistance. Once the types of messages posted by students in distress are identified, appropriate scaffolding tools should be implemented. Some researchers have noted that certain types of courses (those involving undergraduate students with lower GPAs or students with various learning styles) would be better served in a face-to-face learning environment (Carr, 2000). However, the face-to face environment is not always a viable alternative, especially in rural and typically underserved or underrepresented groups.

Instruction in most online courses is primarily textual. However, online courses offer a unique platform for extended critical discourse. Bohrer, Colbert, and Zide (1998) noted that students in online courses were more actively involved in classroom dialogue than in a traditional face-to-face class, fostering meaningful learning through active involvement in extended critical discourse (Stephans, 1994; Sunal & Sunal, 2001; Wheatley, 1991). Vygotsky postulated language between novices and mentors is used to increase cognition (Lee & Smagorinsky, 2000) and provides scaffolding for the learner, while offering an opportunity for renewal for the mentor (John-Steiner & Meehan, 2000). Learner-learner and instructor-learner dialogue are both important in the development of meaningful learning, because the critical dialogue encourages reflection and creates disequilibrium (Vygotsky as cited in Glasson & Lalik, 1993; Hoffman & Krajcik, 1999; Jonassen, Davidson, Collins, Campbell, & Haag, 1995; McLellan, 1997; Piaget, 1976). Hall (1997) and Bos, Krajcik, and Patrick (1995) indicated online dialogue is more thoughtful and reflective because of four factors:

1. The asynchronous nature of the medium allows additional time for thought.

2. Written dialogue is generally more reflective (Glasson & Lalik, 1993).

3. Online discourse is generally more student-centered (Smith, Lane, & Enfield, 1989) with less teacher talk. Often excessive teacher talk consists primarily of question-answer recitation of facts (Goodlad, Soder, & Sirotnik, 1990) and is linked to student boredom and reduced student cognition (Gallimore & Tharp, 1990; Glasson & Lalik, 1993).

4. Dialogue in online discussions can be immediately archived allowing the instructor to assess prior knowledge and develop appropriate intervention (Dillion, 1986; Gallas, 1995; Ollerenshaw & Ritchie, 1997; Thornley-Hall, 1991).

In a case study of an online course designed for the purpose of determining "current issues and problems in educational media and computers," Vrasidas and McIsaac (2000, p. 108) concluded that planning is crucial in online learning environments. In particular, planning is needed to promote student discourse and interaction. In their reflection on the course dialogue, Vrasidas and McIsaac stated that the role of the instructor in an online course should be as a facilitator to encourage rich discourse, and not as an authoritarian figure.

Critical discourse in collaborative is important to support the development of conceptual change. Research supports the use of online learning experiences involving group collaboration (DeSimone, Schmid, & Lou, 2000; Jiang & Ting, 1998; McLellan, 1997; Vrasidas & McIsaac, 2000). Students confront naive conceptions through collaboration, in which the ensuing dialogue fosters a rich learning environment and in which the learners reconstruct their knowledge (Fensham, 1995; John-Steiner & Meehan, 2000; Lee & Smagorinsky, 2000; Vygotsky, as cited in Glasson & Lalik, 1993, and in Moll, 1990). Collaborative conversation is beneficial to all students (Johnson & Johnson, 1979). However, Vrasidas and McIsaac found the interaction was not as extensive as expected in some online settings and, therefore, they emphasized the importance of planning group activities to elicit more extensive learner-learner interaction and critical dialogue.

Online learning has been touted as the panacea for several emerging problems in higher education, including a lack of access to a university due to distance to campus or the high cost of the infrastructure needed for additional on-campus students. However, concern has been voiced on the quality of online learning. In the past, much research in online learning was primarily pre-experimental (Sunal et al., 2003). Recently, studies have compared learning in online settings with learning in different settings and contexts, such as face-to-face instruction. In a study of preservice and in-service undergraduate and graduate students enrolled in an educational media and technology course, Ali and Elfessi (2004) found no significant differences in student performance when comparing the online group to the traditional face-to-face classroom group. Meyer (2003) reported evidence to support the development and use of higher order thinking in threaded discussion in an ethnographic study of two graduate-level courses in educational leadership using both online and face-to-face instruction. Katz and Yablon (2003) conducted research on achievement of students enrolled in an Internet course on freshman level introductory statistics compared to a traditional face-to-face classroom course. The results indicated no statistically significant difference in performance between groups. Additionally, results from other studies have found little or no significant difference in achievement between online courses and face-to-face instruction (Davies & Mendenhall, 1998; Jewett, 1998; Wegener, Holloway, & Crader, 1997; Wegener, Holloway, & Garton, 1999).

Online learning environments are not barrier-free. Technological problems cited as the most common obstacle to effective use of the medium (Davies & Mendenhall, 1998; Jewett, 1998; Russett, 1994; Saunders et al., 1997; Wegener et al., 1997). While simple access to the online learning environment is often problematic, students also typically complain about a lack of personal contact with their peers and mentors (Bohrer et al., 1998; Bos et al., 1995; Guy & Lima, 1999; Saunders et al., 1997; Schlough & Bhuripanyo, 1998). Both students and instructors indicated sufficient time is a barrier (Kroder, Suess, & Sachs, 1998; Mende, 1998; Teeter, 1997). Instructors can be overwhelmed with the number of online postings by students. Instructors noted limited planning time negatively impacted the development of exemplary online learning environments (Saurino, Bentley, Glasson, & Casey, 1999). All of the above barriers negatively impact online discourse, effectively silencing the voices of the participants.

# RESEARCH DESIGN

## Purpose

The purpose of the case study was to investigate the effectiveness of an online graduate science course for in-service middle school teachers. The research question investigated was, "What problem-solving techniques and coping strategies did students use in an online science course to achieve success?"

## Participants, Setting, and Methodology

The participants were enrolled in a graduate online earth science course for in-service middle school teachers, team-taught in a reciprocal manner at three major research universities located in the Northwest, Midwest, and Southeast United States (Sundberg, Odell, Sunal, Mays, & Ruchti, 2004). The study was conducted in Fall 2000. Students were divided into cross-university cooperative groups with colleagues across the country. Each university was responsible for the facilitation of one of the course content topics. The course content in earth system science involved inter-actions among the earth's major systems or spheres: biosphere, hydro-sphere, atmosphere, and lithosphere. The students collaboratively completed the course assignments through a jigsaw strategy in which mutual interdependence was fostered (Slavin, 1990).

The course materials were developed originally through a grant from the National Aeronautics and Space Administration (NASA). The universities involved in the research, in a second project funded through NASA, were asked to evaluate the online course through several course administrations, providing suggestions for course improvement. The curricular materials were designed to be highly interactive and inquiry oriented. During the course, the in-service teachers were required to apply higher order teaching skills within cooperative groups to understand interactions in earth systems and to subsequently implement what they have learned in their own classrooms. The learning fully utilized the online environment and was organized through course management application software. The course content was delivered from links to other Internet sites, including many from online databases maintained by NASA, the United States Geological Survey, and United States Naval Observatory. The course content was delivered in what was termed the "classroom." On the Web site, students interacted in collaborative groups of four with their peers and instructors via a threaded discussion board "classroom application space" and each student had a personal "journal space" where summaries of the discussion and lesson plans were posted. The students could view their own journals; however, only the instructors could view the journals of all of the students. Additionally, students could e-mail their peers or instructors and find other needed contact information like telephone numbers of the instructors in the "classroom application space."

The course was split into modules on earth systems science: deforestation, hurricanes, volcanoes, and sea ice. During the first week of each module, each participant researched the topic along one of the components of the spheres of the earth: atmosphere, biosphere, hydrosphere, and lithosphere. For example, each group of four in-service teachers researched deforestation. In Week 1 of the deforestation module, one teacher studied the impact of deforestation on the atmosphere, another on the biosphere, and so forth. Subsequently, in Week 2, each participant in the group shared the results of the research. After group discussion, consensus was formed and then shared with the entire course in an interactive, online discussion. During Week 3, each group designed and implemented a lesson on the topic (e.g., deforestation) and posted the results of the classroom implementation to the discussion board. At the end of the course, as a final evaluation activity, each in-service teacher developed and posted to the discussion board a lesson on another earth science topic. Subsequently, each teacher implemented the lesson and posted a reflection to the discussion board on the implementation (Sundberg et al., 2004).

During the course, each instructor facilitated one of the modules. Jonathan facilitated deforestation, Julie was the primary instructor for the hurricane module, Tina moderated the volcanoes module, and Jonathan the sea ice module. While each instructor was the primary teacher of one of the modules, the other instructors provided scaffolding as needed when not tasked with leading the discussion. Jonathan was the most experienced online learning instructor and took the lead during the beginning of the semester. Jonathan served to model the online instruction for other instructors. However, throughout the semester, all the facilitators provided students with needed scaffolding. Jonathan primarily focused on technical problems. The other instructors worked more with content questions. The research methodology involved qualitative analysis using naturalistic research of artifacts collected in the course, including e-mail dialogue, transcripts of telephone interviews, and field notes of course facilitators. All data were collected at the same time and in the same manner at all universities. Permission to participate in the research was obtained from all students and instructors. All names are pseudonyms. "Investigator triangulation" was established through the use of the multiple data sources (Craft, 1996; Denzin, 1978; Joyce & Showers, 1995; Patton, 1990). "Methodological triangulation" was obtained through analysis of the data over the course of the semester (Cohen & Manion, 1989; Craft, 1996; Denzin, 1978; Patton, 1990).

Prior to the first class meeting, students completed a self-reported technology survey. E-mail messages were analyzed throughout the course of the semester. At midterm, telephone interviews were conducted of all the participants and the instructors. Throughout the course, the instructors made field notes and periodically (about every 2 to 3 weeks) met with each other in a telephone conference to maximize moderation of the course and address common concerns. Additionally, each instructor made field notes of faxes and telephone calls from students who were struggling with the technology.

## FINDINGS

The students used a variety of problem-solving strategies as they grappled with barriers to effective communication within the small cooperative groups and the class as a whole. Table 10.1 is a summary of the definition of the strategies used by the students to cope with problems in the online learning environment or with group members. In addition, Table 10.1 outlines some of the problems the strategies caused.

**Table 10.1.   Strategies, Definitions, and Problems**

| Coping Strategies Required | Definition | Problem |
|---|---|---|
| Side Groups | Various subgroups of students within the class either physically met together or e-mailed each other directly, avoiding the discussion board. | Instructor may or may not be aware there is a problem. Other students are left out of the conversation. |
| Time Constraints | Barriers related to a lack of sufficient time to complete course assignments in a reasonable amount of time. | Most of the difficulties were related to technical problems. |
| Technology | Some members lacked the technical expertise, consistent access, or adequate equipment. Facilitators were answering the same technical questions multiple times. | Facilitators spent considerable time assisting students with basic technical questions. |
| Venting Frustration and Humor | Students sent e-mail or discussion messages indicating frustration using the equipment or accessing the server. | Encouraging the students was very time consuming for the instructors. |

## Online Coping Strategies to Solve Problems Encountered

### *Side Groups*

Sometimes the students from the same locality or near the same university would physically meet at a central location to work on course assignments. Since the students were assigned to work cooperatively with students from the other universities, this coping mechanism was both beneficial and problematic. A researcher noted that students often create their own classroom at a centrally located school, coffee shop, restaurant, or home (C. S. Sunal, personal communication, December 2000). For example, Stephanie and Cindy created their own classroom in Cindy's kitchen.

> Stephanie is having computer troubles so we worked together to post one thing tonight. We spent hours at the kitchen table eating approximately one ton of Smarties...~☺ (Cindy, e-mail, Southeastern university, as cited in Sundberg, 2004, p. 190)

Using side groups to physically meet at a central location bypassed the discussion board and send e-mail to group collaborative members. While the students could maintain contact with their group members, the entire class did not have access to the discourse.

> We communicate several times through e-mail and also, on the web. I think e-mail is a "key" factor because too often the web site is becoming "cluttered" if you know what I mean. (Joe, e-mail)

> I would encourage more people to e-mail each other with questions, more connection. (Lynn, midterm evaluation)

At the Southeastern university in the study, many of the course participants were previously and concurrently involved in a statewide professional development project. Therefore, the participants were comfortable utilizing alternative means of communication. Julie noted:

> One problem in particular was people dropping out of the course and [group members who were] non-participators. 6 of the original 8 from [Southeastern university] ended up completing the course. Of the remaining 2, one did not participate at all and the other participated on a limited basis. The [Southeastern university] students were somewhat familiar with me, having met me at prior P.E. workshops. Therefore, I feel that they were somewhat reluctant to let me down. They also knew that I would help them as needed if they encountered any problems. They also knew each other from classes at [Southeastern university]. I think this "personalization" had a positive effect on the 6 active [Southeastern university] participants. They also seemed to be e-mailing one another, regardless of group assignment and

I know of 2 that worked together on at least one assignment. (field notes, December 13, 2000)

While the "personalization" was advantageous in this particular setting, it is not always possible to meet face-to-face or in another manner such as a teleconference.
Even though the students recommended using e-mail as noted above, e-mail was not always the solution.

Have been checking the ESSC site on a daily basis trying to catch up with my group mates. Today I did try to e-mail them at home, but 2 of the 3 e-mails came back as not being deliverable ☹. (George, e-mail)

As indicated by the above posting via e-mail, some of the students became discouraged when they were unable to communicate with their colleagues.

In order to address concerns about the difficulty of maintaining contact solely through the use of a discussion board, the students offered suggestions to use alternative communication technologies. One participant wrote that telephone numbers of class members would have been helpful when the Internet service was down: "Maybe I should have gotten phone numbers for my classmates so I could communicate with them" (June, e-mail). Another student indicated the use of a teleconference would assist in attaining and maintaining contact with other students and the course facilitators: "Something like a teleconference would be nice either at the start of the course, each section or each week" (Bill, midterm evaluation). In addition, the use of a synchronous discussion or instant messaging was offered to address concerns about classroom dialogue. For example, Lynn noted, "What I think would be beneficial is to have some sort of an online conference, where everybody is online at the same time. So, you can have a question/answer time with the facilitator" (midterm evaluation).

### Time Constraints
The amount of time needed to complete the course was problematic and time constraints impacted both students and teachers. One student later dropped the course because of the time-intensive nature of the course: "really wanted to do this but now I find that the research class is totally going to take soooo much time....I am sorry that this isn't going to happen for me...cause I want to take this class." Some students spent a large amount of time on the course. However, the amount of time spent in the class was not directly related to success in the class. Jonathan noted in a midterm evaluation:

Some students told me they spent 10–15 hours a week on the class, while others spent 0–5 hours. Obviously some time had to be taken for success, but not all those successful were the mega hour groups. Excellent results came from some of the people who were close enough to interact with classmates.

When probed, Jonathan reported the excessive time spent was more the result of a lack of technical skill than interaction with course content. Most of the time-consuming barriers could be related to one topic: lack of technical expertise. Jonathan answered most of the technical questions because that was his area of expertise. He complained, "For example, I was responsible for the first few weeks, but also for setting up the groups, and trying to coordinate the tech portion. This totally overwhelmed me at the start" (field notes, December 11, 2000). The amount of time to assess the Internet also took considerable time for the students. For example, one student e-mailed Jonathan requesting assistance: "It took me until about an hour ago to get everything working well." Another indicated difficulty posting a journal entry: "I am slowly getting the system. I wish I had saved a copy of my previous journal entry." In addition to the time spent using the technology, the students were not sure how much time they should spend in completing course assignments. The following e-mail sums up concerns about the amount of time needed to successfully complete the course: "I am somewhat concerned about the time investment with this class. Could you give me an estimate as to how much time you think the class will require on a weekly basis?" (Rita, personal communication). In short, the course was very time intensive for both the students and the facilitators.

## Technology

A lack of technical expertise is often cited as problematic in online courses and the problems noted by the facilitators and students indicated similar problems (Davies & Mendenhall, 1998; Jewett, 1998; Russett, 1994; Saunders et al., 1997; Wegener et al., 1997). Although the majority of the students indicated they had adequate skill using the technology in the pretest (Table 10.2), the problems they encountered and were unable to solve by themselves indicated a need for basic instruction in the use of the technology. For example, one student wrote:

> I need help. I thought I knew what I was doing. Turns out I haven't a clue. I tried working on the assignment yesterday and got more and more confused, and I don't think that I got anything posted. I couldn't find it anyway. And now I am not even sure if I am on the right week!! Please help me. I am trying and really want to do this class....I am sorry I am putting everyone else behind. I will get it. (Holly, e-mail)

As indicated above, students were concerned about using e-mail. The following is another example of the difficulty the students had with e-mail: "I am thrilled that went through. My computer told me I had made an error" (Donnie, e-mail).

**Table 10.2.  Technology Survey Results**

| | $N = 27$ |
| --- | --- |
| I feel comfortable using... | |
| E-mail | 26 |
| Word-processing | 27 |
| Internet | 27 |
| Electronic grade book | 25 |
| Presentation software | 22 |
| Digital camera | 20 |
| Spreadsheet software | 21 |
| Scanner | 18 |

Not only e-mail, but also basic navigation using the Internet was a problem for some of the course participants. As one wrote, "I tried again to copy and paste URL or content passages from Web sites, and they just wouldn't paste. Any further ideas, or am I just going to have to deal with it? ☺" (Tory, e-mail).

Not all technical problems were due to a lack of expertise; the format of the course and navigation of the Web site did not appear to some students to be user friendly. In her midterm interview, Katie noted:

> I had to learn how to use the site, especially when we had to switch back and forth between groups and spheres and the journal space. It was not that easy, I just struggle with the technology. The journal space was the hardest one to find, and it is very difficult to go back from the journal space. I did not know the journal space existed until I got help, but it was already week 4 before that happened. (midterm interview)

Another problem area in technology involved a lack of consistent and adequate server access. "Many little things...the server down, too busy online, AOL acts up. Little technical problems that were normal" (Valerie, midterm interview). Server access was problematic for some students at all three of the university sites. "We are on Novell system. When it goes down at the main office, everybody is cut off. We can't get [...] on the Internet" (Ann, midterm interview). In summary, technical difficulties with effective utilization of the technology, course design, and adequate access were barriers.

## Venting Frustration and Use of Humor

In addition to problem-solving solutions designed to deal with technical difficulties, coping techniques like venting frustration or humor were observed among students. Frustration was evident in communiqués to the course facilitators: "Still having problems sending. Oh, *)Y&&^$&$#^^ I hate tech. Oh, Well!" (Sam, e-mail). "Stupid servers" (Tory, e-mail). However, most participants revealed a sense of humor when confronted with difficulties, often technical in nature: "Whatever voodoo happened on the computer, it eventually opened up where I could read. Sometimes I feel like I have to sacrifice a chicken and sprinkle blood over the top of it to get the computer to work right" (Tory, midterm evaluation). "I'm not sure what the problem with the deforestation site was—it just started working after my e-mail with you. (Murphy's Law is always enforced by some unseen entity that hovers around me.)" (Tory, e-mail). "About my CD problem....I borrowed a friend's new laptop to try the CD and I am getting the same message...are there any alternate plans??? This is one of those 'drop back and punt' days" (Rita, e-mail). "I have been out of circulation lately. I plan to get into the work starting today. Happy Hurricane Hunting" (e-mail). From the e-mail communiqués, the discussion board, and interviews, there is some indication that the students who expressed a sense of humor, along with venting their frustration, were more successful in the course. Hiss (2000, p. 28) noted the use of humor in the online class reduces stress and the evidence in the dialogue confirms students who used humor or vented did not drop the course or unofficially drop from the course by a lack of participation in the online dialogue. In contrast, students who posted messages coded as "failure to cope" either dropped the course or simply stopped posting messages for a portion of the semester. The course facilitator contacted the following student and asked if she required assistance. She wrote:

> YES I NEED HELP! As I said before I have not done this before. PLEASE walk me through it. If I cannot get the help I need I feel I will have to drop out of the class. (Carol, e-mail)

Her inability to cope with the frustration, as indicated in the e-mail resulted in her dropping the course.

## Online Facilitator Strategies

The students in the course exhibited problem-solving abilities and coping strategies as they struggled to be successful in an online learning environment. Even though this is admirable, some students (10%) did drop because they were unable to deal successfully with their difficulties. Eliminating or reducing barriers are important to creating online learning environments. Julie, a course facilitator, offered these suggestions:

1. Ask students to cc: or bcc: copies of e-mails to their instructors concerning questions involving course or questions about assignments and due dates.
2. Remind student to use the discussion board so everyone can have access to the information.
3. In order to register for an online course, require students to have access to adequate equipment and a reliable Internet server.
4. Hold a face-to-face meeting, teleconference, or videoconference to personalize the course and ascertain if students have the basic skills needed to be successful in an online course.
5. Prepare a module to guide students through the technology.
6. Encourage students to maintain a sense of humor. Students who maintained a sense of humor with technical difficulties were better able to cope with the problems and find alternative solutions.

## Evaluation of Course Capstone Project

Finally, part of the purpose of the research was to evaluate the effectiveness of the online course. In particular, the designers of the online course were interested in modeling earth system science principles using Internet databases and Web sites. The research was also focused on modeling effective science instruction. At the end of the semester, Julie prepared a summary of problems related to course objectives, content, assignments, and assessment.

As a course capstone project, the in-service teachers prepared a lesson plan on an earth science topic using the earth system science principles modeled in the course. Analysis of the lesson plans submitted by the in-service teachers revealed the expectations for the assignment were poorly articulated.

It appeared some of the lesson plans were simply submitted because they were a part of the class assignment. It was not clear if the lesson plans were actually used in the classroom and how effective/ineffective the lesson plans were in an actual classroom setting. (Julie, field notes)

First, course participants reported difficulty in locating the criteria for the assignments.

> The rubrics were very good. I like the rubrics. I thought they were excellent, and they were very clear in what needed to be in the assignments, but by the time I figured out where they were, I had already posted stuff. We had to do a classroom application for week 6 or somewhere out there, and I got behind, and after I had posted, I found the rubric for it, and I thought Wow. (Angela, midterm interview)

Second, the parameters for the capstone assignment, a lesson plan using earth system science principles, were not clear.

> We need to clearly specify assignments. For example, many of the students had differing ideas about what the final project entailed. Classroom applications varied significantly student to student. As this is a content/professional development course, we should expect that all classroom applications are inquiry based. In fact, it would be preferable if they were learning cycle lesson plans. Maybe this is something we could address early in the course. (Julie, field notes)

Finally, no general format for the lesson plan was delineated. The course participants indicated a basic outline for the lesson plan would make planning and classroom application easier.

> There was no general format to the lesson plans and final project submitted to the discussion board. Recommendation: Include a general format to be used in designing the lesson plans. It makes it easier for the teachers to utilize effective lesson planning and easier for the instructor to grade. The format should be in a learning cycle format. (Mary, final interview)

## Earth System Science Online Course

The course developers were also concerned with the appropriateness of the science content for middle school students and if the in-service teachers had any concerns about their own preparation in terms of earth science content. First, it appears the content is more appropriate for seventh- and eighth-grade students. The configuration of middle school varies from location to location, grades 5 to 8, grades 6 to 8, and so on. Howard, a fifth-grade teacher, considered the content to be a bit too advanced for most of his students.

> A little too high for the fifth grade level but follows the curriculum agenda because it filters down from the National and then the states. We just redid our Science curriculum a couple years ago. (midterm interview)

Secondly, some of the in-service teachers had a strong science content background, which was apparent from the depth of the online postings.

> Many of the students had a very strong Earth Systems Science background and the depth of their postings was evident. I had some concerns about the impact this might have had on students with weak Earth Systems Science backgrounds. I think assessing prior knowledge in the very beginning of the course (e.g., concept map) would be useful and could be used in assigning group members. (Valerie, final evaluation)

The primary focus of the case study centered on typology of online communication indicating the student was unable to cope. However, other themes emerged, including poor technology skills and limited experience with earth system science concepts. Barriers that limit online communication negatively impacted learning in terms of students who dropped the course or failed to interact online in a timely manner.

## CONCLUSION

From the discussion board, e-mails, and interviews, the students were found to be quite creative in developing problem-solving techniques and coping strategies in the online course. The first strategy involved the creation of a side group or study group, a common technique used by students in traditional face-to-face courses. However, the unique nature of the online course dialogue means the creation of side groups can be problematic because not all of the students or even the course instructor have access to the discourse. In a traditional course, the discussion in a side group or study group may become part of the next discussion in class. To address this issue in the future, the course facilitators plan to implement a plan where course participants are drawn from cadres of teachers in close proximity to each other, possibly from the same building or at least the same district. This should provide needed scaffolding for the individual student and reduce isolation, a common complaint (Bohrer et al., 1998; Bos et al., 1995; Guy & Lima, 1999; Saunders et al., 1997; Schlough & Bhuripanyo, 1998). In addition, the facilitators plan to require each group to elect a secretary; the secretary will forward a summary of the face-to-face discussion in the small groups to the discussion board. Thus, the discussion in the side group will become a part of the whole class discussion and enrich the dialogue.

Previous studies have revealed most problems with online dialogue are technical (Davis, 1998; Jewett, 1998; Russett, 1994; Saunders et al., 1997; Wegener et al., 1997). From this study, it appears the solution suggested was to use some form of alternative communication (e-mail, telephone, and personal) to interact with other class members. Students have always formed study groups. Today, along with the traditional coffee shops, e-mail, instant messaging, and the telephone are alternative ways to create a classroom, as students commented: "One thing you might think about in these classes is having one day a week when everybody just gets on and starts chatting" (Sam, midterm interview). "Maybe videoconferencing that would give some structure" (Carol, midterm interview). Students indicated a need for a personal touch in communication: "At the end, instead of posting on the board, the e-mails seemed like it worked better, even though we still posted. Made it more personal" (Valerie, midterm evaluation).

Thus, instructors in online courses might consider the use of alternative forms of telecommunications to meet communication needs and barriers. However, the use of other forms of communication besides a discussion board might be problematic. While the participants are able to collaborate within their groups, the classroom dialogue as a whole may suffer. If corporate, critical dialogue is important to learning, then course developers should incorporate a mechanism to encourage more whole-group discussion. Sam offered a solution: "A phone conference could be possible....It would be great to telephone the people and ask how things were going" (midterm evaluation). Julie, course facilitator, indicated the facilitator could remind participants to post questions to the discussion board so all students would benefit (field notes, December 13, 2000). Additionally, participants indicated teleconferencing with the entire group or a group chat would provide a conduit for a more rich, corporate discussion with the entire class.

Time constraints were a barrier. One student noted actual dates, rather than Week 1, Week 2, and so forth, would have helped by providing a time frame for due dates. This was an excellent suggestion, considering each of the universities operated by a different scholastic calendar and could be useful for many online courses where the student body is global. "Maybe if we'd have put dates, like you did this last time instead of week one and week two, put October and the date, it would have been better" (Kelly, midterm interview). Since most of the time constraints were related to the use of technology, it should be helpful to use a face-to-face meeting, teleconference, or videoconference to make sure all of the students know how to access the Internet, what type of equipment is needed to successfully complete the course, and what the basic requirements of the course are.

As previously mentioned, effective use of the technology was problematic for the students. Students completed a technology survey at the beginning of the course. The instrument was a typical self-reporting assessment of technical skills. Although the students reported they had a basic understanding of the technology, the numerous postings of technology questions indicated a lack of prerequisite skill. One possible solution suggested was to hold a face-to-face meeting as discussed above or to develop online manuals guiding the students through the use of the technology. In addition, creating a cadre of teachers in close proximity should provide individual students with technical assistance from their local group. Finally, the course facilitator could help the student find or suggest technical assistance from a local source, for example, the technical advisor for the local school                                                                                              system.

The students vented frustrations and wrote humorous messages to the course facilitators and other class participants. The course facilitators addressed the concerns of the individual in several ways: providing general instructions via the discussion board to all participants on how to solve a particular technical problem, sending encouraging messages to the individual and all participants, and noting future improvements in the course design. The evidence of frustration and humor in the dialogue indicates the course design should be improved. In addition, the use of a cadre of teachers in close proximity to each other should aid in reducing the frustration of the individual student. More importantly, the students who either vented or resorted to humor finished the course, in contrast to the three students (out of 30 participants) who repeatedly posted messages categorized as "failing to cope."

In reference to improving the final capstone project, Mary proposed a format for the lesson plan that would provide needed scaffolding.

> Include a general format to be used in designing the lesson plans. It makes it easier for the teachers to utilize effective lesson planning and easier for the instructor to grade. The format should be in a learning cycle format. (Mary, final interview)

In summary, if we believe learning takes place in a classroom setting with corporate, critical dialogue, we must address problems with online discourse. Table 10.3 provides a summary of possible solutions to the problems the students and facilitators encountered in the course. In a similar study previously described, Vrasidas and McIsaac (2000) reflected that:

> In the traditional classroom there are several ways that the teacher can use to evaluate students. A confused face or head nodding can communicate a lot to the teacher....In the online classroom, the teacher can only evaluate what he/she has access to; there is no access to facial expressions, voice intonation or body language. Therefore, a variety of methods are essential for evaluating students and educational programs delivered online. (p. 110)

From the problem-solving and coping strategies used by the course participants, we have learned students are creative in finding alternative ways to communicate and students that maintain a sense of humor or have superior problem-solving abilities are more able to cope with difficulties in an online learning environment. More importantly, detailed analysis should be conducted during the course to evaluate the dialogue for clues that indicate a student is not coping well in the online environment, which is congruent with the reflections of Vrasidas and McIsaac (2000). In this manner, effective interventions can be designed to provide needed scaffolding for students. This is a critical issue in online courses because the drop rate and failure rate have been much higher than in typical face-to-face courses (Carr, 2000).

**Table 10.3.   Strategies, Problems, and Possible Solutions**

| Strategy | Problem | Solution |
|---|---|---|
| Side Groups | Instructor may or may not be aware there is a problem. Other students are left out of the conversation. | Create a cadre of teachers in close proximity. The secretary for the group will forward a summary of the group discussion to the whole class. |
| Time Constraints | Most of the difficulties were related to technical problems. | Provide a face-to-face class, teleconference, or videoconference illustrating the basic technical protocols used in the course. |
| | | Provide a calendar with due dates. |
| Technology | Facilitators were answering the same technical questions multiple times. Facilitators spent considerable time assisting students with basic technical questions. | Provide a face-to-face class, teleconference, or videoconference illustrating the basic technical protocols used in the course. |
| | | Provide a FAQ section on the Web page with step-by-step instructions. |
| | | Create a cadre of teachers in close proximity. |
| | | Encourage students to use local technical assistance, the school system technical assistant, for example. |
| Venting Frustration and Humor | Encouraging the students was very time consuming for the instructors. | Create a cadre of teachers in close proximity to offer encouragement and support to frustrated individual students. |
| Articulate Assignments | Students indicated the assignments and expectations were poorly delineated. | Change the navigation so finding the assessment criteria is easier. |
| | | Include a general format for the lesson plan in the capstone project. |

# REFERENCES

Ali, A., & Elfessi, A. (2004, Winter). Examining students' performance and attitudes towards the use of information technology in a virtual and traditional setting. *Journal of Interactive Online Learning, 2*(3). Retrieved June 14, 2004, from http://www.ncolr.org/jiol/archives/2004/winter/05/index.pdf

Bohrer, G. J., Colbert, R., & Zide, M. (1998, February). *Professional development for Bermudian educators*. Paper presented at the annual meeting of the Association of Teacher Educators, Dallas, TX. (ERIC Document Reproduction Service No. ED417140)

Bos, N., Krajcik, J., & Patrick, H. (1995). Telecommunications for teachers: Supporting reflection and collaboration. *Journal of Computers in Mathematics and Science Teaching, 14*(1/2), 187–202.

Carr, S. (2000, February 11). As distance education comes of age, the challenge is keeping the students. *The Chronicle of Higher Education*, A39. Retrieved May 10, 2003, from http://chronicle.com/free/v46/i23/23a00101.htm

Cohen, L., & Manion, L. (1989). *Research methods in education* (3rd ed.). London: Routledge.

Craft, A. (1996). *Continuing professional development: A practical guide for teachers and schools*. London: Open University Press.

Davies, R., & Mendenhall, R. (1998). *Evaluation comparison of online and classroom instruction for HEPE 129-fitness and lifestyle management course* (Evaluation project). Provo, UT: Brigham Young University, Department of Instructional Psychology and Technology. (ERIC Document Reproduction Service No. ED427752)

Davis, N. (1998). Developing telecommunications within European teacher education: Progress, plans, and policy. *Proceedings of SITE 98: Society for Information Technology & Teacher Education International Conference*, 1148–1152. (ERIC Document Reproduction Service No. ED421160)

Denzin, N. K. (1978). *The research act: A theoretical introduction to sociological methods*. New York: McGraw-Hill.

DeSimone, C., Schmid, R., & Lou, Y. (2000, April). *A distance education course: A voyage using computer-mediated communication to support meaningful learning*. Paper presented at annual meeting of the American Educational Research Association, New Orleans, LA.

Dillion, J. (1986). Student questions and individual learning. *Educational Theory, 36*, 333–341.

Fensham, P. (1995). Beginning to teach chemistry. In R. White (Ed.), *The content of science: A constructivist approach to its teaching and learning* (Reprint ed., pp. 14–28). London: Falmer Press.

Gallas, K. (1995). *Talking their way into science: Hearing children's questions and theories, responding with curricula*. New York: Teachers College Press.

Gallimore, R., & Tharp, R. (1990). Teaching mind in society: Teaching, schooling, and literate discourse. In L. Moll (Ed.), *Vygotsky and education: Instructional implications and applications of sociohistorical psychology* (pp. 175–205). New York: Cambridge University Press.

Glasson, G., & Lalik, R. (1993). Reinterpreting the learning cycle from a social constructivist perspective: A qualitative study of teachers' beliefs and practices. *Journal of Research in Science Teaching, 30,* 187–207.

Goodlad, J., Soder, R., & Sirotnik, K. (Eds.). (1990). *Places where teachers are taught.* San Francisco: Jossey Bass.

Guy, F., & Lima, J. (1999). WorldClass system. *Educational Media International, 36*(1), 68–73.

Hall, D. (1997). Computer mediated communication in post-compulsory teacher education. *Open Learning, 12*(3), 54–57.

Hislop, G. (2000, September). Working professionals as part-time on-line learners. *Journal of Asynchronous Learning Networks, 4*(2), Article 4. Retrieved June 13, 2004, from http://www.aln.org/publications/jaln/v4n2/v4n2_hislop.asp

Hiss, A. (2000). Talking the talk: Humor and other forms of online communication. In B. H. Weight (Ed.), *The online teaching guide: A Handbook of attitudes, strategies, and techniques for the virtual classroom* (pp. 24–36). Boston: Allyn and Bacon.

Hoffman, J., & Krajcik, J. (1999, March). *Assessing the nature of learners' science content understandings as a result of utilizing on-line resources.* Paper presented at the meeting of the National Association for Research in Science Teaching, Boston.

Jewett, F. (1998). *Course restructuring and the instructional development initiative at Virginia Polytechnic Institute and State University: A benefit cost study.* (ERIC Document Reproduction Service No. ED423802)

Jiang, M., & Ting, E. (1998). *Course design, instruction, and students' online behaviors: A study of the instructional variables and students' perceptions of online learning.* (ERIC Document Reproduction Service No. ED421970)

Johnson, D., & Johnson, R. (1979). Conflict in the classroom: Controversy and learning. *Review of Educational Research, 49*(1), 51–70.

John-Steiner, V., & Meehan, T. (2000). Creativity and collaboration in knowledge construction. In P. Smagorinsky (Ed.), *Vygotskian perspectives on literacy research: Constructing meaning through collaborative inquiry* (pp.31–50). Cambridge, England: Cambridge University Press.

Jonassen, D., Davidson, M., Collins, M., Campbell, J., & Haag, B. B. (1995). Constructivism and computer-mediated communication in distance education. *American Journal of Distance Education, 9*(2).7–26.

Joyce, B., & Showers, B. (1995). *Student achievement through staff development: Fundamentals of school renewal* (2nd ed.). White Plains, NY: Longman.

Katz, Y. J., & Yablon, Y. B. (2003). Online university learning: Cognitive and affective perspectives. *Campus-Wide Information Systems, 20*(2), 48–54.

Koory, M. A. (2003, July). Differences in learning outcomes for the online and F2F versions of "An Introduction to Shakespeare." *Journal of Asynchronous Learning Networks, 7*(2), Article 3. Retrieved June 13, 2004, from http://www.aln.org/publications/jaln/v7n2/v7n2_koory.asp

Kroder, S., Suess, J., & Sachs, D. (1998). Lessons in launching Web-based graduate courses. *T.H.E. Journal, 25,* 66–69.

Lee, C., & Smagorinsky, P. (2000). Introduction: Constructing meaning through collaborative inquiry. In P. Smagorinsky (Ed.), *Vygotskian perspectives on literacy*

*research: Constructing meaning through collaborative inquiry* (pp. 1–18). Cambridge, England: Cambridge University Press.

McLellan, H. (1997). Information design via the Internet. In R. E. Griffin, J. M. Hunter, C. B. Schiffman, & W. J. Gibbs (Eds.), *VisionQuest: Journeys toward visual literacy. Selected readings from the annual conference of the International Visual Literacy Association* (pp. 11–16). State College, PA: International Visual Literacy Association. (ERIC Document Reproduction Service No. ED408942)

Mende, R. (1998, May). *Hypotheses for the virtual classroom: A case study.* Paper presented at the IT97 Conference, St. Catharines, Ontario, Canada.

Meyer, K. A. (2003, September). Face-to-face versus threaded discussions: The role of time and higher-order thinking. *Journal of Asynchronous Learning Networks,* 7(3), Article 4. Retrieved June 13, 2004, from http://www.aln.org/publications/jaln/v7n3/v7n3_meyer.asp

Moll, L. (1990). Introduction. In L. Moll (Ed.), *Vygotsky and education: Instructional implications of sociohistorical psychology* (pp. 1–27). Cambridge, England: Cambridge University Press.

Ollerenshaw, C., & Ritchie, R. (1997). *Primary science: Making it work* (2nd ed.). London: David Fulton.

Patton, M. Q. (1990). *Qualitative evaluation and research methods* (2nd ed.). London: Sage.

Piaget, J. (1976). *The grasp of consciousness: Action and concept in the young child* (S. Wedgewood, Trans.). Cambridge, MA: Harvard University Press.

Russett, J. (1994 March). *Telecommunications and pre-service science teachers: The effects of using electronic mail and a directed exploration of Internet on attitudes.* Paper presented at the annual meeting of the National Association for Research in Science Teaching, Anaheim, CA. (ERIC Document Reproduction Service No. ED368571)

Saunders, N., Malm, L., Malone, B., Nay, F., Oliver, B., & Thompson, J. C., Jr. (1997, October). *Student perspectives: Responses to Internet opportunities in a distance opportunities environment.* Paper presented at the annual meeting of the Mid-Western Educational Research Association, Chicago. (ERIC Document Reproduction Service No. ED413816)

Saurino, D., Bentley, M., Glasson, G., & Casey, D. (1999, March). *Preparing science teachers using distance learning: Urban and rural students collaborate using video teleconferencing (VTEL) technology.* Paper presented at the National Association for Research in Science Teaching, Boston.

Schlough, S., & Bhuripanyo, S. (1998, March). *The development and evaluation of the Internet delivery of the course "Task Analysis."* Paper presented at SITE 98: Society for Information Technology & Teacher Education, Washington, DC. (ERIC Document Reproduction Service No. ED421089)

Slavin, R. (1990). *Cooperative learning: Theory, research and practice.* Englewood Cliffs, NJ: Prentice-Hall.

Smith, E., Lane, P., & Enfield, M. (1989, March). *Embracing reforms for the future: A case of an Internet-based application facilitating professional development.* Symposium presented at the National Association for Research in Science Teaching, Boston, MA.

Stephans, J. (1994). *Targeting students' science misconceptions: Physical science activities using the conceptual change model.* Riverview, FL: Idea Factory.

Sunal, D. W., & Sunal, C. S. (2001). *Science in the elementary and middle school.* Upper Saddle River, NJ: Merrill.

Sunal, D. W., Sunal, C. S., Odell, M., & Sundberg, C. W. (2003, Summer). Research-supported best practices for developing online learning. *Journal of Interactive Online Learning, 2*(1), Article 1. Retrieved June 2, 2004, from http://www.ncolr.org/jiol/archives/2003/summer/1/index.asp

Sundberg, C. W. (2004). Teaching undergraduate science online. In D. W. Sunal, E. L. Wright, & J. Bland Day (Eds.), *Reform in undergraduate science teaching for the 21st century* (pp. 181–198). Greenwich, CT: Information Age.

Sundberg, C. W., Odell, M. R. L., Sunal, D. W., Mays, A., & Ruchti, W. P. (2004). Team teaching in an online environment: Effects on instructors and students. *Northwest Passage: Journal of Educational Practices, 3*(1), 39–48.

Teeter, T. (1997, October). *Teaching on the Internet. Meeting the challenges of electronic learning.* Paper presented at the fall conference of the Arkansas Association of Colleges of Teacher Education, Little Rock, AR. (ERIC Document Reproduction Service No. ED418957)

Thomas, J., Jr. (2004, February 16). *Practice: Online mentor performance reporting.* Retrieved May 10, 2004, from the Sloan Consortium Web site: http://www.aln.org/effective/details2.asp?ACC_ID=60

Thornley-Hall, C. (Ed.). (1991). *Classroom talk.* Portsmouth, NH: Heinemann.

Vrasidas, C., & McIsaac, M. S. (2000). Principles of pedagogy and evaluation for Web-based learning. *Educational Media International, 37,* 105–111.

Wegener, S., Holloway, K., & Crader, A. (1997). *Utilizing a problem-based approach on the World Wide Web.* (ERIC Document Reproduction Service No. ED414262)

Wegener, S., Holloway, K., & Garton, E. (1999). The effects of Internet-based instruction on student learning. *Journal of Asynchronous Learning Networks, 3*(2), Article 7. Retrieved, from http://www.aln.org/publications/jaln/v3n2/pdf/v3n2_wegner.pdf

Wheatley, G. (1991). Constructivist perspectives on science and mathematics learning. *Science Education, 75*(1), 9–21.

## CHAPTER 11

# CONCEPT MAPPING AND E-LEARNING: A PATHWAY TOWARD THINKING DISPOSITIONS

**Craig S. Shwery**
*University of Alabama*

## INTRODUCTION

The nation's evolutionary progress from a 20th century Industrial Age to that of a 21st century Information Age has dramatically changed the perceptions of teaching and learning. The evolution, fueled with technological multimedia innovations, in turn, has fueled the current educational reform movement into rethinking purpose and direction about how teaching and learning can effectively match the technological innovations of the 21st Century (Leem, 2002; Northrup, 2002).

In response, many higher education institutions in general and teacher education colleges in particular, have been acknowledging the burgeoning demand from their clients to incorporate distance education into their curricula programs (National Center for Education Statistics, 1999). While

*Research on Enhancing the Interactivity of Online Learning*, pages 197–228
Copyright © 2006 by Information Age Publishing
All rights of reproduction in any form reserved.

those clients may prefer face-to-face learning, nonetheless, those same clients are demanding to be permitted the choice, flexibility and opportunity to e-learn through distance online courses (Allen & Seaman, 2003; Simonson, Smaldino, Albright, & Zvacek, 2003). And, while students do not learn any better through distance courses (Schweizer, 1999), ongoing studies have indicated they do not learn any less (Allen et al., 2004; Northrup, 2002). Thus, the once general tension between which format—online verses face-to-face—outperforms the other, has converged toward a more academic issue; that is, exploring the quality in teaching and learning that would be provided in each format (Grasel, Fischer, & Mandl, 2001; Royer, Cisero, & Carlo, 1993; Shin & Chan, 2004).

This same convergence has recently added a new dimension for consideration. Namely, what impact does the design of an online course have on a virtual e-learning environment (Clark, 1994; Noble, Shneiderman, Herman, Agre, & Denning, 1998; Simonson, Schlosser, & Hanson, 1999; Tompkins, 1993)? Regardless of delivery, conceptual learning is exponentially facilitated by activities that confront student misconceptions through direct experience, self-regulated learning, timely feedback, social interaction, and guided scaffolding (Penner, 2001; Sousa, 2001; Vygotsky, 1978; Wadsworth, 1996). In response to this consideration, this chapter discusses how the design of one virtual course challenged, asynchronously, learners to interactively use higher order thinking strategies during a problem-oriented e-learning environment. A major consideration for designing an online course is to replicate a challenging, interactive learning experience that is in line with current educational reform movement considerations. Specifically, the study under discussion attempted to identify individuals' intellectual thinking dispositions and whether the application of systemic scaffolding experiences enhanced those dispositional strategies when challenged in an asynchronous learning environment.

## BACKGROUND

In response to online learning considerations, many higher education educators are attempting, albeit some reluctantly, to develop either synchronous (same time, different-place education) or asynchronous (different time, different-place education) distance learning networks that simulate an equivalent learning opportunity to those experienced in a regular classroom setting. Realizing the need for alternative but equivalent instructional strategies, as well as equivalent learning experiences, designers of virtual courses struggle to make a virtual course just as mindful and challenging as that in a traditional face-to-face classroom (Simonson et al., 2003). One consideration during the design structure of a virtual content course is how the technological multimedia networks can be incorporated, rather than just applied, to help condense time and space that would provide far greater presentation of information and application to meet or exceed the equivalence used in a traditional course (Doyle, 1999). Referencing current brain-learning research, virtual classrooms can enhance an e-learner's preference in making mindful decisions as an active, self-directed, highly situated learner that can use higher order critical thinking skills (Grasel et al., 2001; Jensen, 2000). Such thinking skills are learned over time, leading the need to provide at multiple occasions the opportunity to practice higher order thinking during problem oriented situations (Costa, 2001).

Thus, the consideration to enhance multimedia opportunities in virtual learning parallels a key consideration toward maintaining an increasingly challenging level of learning to occur in this dimension. From a constructivist perspective, one e-learning consideration is how the applications of intellectual thinking strategies are used during a learner's construction-deconstruction-reconstruction restructuring. The challenge occurs when multiple opportunities are systemically provided to visually identify, as well as to compare and contrast, one's developing constructs from a concrete learning level to a more abstract quality of thinking, what Tishman (2001) refers to as *thinking dispositions*. Defined, those thinking dispositions are broad intellectual behaviors that, while including skill constructs, also include attitudinal, motivational and emotional constructs (Costa, 2001; Tishman, 2001). To increase the awareness between concrete and abstract thinking, the study under discussion used graphic organizers to scaffold cognitive experiences with visual experiences during those e-learning construct challenges.

## The Concrete-Abstract Continuum

Used appropriately, instructional media can incorporate concrete experiences to help learners identify and integrate their prior experience with intellectually higher order abstract thinking concepts and in the process alter previous knowledge interpretations (Brush & Saye, 2002; Carr, Gardner, Odell, Munsch, & Wilson, 2003; Royer et al., 1993). Used inappropriately, instructional media may be viewed as requiring necessary trade-offs between the breath and depth of learning experiences, since learning must somehow be "felt" by the teacher, and virtual classrooms are often seen as lacking that affective dimension (Easton, 2000; Smith & Winking-Diaz, 2004). However, is it possible to develop a more responsible learning perception with virtual courses without manufacturing unnecessary trade-offs, when using multimedia to provide similar learning experiences?

Provisions for enhancing effective learning curve experiences are perhaps one of the most sought-after research studies to date (Costa, 2001). For instance, Dale's (1969) inverted *Cone of Experience* was one of the early works to identify learning cycles from a personally-held concrete interpretation to a more worldwide abstract interpretation. The Cone of Experience theory suggests effective learning is tied to systemic experiences that provide developmentally appropriate learning gains over time. Such learning first occurs with the learner in a cycle as a participant in the actual experience. Those experiences internalize a concreteness learning related to those experiences, similar to Piaget's theory concerning assimilation and accommodation learning (Wadsworth, 1974). As the learner continues engaging within this learning event, the learner's interpretation of the event spirals upwards as both a participant and as an observer of the actual event.

At the next learning event experience, the learner is thought to be connecting new learning with existing learning, what Langer (1995) views as stepping in and stepping out of a learning experience. As those learning opportunities increase use of and adapt the learned information, the learner becomes challenged with the experience, moving up the Cone of Experience from both a participant and an observer of those past learned information, to accommodating the information through some other medium than was first used to experience the past learned event. Dale posits that it is at this learning event when a learner begins the process of moving from concrete to more intellectual abstract thinking. The learner observes symbols that represent past learning experiences as they are applied to other situations or events (medium), what Vygotsky (1978) describes as the Zone of Proximal Development, and Bruner (1966) describes as learning that moves from enactive (direct) experiences to iconic representations of experiences (multimedia), to symbolic representations.

Von Glasersfeld, (1984) distinguishes between those concrete and abstract construct events as being either a *trivial* construct or a *radical* construct. A trivial construct refers to the building of new ideas on the foundation of prior ideas (concrete information). For von Glasersfeld, mere psychological constructs that add layers to prior ideas (connections) are trivial, whereas radical constructs suggest there is not an end point to evolutionary development within the explanatory constructs that are mindfully reconceptualizing prior knowledge (abstract information). By having learners review those two types of constructs through self-regulating reflection, a learner can make mindful decisions as to where their personal theories and beliefs fall. Such an opportunity to reconstruct previously rote knowledge (trivial constructs) with more mindfully active knowledge (radical constructs) seems to have helped learners reconceptualize their own thinking approaches toward more meaningful (and less rote) thinking (Costa, 2001; Sousa, 2001; von Glasersfeld, 1984). The equivalent e-learning environment of a virtual course allows similar mindfulness to occur as well as the opportunity to systematically review and recognize the legitimacy of other points of view (Smith & Winking-Diaz, 2004).

What is most thoughtful is that each of those cyclical experiences applies to all learners, not just to young learners. When a learning task is presented to adults who have no relevant experiences on which to draw, applying past concrete experiential learning events to an abstract representation can facilitate higher order thinking dispositions (Bruner, 1966; Langer, 1995; Vygotsky, 1978; Wadsworth, 1974). Post-Piagetians, such as Flavell (1985), support such a view about cyclical learning, suggesting that while older minds may appear to be qualitatively different from younger, more novice minds, their constructs may be closer in design to those novice minds than previously thought within many of those older minds' constructs. Such constructs seem to suggest that older minds look almost as immature as younger ones when operating in relative novice knowledge domains such as teacher pedagogy. Thus, the impact that the design of an online course has on e-learners' trivial and radical constructs would seem to suggest the application of deconstructing/reconstructing is far more telling than a student's learning experiences.

Because it can take time for students to engage in learning that moves from trivial to radical higher order construct restructuring, virtual courses can accommodate such learning by providing multiple layers of media to be associated in the investigation of a topic's information. The greatest amount of information can be presented in the least amount of time through printed or spoken words (the top of the concrete-abstract continuum). In general, as an engaged learner moves up the Cone of Experience toward the more abstract media, more information can be compressed into a shorter period of time than may be possible within a traditional university classroom. Such an online course design would refute the notion that any trade-offs are needed for e-learning.

## Conceptually Constructed Thinking Dispositions

Several decades of cognitive research has provided support for educational reforms investigating how personally-held beliefs and theories influence thinking about learning (Costa, 2001; Marzano & Pollock, 2001; Nespor, 1985; Resnick, 1999; Resnick, Levine, & Teasley, 1991; Rumelhart, 1981; Schon, 1983; Shipman, 1967, 1969; von Glasersfeld, 1989; Zeichner & Tabachnick, 1981). Within many of those studies, researchers advocate that thinking is an incremental task, dependent on the cyclical learning process. That is, learning consists of strategies and skills that are continuously being expanded throughout one's life in the effort toward understanding and mastery of worldviews (Fogarty, 2001; Kozulin, 1998; Resnick, 1999). In addition, there is a growing shift to reflect how the constructed actions associated with classroom teaching are being influenced by existing individual thinking dispositions, what those thinking dispositions look like, and whether the construction-deconstruction-reconstruction actions may, as part of the process, develop higher order critical thinking dispositions among teacher candidates (Kagan, 1992; Katz & Raths, 1985; Kincheloe, Slattery, & Steinberg, 2000). Two converging lines of research—one from cognitive science, one from social psychology—now give us reason to view incremental learning as *intelligence-in-practice* thinking dispositions (Caine & Caine, 1994; Costa, 2001; Feuerstein, 1969, 1982; Fogarty, 2001; Gardner, 1999; Jenson, 2000; Vygotsky, 1978).

Because both intelligence and dispositions are functions considered to be higher order cognitive processes, reason would suggest both can be taught concurrently. If intelligence is a profile of capabilities, and thinking is incremental learning, then thinking dispositions become a habit of persistently trying to understand things and make intellectual thinking function better (Costa, 2001). Following this line of reasoning, one could hypothesize that e-learners can be taught to become incremental thinkers who apply self-regulatory and metacognitive skills when encountering task challenges rather than treating such tasks as being out of their reach (Allen et al., 2004; Smith & Winking-Diaz, 2004; Zimmerman, Bonner, & Kovach, 1996). These provisions would also allow e-learners to think of themselves as learners and bounce back in the face of short-term mistakes and failures.

Cognitive psychologists have been studying incremental thinkers for some time to see how systemic actions and dispositions promote higher levels of incremental intelligence. The research has uncovered incremental intelligence to be more than techniques and skills. Since the stance is that intelligence reflects a higher order cognitive process, the actions from higher order thinking are regarded as a particular mental set that calls for distinct, habitual ways of behaving. Called *dispositions* by Ennis (1962, 1986), and *passions* by Paul (2001), these habitual ways of behaving constitute the spirit, or the affective dimension, of incremental thinking, making learning much less mechanistic than is customarily portrayed (Dabbagh, 2001; Jackson, 2001; Langer, 1989; Tishman, 2001).

Messy and admittedly more complex forms of habitual incremental thinking are those attitudinal, motivational, and emotional thinking dispositions that are typically not celebrated as intelligence and are left out of the many ability-centered academic activities that are usually targeted to classify and assess what good intellectual thinking represent (Langer, 1989;

Tishman, 2001). Unfortunately, leaving those particular intellectual thinking characteristics out of many academic assessments misses the mark in underscoring the complexity that represents critical and thoughtful thinking among individuals; factors that frame references from which all meaning is constructed and communicated—and on which all perceived achievement depends (Caine & Caine, 1994; Feuerstein, 1969, 1982). For e-learners, leaving these complex thinking characteristics out of the online design could reduce the self-regulating constructions to just by-products for an end product to the assignment.

Interestingly, McDermott (1984) has suggested a learner's progress in school is less influenced by the instructional activities than by the social relationship the learner has developed with teachers and peers. Implicit from McDermott's theory is the idea that for e-learners, learning is as much an influential by-product of cultural, linguistic, and cognitive social events as are academically involved activities. Wolf and Reardon (1996) concur, suggesting "developing achievement" supported through meaningful classroom practices while learners are engaged at various levels of competencies (writing an essay, piecing together historical evidence, or conducting an experiment online) result in higher proficient performance when faced with a variety of challenging goals.

## Concept Mapping: From Theoretical to Visual

Concept mapping research can be traced to investigative works from the 1950s to the present (Ausubel, 1963, 1968; Deese, 1962, 1965; Edmondson, 1995; Kelly, 1955; Novak, 1993). Kelly's (1955) personal construct psychology saw prior learning as resulting in a repertory grid of generic character traits or personal constructs that influenced how a person thinks and/or responds to a new experience. Ausubel (1963, 1968) showed how school learning tasks could be made more challenging and meaningful without creating academic rote memorization constructs. His idea of advance organizers as a kind of cognitive bridge between learning and existing episodic concepts in the learner's cognitive structure has become one of the most researched ideas. Other studies exploring personal constructs have designed similar associationist memory models that help to reveal significant correlations between the similarity of students' and experts' cognitive structures and measures of achievement (Boxtel, van der Linden, Roelofs, & Erkens, 2002; Diekhoff, 1983; Fenker, 1975; Goldsmith, Johnson, & Acton, 1991; Herl, Baker, & Niemi, 1996; Preece, 1976a, 1976b, 1976c; Shavelson, 1972, 1974; Shavelson & Stanton, 1975).

Novak, the preeminent figure in concept map design, is credited with spawning the human constructivist model to illustrate the cognitive psychology of human learning and the epistemology of knowledge production

(Novak, 1972, 1993). His work focuses on how meaningful learning is bridged from new ideas or concepts that are anchored by previously acquired knowledge in a nonarbitrary way, supporting von Glasersfeld's (1989) theory of trivial and radical learning.

Novak and Gowin (1984), working from Ausubel's (1968) assimilation theory, developed a type of advance organizer, the concept map, to describe how individuals construct new forms of epistemological meanings within a particular discipline. Their results found that novices essentially developed the same forms of epistemological constructs as those constructed by many professionals of that same discipline, supporting Flavell's (1985) theory that older minds might look as immature and novice as any other mind when being challenged by new knowledge.

Supporting research in the area of conceptual mapping, Bean, Singer, Sorter, and Frazee's (1986) work places conceptual mapping as a piece in their designs called graphic organizers, a strategy somewhere between Armbruster's (1982) conceptual frames (mapping expository information), and Geva's (1983) flowcharting (linking relationships). Their research into different graphic organizer designs found learning through the use of graphic organizers to be consistently superior to the use of outlining or simple mapping when administering both multiple-choice tests and short answer tests to students. Darch, Carmine, and Kameenui (1986) expanded the use of graphic organizers to include cooperative learning groupings. They found graphic organizers used within a cooperative group setting provided enhanced learning and a higher retention curve in the information being explored than by those same students exploring information individually without the use of an organizer and interactive learning. For e-learners, the inclusion of graphic organizers and cooperative groups in an online course would add to the incremental thinking dimension.

## The Participants, the Design, and the Method

Since concept mapping is a tool theoretically examining cognitive structures, what are some empirical tools to assess those cognitive structures? By the very nature that concept maps are idiosyncratic representations of an individual's thinking processes, there is no common method to assess and later evaluate a learner's ongoing learning attitudes and thinking dispositions. The most widely used scoring instrument to examine cognitive thinking structures was developed and introduced by Novak (1981) and later modified by others to fit particular social situations. However, those instruments were quantitative in scope, time-consuming, and necessitated judgments be made with regard to global perceptions about the concept map design. Those early scoring instruments also placed numerical scores on each concept node, or categories, as well as the number of branchings within a concept map (Stewart, Van Kirk, & Rowell, 1979; Stuart, 1985). In her closing statements, Stuart issued the charge for a more qualitative instrument to be designed for classroom-friendly usage. The study under discussion took up that charge by designing a *qualitative* rubric and scoring instrument to assess the incremental e-learning intelligence during a virtual online course.

The 43 subjects (40 females, 3 male) who participated in this study were K–12 classroom teachers who attended a mid-sized research university in the southeast United States. Each subject was enrolled in a required master's level core course that covered brain-based learning research, various learning theories, critical thinking strategies, as well as intellectual thinking disposition skills. A number of graduates were unfamiliar with the structure of online courses, the deadline responsibilities, online discussion protocols, or cut/paste procedures. Those subjects found their footing in navigating the course after successfully completing an initial assignment that focused on using the various components required of the online course design. The remaining subjects were fully involved because of past experiences using online courses.

The course was designed to incorporate a type of advance organizer (Ausubel, 1963, 1968, 1981), referred to in education as concept mapping, to visually represent individual interpretations about the course information (Novak, 1990, 1993; Novak & Gowin, 1984). The visual course outline design was arranged into five sessions. The first, third and fifth sessions required individuals to create a concept map that revealed a personal interpretation of introduced information that built upon previous information. The first map was used as the benchmark in the study for the other two concept maps in order to reveal a level of thinking disposition structure development between the subjects' ongoing visual interpretations and the established global view of the same information (see Table 11.1).

For instance, the first map required subjects to organize the *Information Learning Processing Model* that would show practical application in the classroom; the second map required organizing the concept topic, *Transfer Higher Order Strategies,* into the first map, recreating a new concept map design if needed; the third map required organizing Bloom's *Taxonomy and Intellectual Thinking Dispositions,* as well as various contemporary learning theories into the second map, again recreating a new concept map design if needed. Each completed map was posted in an online "drop box" designated specifically for that map.

Each of five online sessions where designed to build upon the last session's information, with the assignments referring to past readings, discussion questions, and other topics that would help e-learning transfer and interactive accountability. Within each session there were approximately

**Table 11.1.   First Concept Map Data Set Structure Parameters (N=43)**

| Number of Simple Maps | Number of Sequence Maps | Number of Outside Influences Maps | Number of Meaningful Maps |
|---|---|---|---|
| 19 | 18 | 4 | 2 |
| Related Characteristics | Related Characteristics | Related Characteristics | Related Characteristics |
| Simple cause/effect supporting attribute association; few categories; loosely organized; little causal relationships; minimal development; simple problem solving thinking. | Temporal, Chaining or Linear sequencing. Little cause/effect supporting attribute association; few categories; linking organization problematic; narrow distinctions; identification of order (form) over placement of information (function). | Major supporting attribute association with cause/effect pattern; thoughtful categories; linking organization with categories maintains integrity of map; complex linkage; expanding relationships; expanding analysis, synthesis with facts; expanding world-wide views. | Complex supporting attribute association; infers cause/effect interactions; uniquely organized categories; complex/creative linkage; complex causal relationships; sound map integrity; complex usage of judgment and evaluation; unique world-wide views. |
| Map Represents | Map Represents | Map Represents | Map Represents |
| A Simple Information Concept Structure | A Sequence of Concept Structure | An Outside Influence on Concept Structure | A Meaningful Learning Concept Structure |

7–8 embedded assignments required to be completed within 2–3 week intervals, plus a short answer essay organized to be taken in pairs or sometimes in groups of three, depending on the essay questions. Each assignment usually included five or more questions that required subjects to post on discussion boards with responding requirements to other subjects' response postings. The online course design prohibited individuals from moving too far ahead of others by requiring posting responses in a timely manner. Also, in order that each subject remained an asynchronous e-learner, sessions were not posted on the outline earlier than 4 days prior to the beginning date for that session. The purpose for this design was to maintain the subjects' e-learning as close to an interactive reflective problem-solving mode as possible within the confines of a virtual course. The design and purpose for the framework were explained in an open letter sent to those enrolled in the course before the first starting date. This information was also placed in the e-syllabus and posted on the course's Web site.

The course had been redesigned a number of times over the past three semesters. Using a pedagogical constructivist perspective, the Cone of Experience format, as well as systematic and challenging learning experiences, the framework that was utilized in the present design was to provide practical applications in which the presented theories could be explored and tested in current classroom settings. As part of each session's requirements, subjects provided online postings from the results of those practiced applications. Thus, each time an assignment and related readings introduced new information, that information was carefully adjusted to align with the cyclical events of theory discussions, practical classroom application and, where applicable, the design of a concept map that visually reflected how the theoretical information was used.

Two qualitative methods were used to analyze data from the maps; a rubric and a concept-map scoring instrument. Neither the rubric nor scoring instrument was provided to the subjects so as to maintain trustworthiness in the process of interpretation (Lincoln & Guba, 1985, 2000). In addition, all concept maps posted were part of a larger assignment and given a pass/fail grade. All maps were graded with a passing score.

Both the rubric and instrument were adapted from Kinchin, Hay, and Adams' (2000) qualitative work in identifying different concept mapping structures. The original structures in Kinchin et al.'s design classification highlighted "three major patterns which are referred to as *spoke*, *chain*, and *net* structures [italics added]" arguing that these patterns can be interpreted as "indicators of progressive levels of understanding" (p. 43). In adapting the concept map structure classifications for e-learning, the author included ways to differentiate conceptual thinking in terms of their complexity, resilience in accommodating additional information, levels of cognitive thinking, as well as the establishment of key concepts, degree of appreciation of wider viewpoints, and its approximant relationship with worldview thinking (Bloom, Englehart, Furst, Hill, & Krathwohl, 1956; Costa, 2001; Kinchin, Hay, & Adam, 2000; Tishman, 2001).

To test the integrity and rigor of the rubric and scoring instrument structure design for use in online learning, the rubric mapping classification and the scoring instrument went through several revisions prior to the current form that includes a fourth structure classification, *branching*, placed between the "chain" and the "net" classifications. The purpose was to delineate a clearer cognitively thinking picture of an individual's use of higher order thinking disposition strategies that seemed fuzzy without the additional classification. The result provided a closer approximation of four major concept map classifications, their parameters, and a scoring instrument that can interpret thinking disposition skills (see Appendix A and B for the rubric and scoring instrument). As research continues in this area, similar designs are expected to refine and include other structure classifications.

## ANALYSIS

Described in Table 11.1 are four distinct thinking disposition designs that represent subjects' interpretations of the presented information to the introduction of *Information Learning Processing Model*. The majority of the subjects' (19) first map's data fell into the *Simple Information Concept Structure* (see Figure 11.1; simple problem solving, compare/contrast simple, minimal development of map, and little linking or causal relationships with categories 1–3 scoring cycle—see Appendix B, Concept Map Scoring Instrument).

**Table 11.2.   Second Concept Data Map Set Structure Parameters (N=43)**

| Number of Sequence Maps | Number of Simple Maps | Number of Outside Influences Maps | Number of Meaningful Maps |
|---|---|---|---|
| 25 | 6 | 9 | 3 |
| Number of New Map Structures | Number of New Map Structures | Number of New Map Structures | Number of New Map Structures |
| 5 moved to Outside Influences Maps from First Map Structure; 1 moved to Meaningful Maps from First Map Structure | 13 moved to Sequence Maps from First Map Structure | 5 moved from Sequence Maps | 1 moved from Sequence Maps |
| Total Sequence Maps | Total Simple Maps | Total Outside Influences Maps | Total Meaningful Maps |
| 25 from original 18 | 6 from original 19 | 9 from original 4 | 3 from original 2 |
| Related Characteristics | Related Characteristics | Related Characteristics | Related Characteristics |
| Temporal, Chaining or Linear sequencing. Little cause/effect supporting attribute association; few categories; linking organization problematic; narrow distinctions; identification of order (form) over placement of information (function). | Simple cause/effect supporting attribute association; few categories; loosely organized; little causal relationships; minimal development; simple problem solving thinking. | Major supporting attribute association with cause/effect pattern; thoughtful categories; linking organization with categories maintains integrity of map; complex linkage; expanding relationships; expanding analysis, synthesis with facts; expanding world-wide views. | Complex supporting attribute association; infers cause/effect interactions; uniquely organized categories; complex/creative linkage; complex causal relationships; sound map integrity; complex usage of judgment and evaluation; unique world-wide views. |

**Table 11.2.   Second Concept Data Map Set Structure Parameters (N=43) (Cont.)**

| Map Represents | Map Represents | Map Represents | Map Represents |
|---|---|---|---|
| A Sequence of Concept Structure | A Simple Information Concept Structure | An Outside Influence on Concept Structure | A Meaningful Learning Concept Structure |

Figure 11.1 shows a representational Simple Information Concept Structure concept map designed by one of the 19 students whose map fell into this category. There are several components to consider in scoring this design. First, the design reveals a simple "spoke" association with few categories reflecting thoughtful cognitive thinking about the topic and the process involved in the topic. While there are visual representations of causes and effects, the information presented is weak in meaning and association. Second, there are no indications that any of the categories and attributes would be linked in any way other than by the topic. Such a design is reminiscent of an elementary brainstorming or webbing of information without thoughtful attention to how and why the information may be linked. Third, most all of the designs were structured similarly and seemed to be more concerned with form (trivial) presentation than with function (radical) interpretation.

The next first map structure, *Sequence of Concept Structure*, had 18 maps; identifying order through ranking sequence, little difference between important and not relevant information, narrow development, and narrow distinctions with supporting attributes (4–6 scoring cycle). Four maps fell into the *Outside Influences on Concept Structure*: use of analysis, synthesis, and evaluation thinking to identify facts with supporting attributes, complex sub-linking with a category, and developing a worldwide view theory of the information (7–9 scoring cycle). Two maps fell into the *Meaningful Learning Concept Structure*: creative thinking in interrelating categories and supporting attributes, nonlinking to inconsistencies among relationships, and sound reasoning to a unique worldwide view theory of the information (10–12 scoring cycle).

These e-learning data were consistent with data collected from a face-to-face course using the same criteria, rubric, and scoring instrument piloted earlier, supporting the stance that e-learners do not learn any better or any worse in distance learning environments when provided higher order thinking interactive activities (Allen et al., 2004; Northrup, 2002; Schweizer, 1999). Equally significant from the e-learning data are how most subjects were thinking about the newly presented information. Most were simply trying to figure out how to build the new information onto existing constructed information.

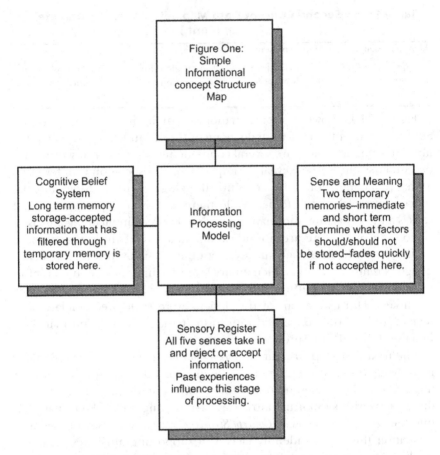

Figure 11.1.   Simple informational concept structure map.

Similar to supporting learning-related cognitive research (Costa, 2001; Dale, 1969; Flavell, 1985; Resnick et al., 1991; von Glasersfeld, 1984), older minds respond to new information in the same way almost all learners' accommodate the information: that is, by trivializing (connecting) the information with prior information. It is not until later, when more practice and reflection on that same information becomes more radically thought out (Routman, 1991). Thus, for asynchronous e-learners, interacting on information is dependent on what one does or is asked to do with the information, rather than the delivery of the information itself.

In addition, the results from the first concept map provided a benchmark for assessing the degree and level of thinking disposition e-learner will exhibit over the course of the semester designed online course. That is, based on the theoretical framework supporting the course design, the e-learning cycle, as well as the measurement protocols, provide strong qualitative advance organizer support "for the information collection by the evaluator" (Lincoln & Guba, 2000, p. 174).

As outlined in Table 11.2, the introduction of *Transfer Higher Order Strategies* to be combined with the past *Information Learning Processing Model* information required subjects to design a concept map detailing their interpretations of the combination information. Six of the original 19 maps in the first concept map structure remained in the *Simple Information Concept Structure*: simple problem solving, compare/contrast simple, minimal development of map, and little linking or causal relationships with categories (1–3 scoring cycle). But, 13 of those maps in the first simple structure map parameters fell into the majority of the second concept map parameters (25), or the *Sequence of Concept Structure* (see Figure 11.2): identifying order through ranking sequence, little difference between important and not relevant information, narrow development, and narrow distinctions with supporting attributes (4–6 scoring cycle).

Figure 11.2 shows a representational Sequence of Concept Structure concept map designed by one of the 13 students whose map fell into this category. Several higher order thinking disposition components were considered in the scoring of this design structure. First, the design reveals a temporal or "chain" association with narrow causal relationships among the presented categories. Second, and perhaps the most telling, is the misinterpretation of new information constructed into the design. At this juncture in the course, new information relating to higher order thinking strategies were introduced, discussed, and practiced through several assignments. Yet, those strategies were not constructed into the map's design. Rather, the term "Environment" was used to incorporate any and all additional information into previous concept map interpretations. Each of the 13 subjects' map designs included some type of broad category that was meant to reflect the newly presented information. Third, the sequencing of categories lost meaning of causal relationships and identified little difference from the important to less important information. Fourth, because of the unique structure design, categories were usually indicated from a top-to-bottom ranking process, resulting in weak meaning association. This type of structure design represented a struggle between trivial constructs and radical constructs, in which newly acquired information no longer seems to fit into the first choice concept map design (spoke). The alternative visual representation chosen reflects a critical reconstruction of past information by trying to develop a more effective interpretation of the presented information. Thus, this design represents an individual who is attempting to make meaning by not simply adjusting information to fit an existing construct. Rather, the construct is being redesigned to fit the information.

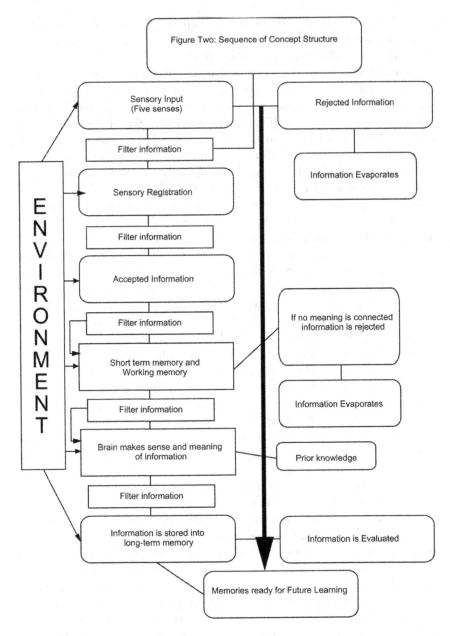

Figure 11.2.   Sequence of concept structure.

Similarly, of the original 18 *Sequence of Concept Structure* maps, five of the maps were redesigned and moved to the *Outside Influences on Concept*

*Structure* parameters, making a total of nine concept maps fitting those map structure parameters (7–9 scoring cycle). Finally, a first concept map that originally fell into the *Sequence of Concept Structure* was redesigned to meet the parameters of the *Meaningful Learning Concept Structure*, making for a total of 3 map designs meeting those map structure parameters (10–12 scoring cycle).

What makes these second map structures so dynamic for an asynchronous online course is how the e-learners had been actively engaged within the presented information for the purpose of making sense of the content. That is, even without direct instruction suggestions from the instructor, all but six subjects reassessed their understanding from a trivial stance that moved them more, if not completely, toward a radical stance. The course provisions of scaffolding, exploration, reflection, deconstruction/reconstruction, as well as discussions about the use of higher order critical thinking strategies, had allowed individual e-learners the opportunity to self-regulate their e-learning.

The third and final concept map was most revealing and supported much of the research with regard to time, reflection, and learning (Eby & Kujawa, 1994; Henderson, 1992). Eby and Kujawa suggest that active learning time, the amount of time spent working at one's own learning levels in learning something new, is a most important indicator in a student's achievement.

As noted in Table 11.3, the introduction of *Bloom's Taxonomy* and *Intellectual Thinking Dispositions*, as well as various contemporary learning theories with the above Transfer Higher Order Strategies and Information Learning Processing Model information required subjects to design a concept map detailing their interpretations of this final combination information. There were five maps with parameters that fell into the *Simple Information Concept Structure*: simple problem solving, compare/contrast simple, minimal development of map, and little linking or causal relationships with categories (1–3 scoring cycle). That is, from the six map designs that fell into this structure in the second map construction (see Table 11.2), one original map design changed to meet the parameters in the *Meaningful Learning Concept Structure*. Such a change in design suggests this individual continued to have difficulty in making sense of the additional information, until finally the individual needed to change the concept map design. These final five concept maps originated as simple structures at the beginning of the course and changed little throughout the course, except to add-on additional information to the existing structure without concern toward mapping integrity.

**Table 11.3.   Third Concept Map Structure Parameters (N=43)**

| Number of Simple Maps | Number of Sequence Maps | Number of Outside Influences Maps | Number of Meaningful Maps |
|---|---|---|---|
| 5 | 18 | 15 | 5 |
| Number of New Map Structures | Number of New Map Structures | Number of New Map Structures | Number of New Map Structures |
| 1 moved to Meaningful Maps from Second Map Structure | 6 moved to Outside Influences Maps from Second Map Structure; 1 moved to Meaningful Maps from Second Map Structure | 6 moved from Sequence Maps | 1 moved from Outside Influences Maps; 1 moved from Simple Maps |
| Total Simple Maps | Total Sequence Maps | Total Outside Influences Maps | Total Meaningful Maps |
| 5 from original 19 | 18 maps (down) from 25 second maps | 15 maps (up) from 9 second maps | 5 maps (up) from original 2 maps |
| Related Characteristics | Related Characteristics | Related Characteristics | Related Characteristics |
| Simple cause/effect supporting attribute association; few categories; loosely organized; little causal relationships; minimal development; simple problem solving thinking. | Temporal, Chaining or Linear sequencing. Little cause/effect supporting attribute association; few categories; linking organization problematic; narrow distinctions; identification of order (form) over placement of information (function). | Major supporting attribute association with cause/effect pattern; thoughtful categories; linking organization with categories maintains integrity of map; complex linkage; expanding relationships; expanding analysis, synthesis with facts; expanding world-wide views. | Complex supporting attribute association; infers cause/effect interactions; uniquely organized categories; complex/creative linkage; complex causal relationships; sound map integrity; complex usage of judgment and evaluation; unique world-wide views. |
| Map Represents | Map Represents | Map Represents | Map Represents |
| A Simple Information Concept Structure | A Sequence of Concept Structure | An Outside Influence on Concept Structure | A Meaningful Learning Concept Structure |

Eighteen final maps fell into the *Sequence of Concept Structure:* identifying order through ranking sequence, little difference between important and not relevant information, narrow development, and narrow distinctions with supporting attributes (4–6 scoring cycle). As noted in Table 11.1, while there were originally 18 maps that also fell into this structure parameter, only six of these original map structures did not change in design by the end of the course. That is, as map structure designs changed and moved over the course, falling into other parameters, only six individuals kept the same structure throughout. From the 25 maps that fell into this parameter range in the second map (See Table 11.2), seven maps were redesigned to meet other parameters; six of those maps moved to the *Outside Influences on Concept Structure* (7–9 scoring cycle) and one redesigned map structure moved to the *Meaningful Learning Concept Structure* (10–12 scoring cycle). Fifteen final maps fell into the *Outside Influences on Concept Structure* parameters (7–9 scoring cycle). As noted above, six of those new maps came from the *Sequence of Concept Structure*. Finally, five map designs fell into the *Meaningful Learning Concept Structure* (see Figure 11.3).

Figure 11.3 shows the representational Meaningful Learning Concept Structure map designed by one of the five students whose map fell into this category. This map represents a highly developed radical construct. Several important components were considered for scoring this and similar designs into the highest map structure that reflects a more worldwide view than do any of the other concept map designs. First, the design is unique and complex. The "net" design contains justifiable categories linking complex classification that describe creative linking between and categories and supporting attributes. Second, and an important distinction from other map structures, is that additions to the design will have minor consequences to the map's integrity. That is, where other map designs could result in a structure failure from the lack of accommodation to meaning when new information is added (e.g., spoke and chain structures), the net structure can accommodate information additions because of the complex routing of information. Third, the unique design provides an aesthetic structural relationship. Such a consideration allows a novel worldwide interpretation of multilayered information that is not greater or lesser than any of the information. Rather, similar to the Gestalt Theory, the sum of information becomes more than the individual pieces of information when placed together. This type of structure design represented a sound testing of presented information and takes into account the multifaceted information. Such interconnections are recognized by sound reasoning and highly developed thinking disposition.

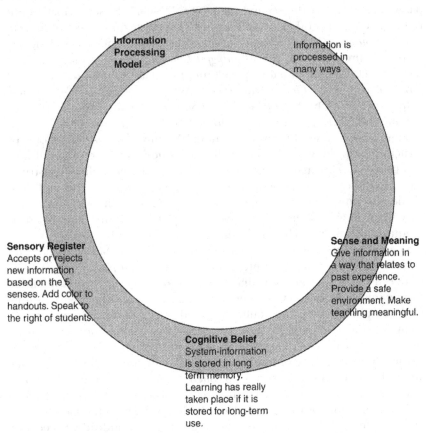

Figure 11.3.   Meaningful Learning Concept Structure.

## DISCUSSION

Reviewing the data from those six students suggests that as more complex information was introduced; construct development remained *trivial* in how that information was interpreted. Rather than expanding the complexity of changing causal relationships design between and among the presented information over time in the course, accommodations were made by simple additions to one existing map design, namely the spoke structure. While these additions did not alter the maps' "spoke" integrity, the lack in reconsidering design alterations does suggest meaningful higher order intellectual considerations were not adopted. In reference both to the rubric and to the scoring instrument (see Appendix A through

B), these six e-learners' *thinking attributes* (simple cause/effect associations), *thinking complexity* (little linking, simple categories), and *thinking relationships* (little causal relationships) were not thought out carefully. As long as causes and effects were kept to a minimum design, there would not be a need for more complex thinking in how the combination of information linked to inform the learner. Unfortunately, this meant there was little thought to worldwide relational-information complexity.The results from data analysis from these three sets of maps suggest several important considerations for e-learners, as well as where e-learners fall along the intellectual thinking disposition continuum and what this means for online course designs. A most interesting and telling set of data that fell out of the analysis came from the six students who chose to retain the same map design (*Simple Information Concept Structure*) throughout their three sets of maps.

These six students also had difficulty adjusting to the e-discussion board interaction requirements, again preferring to be minimalists with their responses. Thus, the maps' visual structure supported a top-down learning belief, similar to a transmission style of teaching and learning. For these e-learners, the learning challenge was reduced to how to meet the course assignment expectations, rather than to challenge their own learning. A major concern with this type of higher order construct teacher/thinker is in how this type of learner may view the learning process in terms of classroom teaching. Another concern is how this type of teacher/thinker will view technology's use in the classroom.

For example, the use of concept mapping, rubrics, and scoring instruments would provide strong evidence for intervention in guiding e-learners to rethink their role as a teacher-learner-teacher-thinker. While sharing the assessment instruments with e-learners would not be advisable, because of mimicking issues, the use of scaffolding alternative thinking strategies would be most appropriate for those e-learners having particular difficultly making meaningful connections with combination information, as well as for those e-learners having difficulty moving from the trivial to radical deconstruction-reconstruction process.

In regard to the remaining two map sets data, which were compared to the benchmark map set (e.g., first map data set), the e-learning process represents similar face-to-face classroom learning development. For instance, many e-learners attempted to redesign their concepts maps for a better interpretation as additional information was presented throughout the online semester. Of the total map designs falling into the *Sequence of Concept Structure* parameter (31), 13 maps were redesigned to fit other higher order thinking strategies. This means that as the information became more complex, these 13 individuals accommodated the information by using higher order thinking disposition strategies. Thus, as the information became more complex, so did the *thinking attributes*, the *thinking complexity*, and the *thinking relationships* strategies. For these e-learners, experimentation in how to visually represent their thoughts was assisted with the use of new thinking information that was presented in stages during the online course (Dale's Cone of Experience). But, for these e-learners, the information was still fuzzy and lacked ownership; the map structure had linkage difficulty, any additions were problematic, and while there was movement between trivial and radical reconstruction, the thinking reflection was still narrow, a lower coping thinking disposition strategy. Developmentally, those e-learners who fell into this category of learning would require additional opportunities to investigate their interpretations of the presented course information. However, because learning is incremental, as is the intellectual thinking dispositions, those e-learners may find this developmental learning "zone" sufficiently challenging. Providing additional opportunities to investigate could bring about frustration leading to downplaying the information to meet an objective for the class rather than for themselves.

The total map designs falling into the *Outside Influences on Concept Structure* parameter (15), as well as those falling into the *Meaningful Learning Concept Structure* parameter (5), suggest a clear inclusion of using intellectual thinking disposition strategies. For those e-learners, the learning challenge was in how to enhance their learning by thinking more outside the box. When using the assessment instrument, what separated these e-learners from e-learners who fell into *Sequence of Concept Structure* parameter was how they used dispositions to learn for learning sake, a rather high-level intellectual thinking disposition characterization. Noteworthy from the data was the individual's ability to rethink the design to accommodate a sophisticated worldwide viewpoint in relation to what the information also meant for teaching and learning.

The result from the course design is worth repeating: during this study the higher order thinking strategies introduced throughout the asynchronous design did not explicitly require e-learners to use the information. Map design changes were the result of various interactive online assignments and discussions. It is the result of this active interaction that so clearly separated the six individuals described first in this discussion with the remaining 37 e-learners of the study. Those remaining e-learners attempted to some degree toward altering their thinking positions to fit a more complex interpretation of the course's complex combination information.

## CONCLUSION

Each map and the related parameters represented a type of thinking that accommodates complex information. The provocative evidence obtained from this study supports the need to provide higher order complex thinking strategies to e-learners in virtual courses. To better approximate how and why information connects, interconnects, develops causal relationships, and influences learning, virtual courses need to be mindful in providing various opportunities not just to build upon existing knowledge (trivial constructs). Rather, for e-learning to be effective, the design of the online course needs to include a consistent deconstruction-reconstruction of information (radical constructs) to be compared and contrasted with a previous learned experience. Evidence collected from this study supports similar investigations concerning the quality of interactive online course design. That is, the location of learning is less important than the quality provided for exploration of the presented information.

The results from this study further support the current reform movement in teacher education to utilize effective, scientifically-based instructional strategies, when designing online courses to promote e-learning the internalization of change in beliefs and dispositions about teaching and learning (Maxwell, 2004). As more individuals in teacher education take on the rigors of online learning, e-learners must be challenged to explore their intellectual thinking dispositions, or continue to contribute to the myth that online learning delimits e-learners' intellectual thinking by not requiring deeper investigations of the existing knowledge they hold or are in the process of learning.

## REFERENCES

Allen, I. E., & Seaman, J. (2003). *Sizing the opportunity: The quality and extent of online education in the United States, 2002 and 2003.* Needham, MA: Sloan-C.

Allen, M., Mabry, E., Mattrey, M. Bourhis, J., Titsworth, S., & Burrell, N. (2004). Evaluating the effectiveness of distance learning: A comparison using meta-analysis. *Journal of Communication, 54,* 402–420.

Armbruster, B. B. (1982). *Idea mapping: The technique and its use in the classroom* (Reading Education Report No. 36). Urbana, IL: University of Illinois, Center for the Study of Reading.

Ausubel, D. P. (1963). *The psychology of meaningful verbal learning.* New York: Grune and Stratton.

Ausubel, D. P. (1968). *Educational psychology: A cognitive view.* New York: Holt, Rinehart and Winston.

Ausubel, D. P. (1981). Schemata, cognitive structure, and advance organizers. A reply to Anderson, Spiro, and Anderson. *American Educational Research Journal, 17,* 400–404.

Bean, T. W., Singer, H., Sorter, J., & Frazee, C. (1986). The effect of metacognitive instruction in outlining and graphic organizer construction on students' comprehension in a tenth-grade world history class. *Journal of Reading Behavior, 15*(2), 153–169.

Bloom, B. S., Englehart, M. D., Furst, E. J., Hill, W. H., & Krathwohl, D. R. (Eds.). (1956). *Taxonomy of educational objectives: The classification of educational goals. Handbook I: Cognitive domain.* New York: Longmans, Green.

Boxtel, C., van der Linden, J. L., Roelofs, E., & Erkens, G. (2002). Collaborative concept mapping: Provoking and supporting meaningful discourse. *Theory Into Practice, 41,* 40–46.

Bruner, J. (1966). *Toward a theory of instruction.* Cambridge, MA: Harvard University Press.

Brush, T. A., & Saye, J. W. (2002). A summary of research exploring hard and soft scaffolding for teachers and students using a multimedia supported learning environment. *The Journal of Interactive Online Learning, 1*(2), 1–12.

Caine, R. N., & Caine, G. (1994). *Making connections: Teaching and the human brain.* Menlo Park, CA: Addison-Wesley.

Carr, K., Gardner, F., Odell, M., Munsch, T., & Wilson, B. (2003). The role of online, asynchronous interaction in development of light and color concepts. *The Journal of Interactive Online Learning, 2*(2), 1–17.

Clark, R. (1994). Media will never influence learning. *Educational Technology Research and Development, 42,* 21–29

Costa, A. L. (Ed.). (2001). *Developing minds: A resource book for teaching thinking* (3rd ed.). Alexandria, VA: Association for Supervision and Curriculum Development.

Dabbagh, N. (2001). Concept mapping as a mind tool for critical thinking. *Journal of Computing in Teacher Education, 17*(2), 16–24.

Dale, E. (1969). *Audio-visual methods in teaching,* (3rd ed.). New York: Holt, Rinehart & Winston.

Darch, C. B., Carmine, D. W., & Kameenui, E. J. (1986). The role of graphic organizers and social structure in content area instruction. *Journal of Reading Behavior, 18,* 275–295.

Deese, J. (1962). *On the structure of associative meaning.* Baltimore, MD: The Johns Hopkins University Press.

Deese, J. (1965). The structure of associations in language and thought. *Psychological Review, 69,* 161–175.

Diekhoff, G. M. (1983). Relationship judgments in the evaluation of structural understanding. *Journal of Science Teacher Education, 1*(4), 66–69.

Doyle, A. (1999). A practitioner's guide to snaring the net. *Educational Leadership, 56,* 12–15.

Easton, S. S. (2000). Clarifying the instructor's role in online distance learning. *Communication Education, 52*(2), 87–105.

Eby, J. W., & Kujawa, E. (1994). *Reflective planning, teaching, and evaluation: K–12.* New York: Macmillan.

Edmondson, K. M. (1995). Concept mapping for the development of medical curricula. *Journal of Research in Science Teaching, 32,* 777–793.

Ennis, R. H. (1962). A concept of critical thinking. *Harvard Educational Review, 32,* 81–111.

Ennis, R. H. (1987). A taxonomy of critical thinking dispositions and abilities. In J. B. Baron & R. J. Sternberg (Eds.), *Teaching thinking skills: Theory and practice* (pp. 9–26). New York: W. H. Freeman.

Fenker, R. M. (1975). The organization of conceptual materials: A methodology for measuring ideal and actual cognitive structures. *Instructional Science, 4*, 33–57.

Feuerstein, R. (1969). *The instrumental enrichment method: An outline of theory and technique.* Jerusalem: Hadassah-Wizo-Canada Research Institute.

Feuerstein, R. (1982). *Instrumental enrichment.* Baltimore, MD: University Press.

Flavell, J. (1985). *Cognitive development* (2nd ed.). Englewood Cliffs, NJ: Prentice-Hall.

Fogarty, R. (2001). Our changing perspective of intelligence: Master architects of the intellect. In A. L. Costa (Ed.), *Developing minds: A resource book for teaching thinking* (3rd ed., pp. 144–149). Alexandria, VA: Association for Supervision and Curriculum Development.

Gardner, H. (1999). *The disciplined mind.* New York: Simon and Schuster.

Geva, E. (1983). Facilitating reading comprehension through flowcharting. *Reading Research Quarterly, 15*, 384–405.

Goldsmith, T. E., Johnson, P. J., & Acton, W. H. (1991). Assessing structural knowledge. *Journal of Educational Psychology, 83*(1), 88–96.

Grasel, C., Fischer, F., & Mandl, H. (2001). The use of additional information in problem-oriented learning environments. *Learning Environments Research, 3*, 287–305.

Henderson, J. G. (1992). *Reflective teaching: Becoming an inquiring educator.* New York: Macmillan.

Herl, H. E., Baker, E. L., & Niemi, D. (1996). Construct validation of an approach to modeling cognitive structures of U. S. history knowledge. *The Journal of Educational Research, 89*, 206–18.

Jackson, T. E. (2001). The art and craft of "gently Socratic" inquiry. In A. L. Costa (Ed.), *Developing minds: A resource book for teaching thinking* (3rd ed., pp. 459–465). Alexandria, VA: Association for Supervision and Curriculum Development.

Jensen, E. (2000). *Brain-based learning: The new science of teaching and training.* San Diego, CA: The Brain Store Publishers.

Kagan, D. (1992). Professional growth among preservice and beginning teacher. *Review of Educational Research, 62*, 197–209

Katz, L., & Raths, J. (1985). Dispositions as goals for teacher education. *Teaching and Teacher Education, 1*, 301–307.

Kelly, G. A. (1955). *The psychology of personal constructs.* New York: Norton

Kennedy, M. (1997). *Defining an ideal teacher education program.* Washington, DC: National Council for the Accreditation of Teacher Education.

Kincheloe, J., Slattery, P., & Steinberg, S. (2000). *Contextualizing teaching.* New York: Longman.

Kinchin, I., Hay, D., & Adams, H. (2000). How a qualitative approach to concept map analysis can be used to aid learning by illustrating patterns of conceptual development. *Educational Research, 42*, 43–57.

Kozulin, A. (1998). *Psychological tools: A sociocultural approach to education.* Cambridge, MA: Harvard University Press.

Langer, E. (1989). *Mindfulness.* Reading, MA: Addison-Wesley.

Langer, J. A. (1995). *Envisioning literature: Literary understanding and literature instruction.* New York: Teachers College Press.

Lapp, D., Flood, J., & Fisher, D. (1999). Intermediality: How the use of multiple media enhances learning. *The Reading Teacher, 52,* 776–780.

Leem, J. (2002). Effects of different types of interaction on learning achievement, satisfaction and participation in web-based instruction. *Innovations in Education and Teaching International, 39*(2), 153–162.

Lincoln, Y. S., & Guba, E. G. (1985). *Naturalistic inquiry.* Newbury Park, CA: Sage.

Lincoln, Y. S., & Guba, E. G. (2000). Paradigmatic controversies, contradictions, and emerging confluences. In N. K. Denzin & Y. S. Lincoln (Eds.), *Handbook of qualitative research* (2nd ed., pp. 163–188). Thousand Oaks, CA: Sage Publications.

Marzano, R. J., & Pollock, J. E. (2001). Standards-based thinking and reasoning skills. In A. L. Costa (Ed.), *Developing minds: A resource book for teaching thinking* (3rd ed., pp. 29–34). Alexandria, VA: Association for Supervision and Curriculum Development.

McDermott, L. (1984). Research on conceptual understanding in mechanics. *Physics Today, 37,* 24–32.

Maxwell, J. A. (2004). Causal explanation, qualitative research, and scientific inquiry in education. *Educational Researcher, 33*(2), 3–11.

National Center for Education Statistics. (1999). *Distance education at postsecondary institutions, 1997–1998* (NCES Report 2000–013). Washington, DC: Author.

Nespor, J. K. (1985). *The role of beliefs in the practice of teaching: Final report of the teacher beliefs study.* (ERIC Document Reproduction Service No. ED 270–446).

Noble, D., Shneiderman, G., Herman, R., Agre, P., & Denning, P. (1998). Technology in education: The fight for the future. *Educom Review, 33,* 22–30.

Northrup, P. T. (2002). Online learners' preferences for interaction. *Quarterly Review of Distance Education, 3*(2), 219–226.

Novak, J. D. (1972). Audio-tutorial techniques for individualized science instruction in the elementary school. In H. Triezenberg (Ed.), *Individualized science: Like it is* (pp. 14–30). Washington, DC: National Science Teachers Association.

Novak, J. D. (1981). Applying learning psychology and philosophy of science to biology teaching. *The American Biology Teacher, 43,* 12–20.

Novak, J. D. (1990). Concept mapping: A useful tool for science education. *Journal of Research in Science Teaching, 27,* 937–949.

Novak, J. D. (1993). Human constructivism: A unification of psychological and epistemological phenomena in meaning making. *International Journal of Personal Construct Psychology, 6,* 167–193.

Novak, J. D., & Gowin, D. B. (1984). *Learning how to learn.* New York: Cambridge University Press.

Paul, R. W. (2001). Dialogical and dialectical thinking. In A. L. Costa (Ed.), *Developing minds: A resource book for teaching thinking* (3rd ed., pp. 427–436). Alexandria, VA: Association for Supervision and Curriculum Development.

Penner, D. E. (2001). Cognition, computers and synthetic science: Building knowledge and meaning through modeling. In W. Secada (Ed.), *Review of research in education* (pp. 1–36). Washington, DC: American Educational Research Association.

Preece, P. F. (1976a). Associative structure of science concepts. *British Journal of Educational Psychology, 46,* 174–183.

Preece, P. F. (1976b). The concepts of electromagnetism: A study of the internal representation of external structures. *Journal of Research in Science Teaching, 13*, 517–524.

Preece, P. F. (1976c). Mapping cognitive structure: A comparison of methods. *Journal of Educational Psychology, 68*(1), 1–8.

Resnick, L. B. (1999). Making America smarter. *Education Week, 8*, pp. 38–40.

Resnick, L. B., Levine, J. M., & Teasley, S. D. (Eds.). (1991). *Perspectives on socially shared cognition.* Washington, DC: American Psychological Association.

Routman, R. (1991). *Invitations: Changing as teachers and learners k–12.* Portsmouth, NH: Heinemann.

Royer, J. M., Cisero, C. A., & Carlo, M. S. (1993). Techniques and procedures for assessing cognitive skills. *Review of Educational Research, 63*, 201–243.

Rumelhart, D. E. (1981). Schemata: The building blocks of cognition. In J. T. Guthries (Ed.), *Comprehension and Teaching: Research Reviews* (pp. 573–603). Newark, DE: International Reading Association.

Schon, D. A. (1983). *The reflective practitioner: How professionals think in action.* New York: Basic Books.

Schweizer, H. (1999). *Designing and teaching an on-line course: Spinning your web classroom.* Needham Heights, MA: Allyn & Bacon.

Shavelson, R. J. (1972). Some aspects of the correspondence between content structure and cognitive structure in physics instruction. *Journal of Educational Psychology, 63*(3), 225–234.

Shavelson, R. J. (1974). Methods for examining representations of a subject-matter structure in a student's memory. *Journal of Research in Science Teaching, 11*, 231–249.

Shavelson, R. J., & Stanton, G. C. (1975). Construct validation: Methodology and application to three measures of cognitive structure. *Journal of Education Measurement, 12*(2), 67–85.

Shin, N., & Chan, J. K. Y. (2004). Direct and indirect effects of online learning on distance education. *British Journal of Educational Technology, 35*, 275–288.

Shipman, M. D. (1969). Participation and staff-student relations: A seven year study of social changes in an expanding college of education. *Journal of Research into Higher Education Monographs, 6*, 1–38.

Shipman, M. D. (1967). Environmental influences on response to questionnaires. *British Journal of Educational Psychology, 37*, 54–57.

Simonson, M., Schlosser, C., & Hanson, D. (1999). Theory and distance education: A new discussion. *The American Journal of Distance Education, 13*, 60–75.

Simonson, M., Smaldino, S., Albright, M., & Zvacek, S. (2003). *Teaching and learning at a distance: Foundations of distance education* (2nd ed.). Upper Saddle River, NJ: Merrill Prentice Hall.

Smith, M C., & Winking-Diaz, A. (2004). Increasing students' interactivity in an online course. *Journal of Interactive Online Learning, 2*(3), 1–25.

Sousa, D. A. (2001). *How the brain learns: A classroom teacher's guide* (2nd ed.). Thousand Oaks, CA: Corwin.

Stewart, J., Van Kirk, J., & Rowell, R. (1979). Concept maps: A tool for use in biology teaching. *American biology Teacher, 41*(3), 171–175.

Stuart, H. (1985). Should concept maps be scored numerically? *European Journal of Science Education, 7,* 73–81.

Tishman, S. (2001). Added value: A dispositional perspective on thinking. In A. L. Costa (Ed.), *Developing minds: A resource book for teaching thinking* (3rd ed., pp. 29–34). Alexandria, VA: Association for Supervision and Curriculum Development.

Tompkins, L. S. (1993). A new light on distance learning: Fiber optics. *Journal of Educational Technology Systems, 21,* 265–275.

von Glasersfeld, E. (1984). An introduction to radical constructivism. In P. Watzlawick (Ed.), *The invented reality* (pp. 17–40). New York: Norton.

von Glasersfeld, E. (1989). Cognition, construction of knowledge and teaching. *Syntheses, 80,* 121–140.

Vygotsky, L. S. (1978). Mind in society: The development of higher psychological processes (M. Cole, V. John-Steiner, S. Scribner & E. Souberman, Eds.). Cambridge, MA: Harvard University Press.

Wadsworth, B. J. (1974). *Piaget's theory of cognitive development: An introduction for students of psychology and education.* New York: David McKay.

Wadsworth, B. J. (1996). *Piaget's theory of cognitive and affective development: Foundations of constructivism* (5th ed.). White Plains, NY: Longman.

Wolf, D. P., & Reardon, S. F. (1996). Access to excellence through new forms of student assessment. In J. B. Baron & D. P. Wolf (Eds.), *Performance-based student assessment: Challenges and possibilities* (pp. 1–33). Chicago: University of Chicago Press.

Zeichner, K., & Tabachnick, B. (1981). Are the effects of university teacher education "washed out" by school experience? *Journal of Teacher Education, 32*(3), 7–11.

Zimmerman, B. J., Bonner, S., & Kovach, R. (1996). *Developing self-regulated learners: Beyond achievement to self-efficacy.* Washington, DC: American Psychological Association.

## APPENDIX A

### *Concept Map Rubric*

(Adapted from Bloom, 1956; Dorough & Rye, 1997; Kinchin & Hay, 2000, Novak, 1993)

| | *Spoke* | *Chain* | *Branching* | *Net* |
|---|---|---|---|---|
| Map Structure Parameters | One level with several categories—not viewed as connecting thoughts. Simple cause/effect problem solving designed structure. | Many sequence levels, but often incorrect supporting attributes. Linear and/or temporal designed structure. | Many category and sub-categories with some supporting attributes attached to each. Developing thoughtful theory to test information. Designed structure complex. | Justifiable categories and linking levels with complex supporting attributes. Sound testing of complex worldwide view theory. Unique designed structure. |

*Cognitive Map Intellectual Thinking Dispositions*

| Scoring Cycle*: | *1–3* | *4–6* | *7–9* | *10–12* |
|---|---|---|---|---|
| Category and Supporting Attributes Thinking | Simple cause/effect association with no category egory connections. Few category qualities. Little supporting attributes to a category. | Show temporal, chaining or linear category sequencing. Little or no cause/effect among categories and supporting attributes. Few common qualities. | Linking supporting attributes to major categories. Thoughtful category classification. Developing cause/effect patterns and order. | Complex classification between and among categories and supporting attributes. Unique categories. Infers cause and effect interactions. Draws sound conclusions. |

*Cognitive Map Intellectual Thinking Dispositions (Cont.)*

| Scoring Cycle*: | 1–3 | 4–6 | 7–9 | 10–12 |
|---|---|---|---|---|
| Category Complexity Thinking | Few categories; little linking among categories. Additions without consequences in changing map structure or plan. Simple supporting attributes to a category. | Linking within categories difficult. Additions difficult; map structure failure particularly near the beginning or end of the chaining sequence. Simple supporting attributes. | Some linking within category and supporting attributes. Additions without map structure failure. Thoughtful attributes to category; can be inferred across categories. Reflects worldwide view. | Describes complex, creative linking between and among categories and supporting attributes. Provides novel and/or aesthetic ideas to relationships. Map structure is unique to world-wide view. |
| Causal Relationships Thinking | Shows little or no causal relationships among categories and supporting attributes. Addition or loss of relationship has little effect maps overview. | Narrow causal relationships among categories and supporting attributes. Narrow understanding. Sequencing can lose meaning of causal relationships. | Expanded causal relationships among categories and supporting attributes. Expanded understanding. Addition of causal relationships has little effect on map integrity. | Complex causal relationships among categories and supporting attributes. Complex understanding. Additions has minor consequences to map integrity; ' "other routes" available because of complex relationship. |
| Thinking Dispositions Strategy and Skill | *Simple Problem Solving* Compare/contrast simple. Classify and defining weak. Multiple thinking perspectives of categories and supporting attributes weak. Minimal development | *Identifying Order* Ranking information; identify some supporting attributes in sequence; little difference from important/not important information. Map sequencing have narrow distinctions. | *Critical Thinking* Use of analysis, synthesis, evaluation thinking. Identify facts, claims with supporting attributes; complex sub-linking; with a category. Developing a more worldwide theory. | *Creative Thinking* Interrelate categories and supporting attributes; identify assumptions that interconnect; recognize inconsistencies in relationships and does not link. Sound reasoning to a unique worldwide theory. |

*Cognitive Map Intellectual Thinking Dispositions (Cont.)*

| Scoring Cycle*: | 1–3 | 4–6 | 7–9 | 10–12 |
|---|---|---|---|---|
| Map Concept Structure Repre- sents | Simple Informa- tion Concept Structure | Sequence of Concept Struc- ture | Outside Influ- ences on Con- cept Structure | Meaningful Learning Con- cept Structure |

\* See Concept Map Scoring Instrument

## APPENDIX B

## *Concept Map Scoring Instrument*

(C. S. Shwery & T. McCormick, 2004)

### Concept Map Thinking Dispositions

| Cognitive Thinking Parameters | Simple Structure————————————————Complex Structure | | | | | | | | | | | |
|---|---|---|---|---|---|---|---|---|---|---|---|---|
| **Defining a Concept** | | | | | | | | | | | | |
| • Concept Structure | 1 | 2 | 3 | 4 | 5 | 6 | 7 | 8 | 9 | 10 | 11 | 12 |
| **Category Thinking Interaction** | | | | | | | | | | | | |
| • Cause and Effect | 1 | 2 | 3 | 4 | 5 | 6 | 7 | 8 | 9 | 10 | 11 | 12 |
| • Classification | 1 | 2 | 3 | 4 | 5 | 6 | 7 | 8 | 9 | 10 | 11 | 12 |
| **Category Thinking Complexity** | | | | | | | | | | | | |
| • Linking Category Integration | 1 | 2 | 3 | 4 | 5 | 6 | 7 | 8 | 9 | 10 | 11 | 12 |
| • Map Structure Additions | 1 | 2 | 3 | 4 | 5 | 6 | 7 | 8 | 9 | 10 | 11 | 12 |
| • Category Attributes | 1 | 2 | 3 | 4 | 5 | 6 | 7 | 8 | 9 | 10 | 11 | 12 |
| **Causal Relationship** | | | | | | | | | | | | |
| • Causal Relation- ships | 1 | 2 | 3 | 4 | 5 | 6 | 7 | 8 | 9 | 10 | 11 | 12 |
| **Thinking Disposition** | | | | | | | | | | | | |
| • Exploring concept relationships | 1 | 2 | 3 | 4 | 5 | 6 | 7 | 8 | 9 | 10 | 11 | 12 |
| • Multiple perspectives | 1 | 2 | 3 | 4 | 5 | 6 | 7 | 8 | 9 | 10 | 11 | 12 |
| • Level of world- wide reflection | 1 | 2 | 3 | 4 | 5 | 6 | 7 | 8 | 9 | 10 | 11 | 12 |

Side One

### Concept Map Thinking Dispositions (Cont.)

**Directions:**
Referencing the rubric, circle the appropriate number within each parameter's **Thinking Disposition** identifier. After responding to *all* identifiers, turn the scoring instrument so "**Side One**" is facing you. Connect the circled numbers with a straight line. Using "**6**" as the baseline, you can determine the student's critical thinking skills strengths and weakness. Numbers that fall **above** the baseline are student's *weaknesses*; numbers that fall **below** the baseline are student's *strengths*. The purpose of the rubric and scoring instrument are to guide you in teaching critical thinking skills identified as weaknesses. The rubric, **nor** the scoring instrument are meant for students' use. You do not want to skew the information by showing students the rubric and/or scoring instrument which may result in mimicking.

| | Map Structure | Simple Concept | Sequence Concept | Outside Influences | Meaningful Global |
|---|---|---|---|---|---|
| First Result | | | | | |
| Second Result | | | | | |
| Third Result | | | | | |

Side One